Oil & Water

Steve Duin | *Author*

Shannon Wheeler | *Artist*

Mike Rosen | *Editor*

Tom Orzechowski | *Letterer*

FANTAGRAPHICS BOOKS
7563 Lake City Way NE. Seattle WA 98115 USA

Written by **Steve Duin**
Illustrated by **Shannon Wheeler**
Edited by **Michael Rosen**
Lettered by **Tom Orzechowski**
Production & Cover Design by **Alexa Koenings**
Associate Publisher: **Eric Reynolds**
Published by **Gary Groth** & **Kim Thompson**

 | To receive a free catalog from Fantagraphics, call 1-800-657-1100 in North America or write to us at 7563 Lake City Way NE, Seattle, WA 98115 USA. Or visit us at www.fantagraphics.com. | Distributed in the U.S. by W.W. Norton & Co. (800-233-4830) | Distributed in Canada by Canadian Manda Group (416-516-0911) | Distributed in the United Kingdom by Turnaround Services (44 (0)20 8829-3002) | Distributed to the comics market by Diamond Comic Distributors (800-452-6642) | First printing: October 2011 | ISBN 978-1-60699-492-4 | Printed in Singapore

Dedications

Dedicated to the 11 men who died in the Deepwater Horizon disaster... and to all those working to ensure that future generations of those Gulf Coast families grow up in a different world.

My thanks to Rani for encouraging me to take on this project and for her support as I struggled through it; to my children, Austin and Berkeley, who are a constant source of reward; to Patricia Wheeler and Richard Epstein; and to Mike Rosen, the linchpin of this entire endeavor. — **Shannon Wheeler**

For the inspiration I found in the Gulf, and the friends I brought home. — **Steve Duin**

"On Aug. 7, Mike Rosen will lead two dozen Oregonians on a 10-day pilgrimage to the Gulf Coast. They want to measure the impact of one of the worst environmental disasters in U.S. history, and encourage the shrimp boaters, hoteliers, beachcombers and off-shore oil workers now soaking in 184 million gallons of spilt petroleum. They hope to return with a painful but powerful story of the strategic changes we all need to make in the landscape of environmental protection and personal responsibility."
— *The Oregonian*, 18 July 2010

Prologue

Our journey – the August 2010 odyssey of two dozen Oregonians to the devastated Gulf Coast – did not begin with a single step or 200 million gallons of oil.

It was greased, instead, by an extraordinary statement of commitment by KEEN.

When PDX 2 Gulf Coast began plotting its 10-day expedition through Louisiana, Mississippi and Alabama in the summer of 2010, KEEN stepped up with financial support that made the trip a reality.

KEEN put it this way: "We cannot change what happened in the Gulf of Mexico, but we would like to help prevent a future disaster by committing to make considered decisions, helping individuals connect the dots on how they can make changes to lighten our collective impact on the earth."

KEEN has a history of supporting communities in need that started with tsunami relief in 2004. PDX 2 Gulf Coast presented itself as a response to the Gulf Coast crisis and its communities with a vision and purpose. Visit www.keenfootwear.com to learn more.

PDX 2 Gulf Coast — and this graphic novel — would not have been possible if KEEN didn't work equally hard to craft a better world.

Mike Rosen | *Project Leader*
PDX 2 Gulf Coast
www.pdx2gulfcoast.com

I'm writing this introduction exactly a year after the Deepwater Horizon blew in the Gulf of Mexico, sending enormous quantities of oil into the ocean and shutting down normal life for at least a summer along the shores of Louisiana and Mississippi. Twelve months later, we know a few things: much of the oil was burned, skimmed, or dispersed with chemicals. Much of it remains, probably along the bottom of the sea. And BP is still in the same business it was before, along with its compatriots around the Gulf.

This book serves a useful purpose, reminding outsiders what the realities of life along the Gulf are like. Through the eyes of a clueless crew of Oregonians on some kind of mission of mercy/voyeurism, Steve Duin and Shannon Wheeler capture a few of the myriad voices speaking in one of America's most distinctive dialects in one of its most distinctive places. They see the very brave people of the region fighting back as best they can. They witness firsthand the economies of seafood and of oil. And they see which one is bigger and more powerful.

Here's one of the real stories of the Deepwater Horizon: the crisis was interpreted so narrowly that the deep and profound questions it raised never really came up. For one, it illustrated quite beautifully the fact that we are running out of oil: Why else would BP have been drilling a mile down, where it had no idea how to control a blowout, all for a field that in the best of cases would have provided a week's worth of American oil consumption?

Even more, the plume of oil that spread across the water was just the visible reminder of an even more deadly plume that spreads each day across the sky. Consider: if the oil leaking from the Deepwater hole had instead made it uneventfully ashore to some refinery, been converted into gasoline, pumped into your car, and then burnt, the resulting carbon dioxide would have produced its own ongoing environmental disaster. The water of the Gulf, and of every other ocean on earth, is about 30% more acid than it was just four decades ago because the seas are absorbing so much CO_2. Already that change in chemistry is enough to cause serious problems for the smallest animals in the food chain; by mid-century, some biologists predict, the more acidic water will be dissolving shells.

Not only that, but as the sea gets hotter, the chance for stronger hurricanes increases — hurricanes, after all, draw their fury from the heat in the first few meters of the sea's surface. The 'one-two punch' of Katrina and the spill that so many characters in this volume remark on are linked in more ways than one.

The best thing that could have come from the spill, then, would have been some real attention to the underlying problem: our addiction to oil, and the havoc that addiction wreaks everywhere. But confronting that addiction would have meant, among many other things, confronting the economy of the Gulf states. Governors along the coast were outraged with the federal government during the crisis, largely because the feds temporarily restricted new offshore drilling. As this book makes clear, the Gulf economy as presently constituted would grind to a halt were it not for oil.

It's clear by now that the Gulf spill was not the wake-up call many imagined. With huge amounts of money (though still small compared to BP's profits), the oil industry managed to hit the snooze button on this alarm clock. The feds tightened the rules a bit on deepwater rigs, but that was never the real issue.

The real issue is oil, and all that it means in our economies and in our lives.

Bill McKibben
Schumann Distinguished Scholar
Middlebury College
Middlebury, VT

April 2011

Bill McKibben is the author of a dozen books about the environment, beginning with The End of Nature *in 1989, which is regarded as the first book for a general audience on climate change. He is a founder of the grassroots climate campaign 350.org, which has coordinated 15,000 rallies in 189 countries since 2009.* Time *called McKibben "the planet's best green journalist," and* The Boston Globe *argued in 2010 that he is "probably the country's most important environmentalist."*

Daddy's Money

Grand Isle. LA

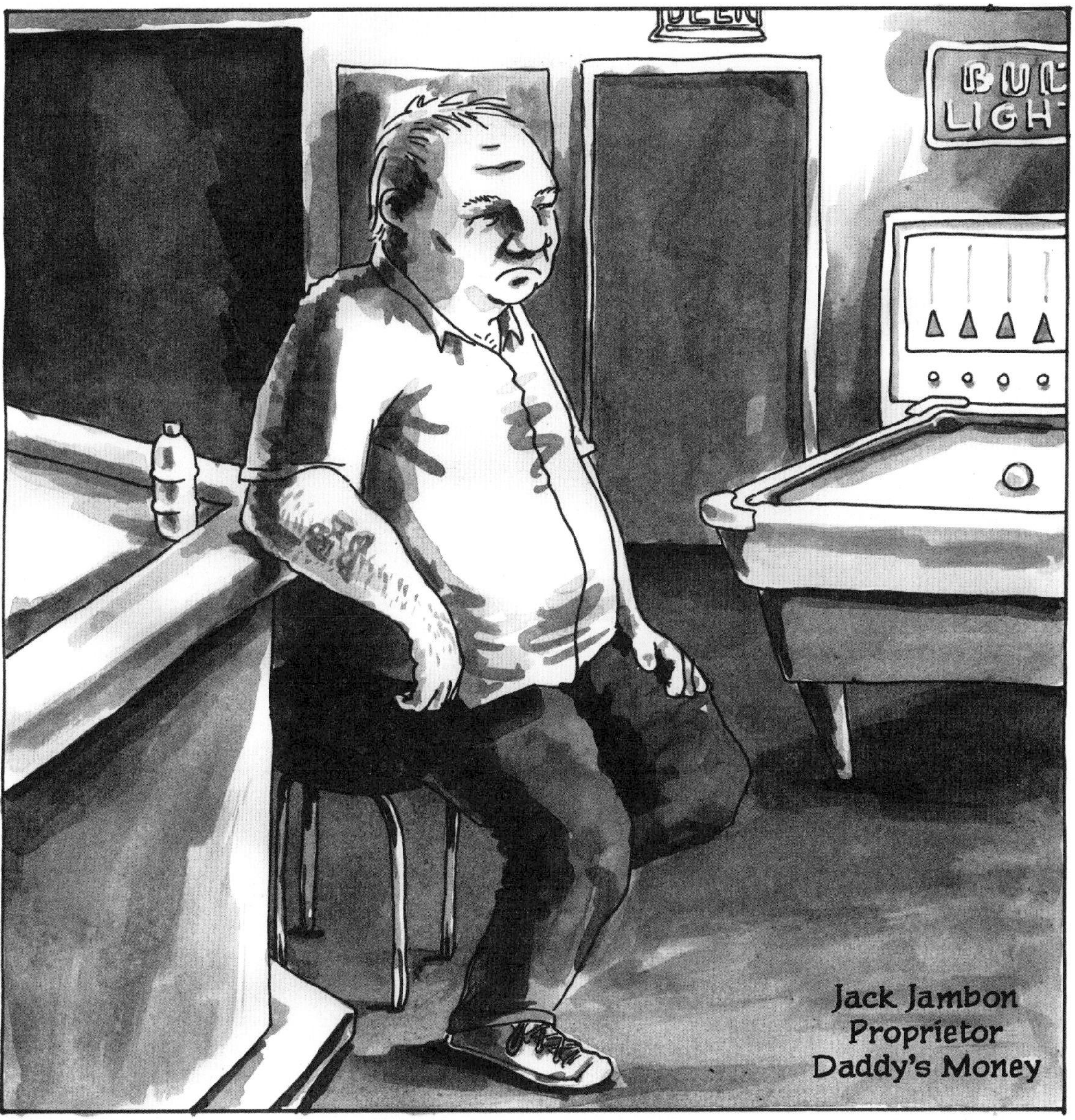

Jack Jambon
Proprietor
Daddy's Money

Oil?
Let's do the math.
ONLY!
SEXY SIRENS
FROM SLIDELL!

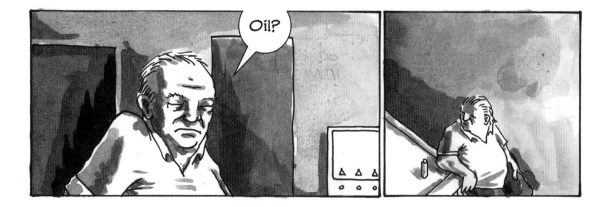

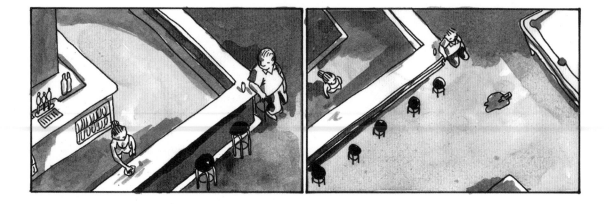

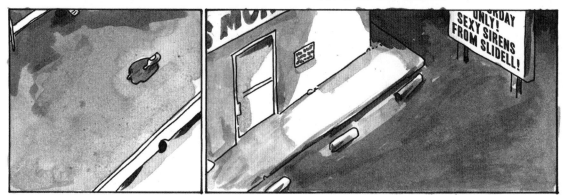

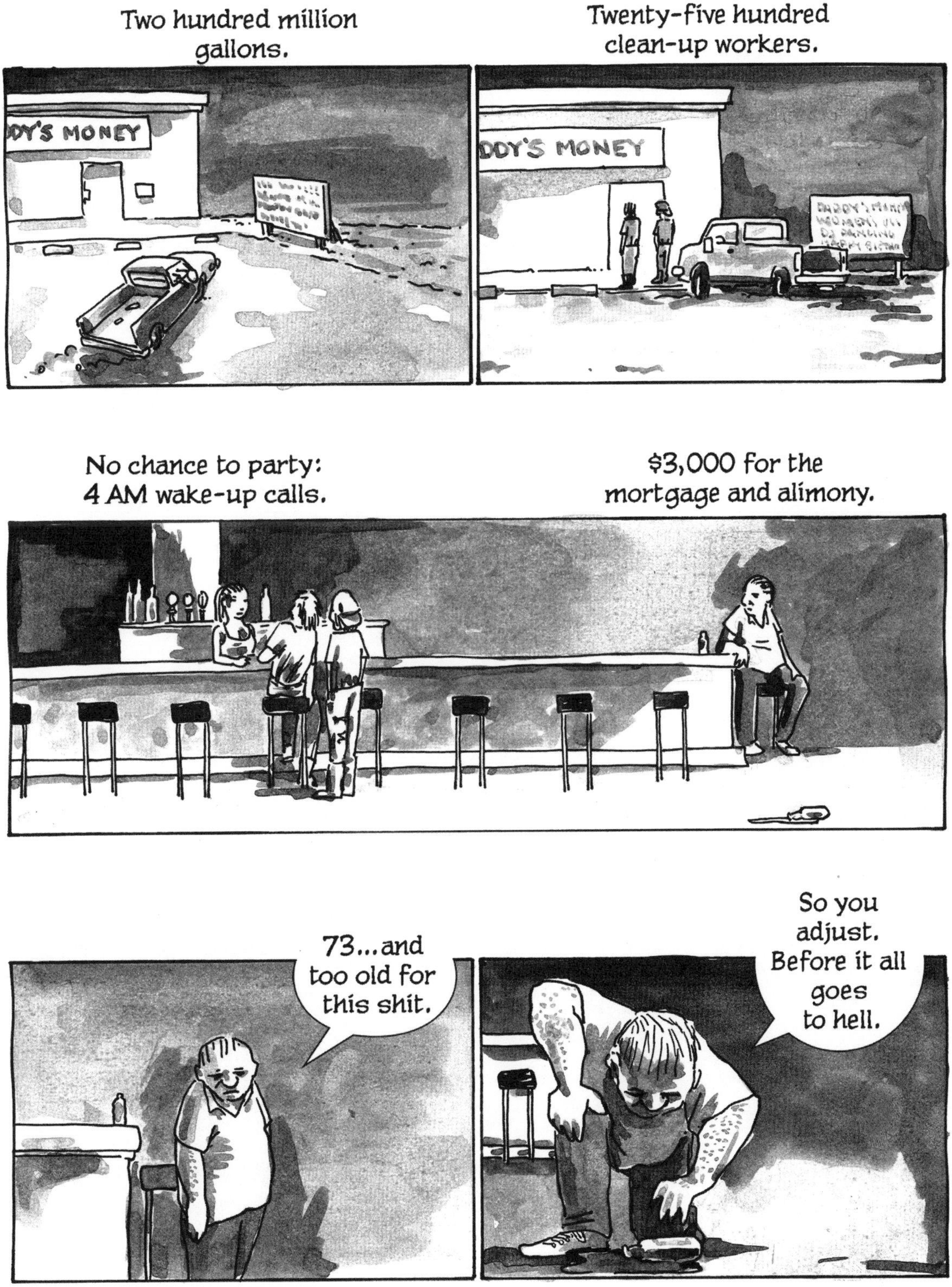
Two hundred million gallons.
DDY'S MONEY
Twenty-five hundred clean-up workers.
DDY'S MONEY
No chance to party: 4 AM wake-up calls.
$3,000 for the mortgage and alimony.
73...and too old for this shit.
So you adjust. Before it all goes to hell.

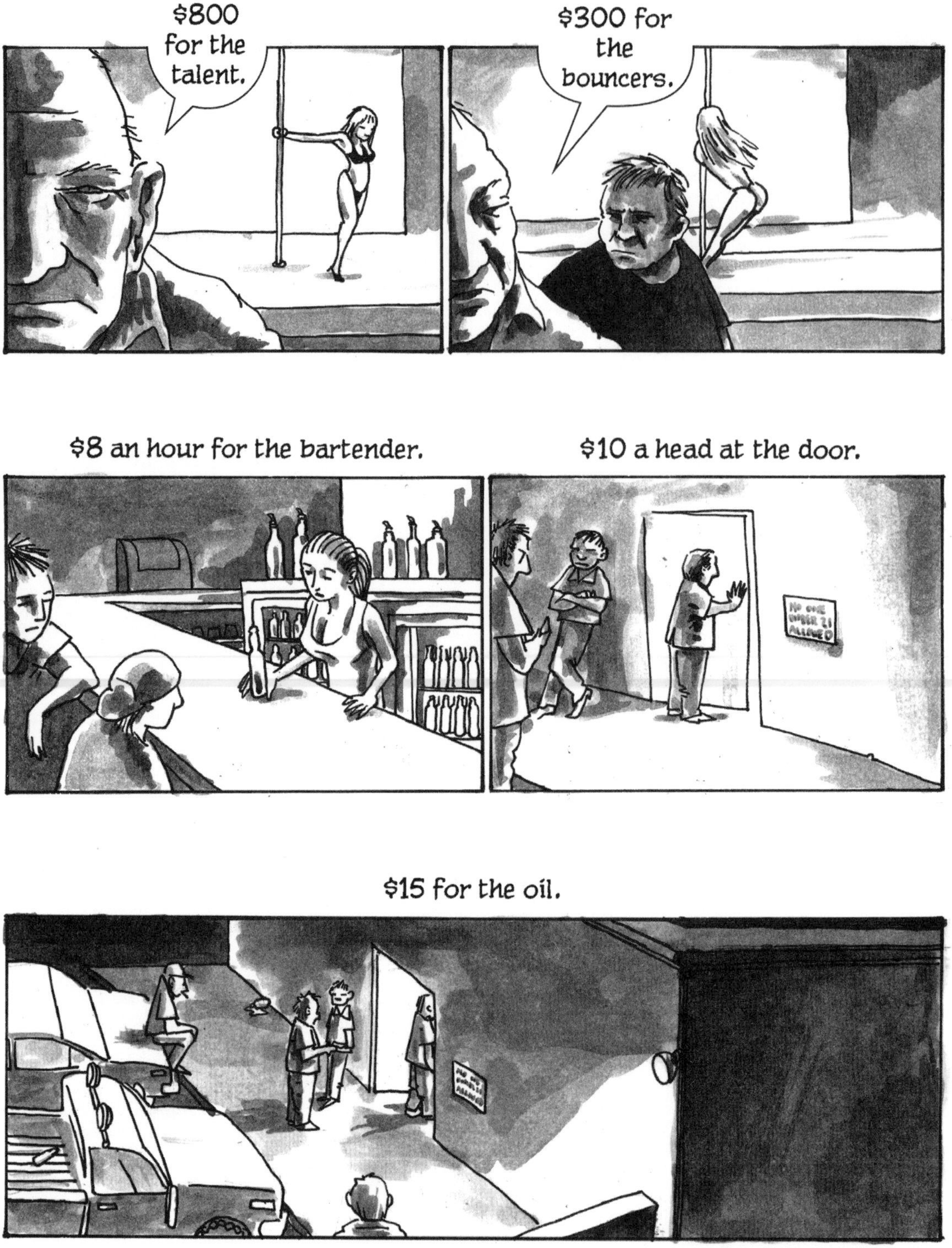
$800 for the talent.
$300 for the bouncers.
$8 an hour for the bartender.
$10 a head at the door.
$15 for the oil.

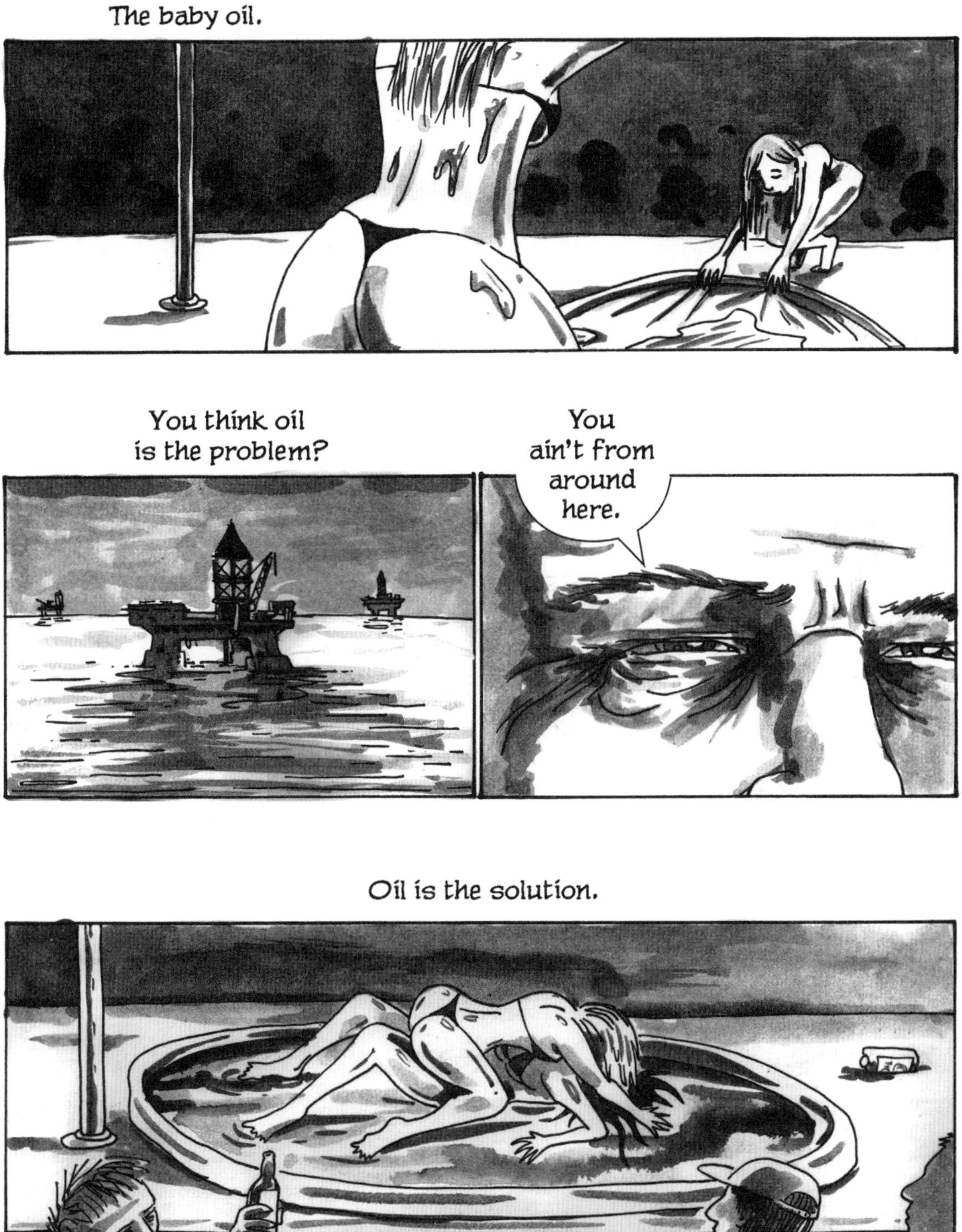
The baby oil.
You think oil is the problem?
You ain't from around here.
Oil is the solution.

Chi sono queste persone?

Portland, OR

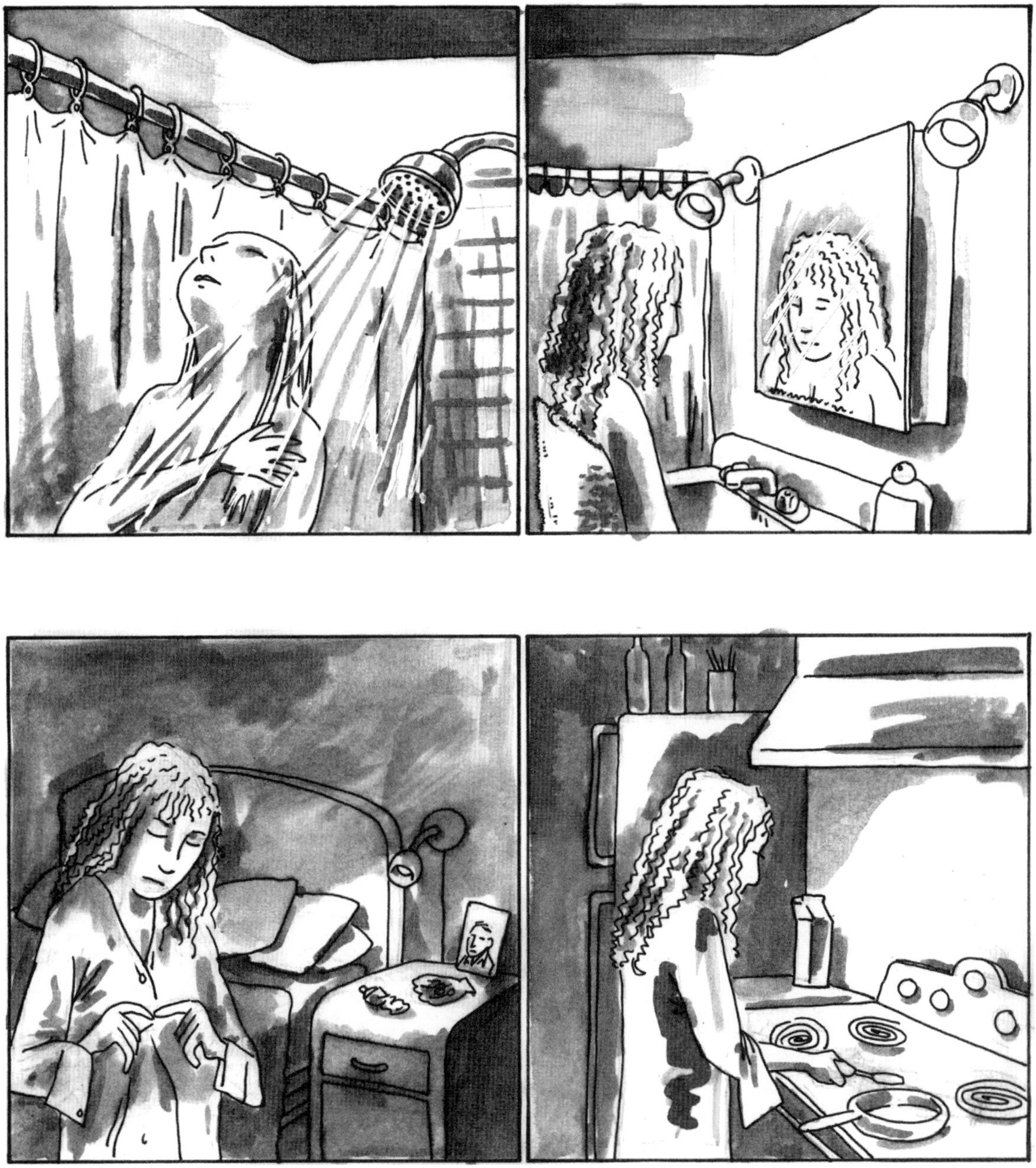

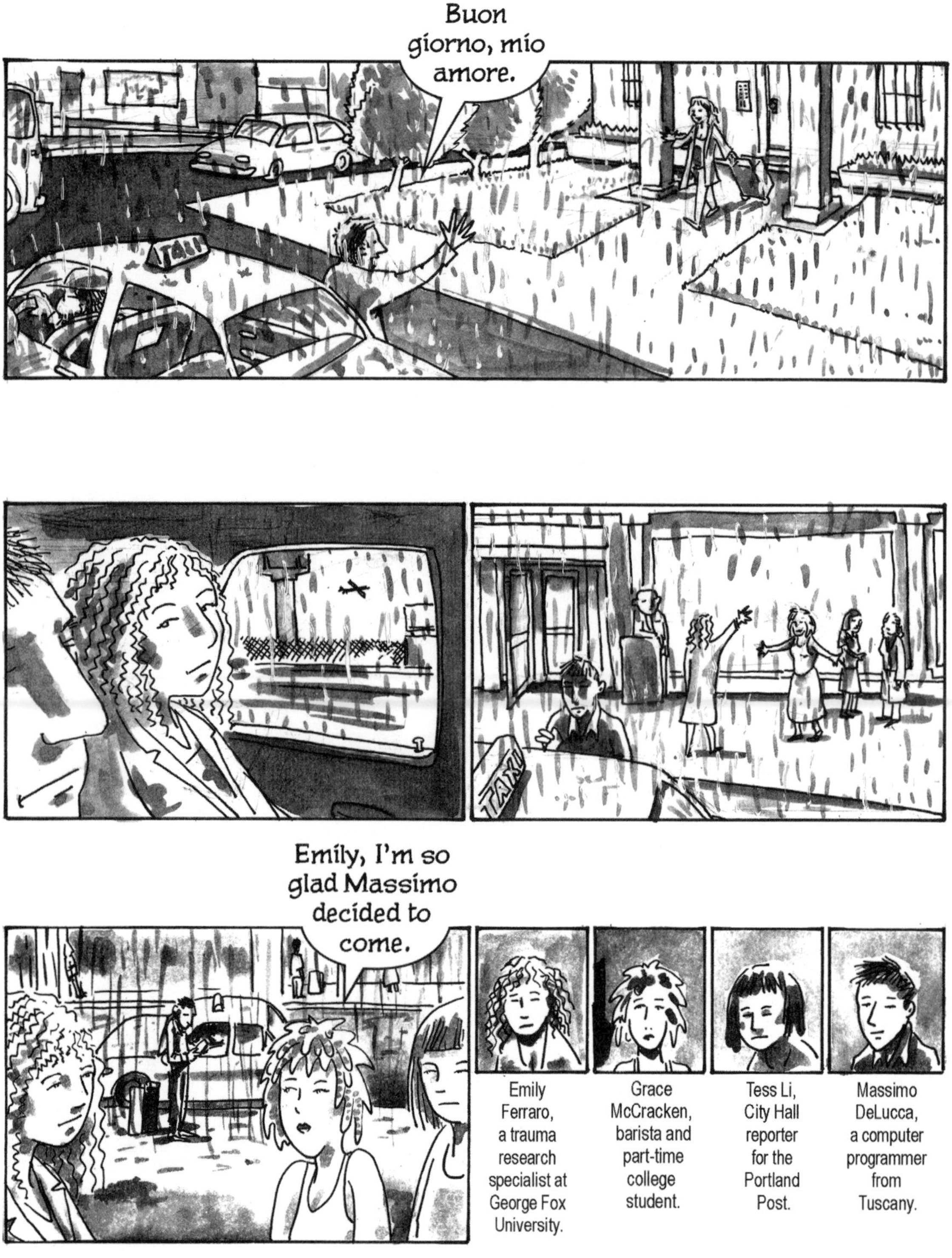

Buon giorno, mio amore.
Emily, I'm so glad Massimo decided to come.
Emily Ferraro, a trauma research specialist at George Fox University.
Grace McCracken, barista and part-time college student.
Tess Li, City Hall reporter for the Portland Post.
Massimo DeLucca, a computer programmer from Tuscany.

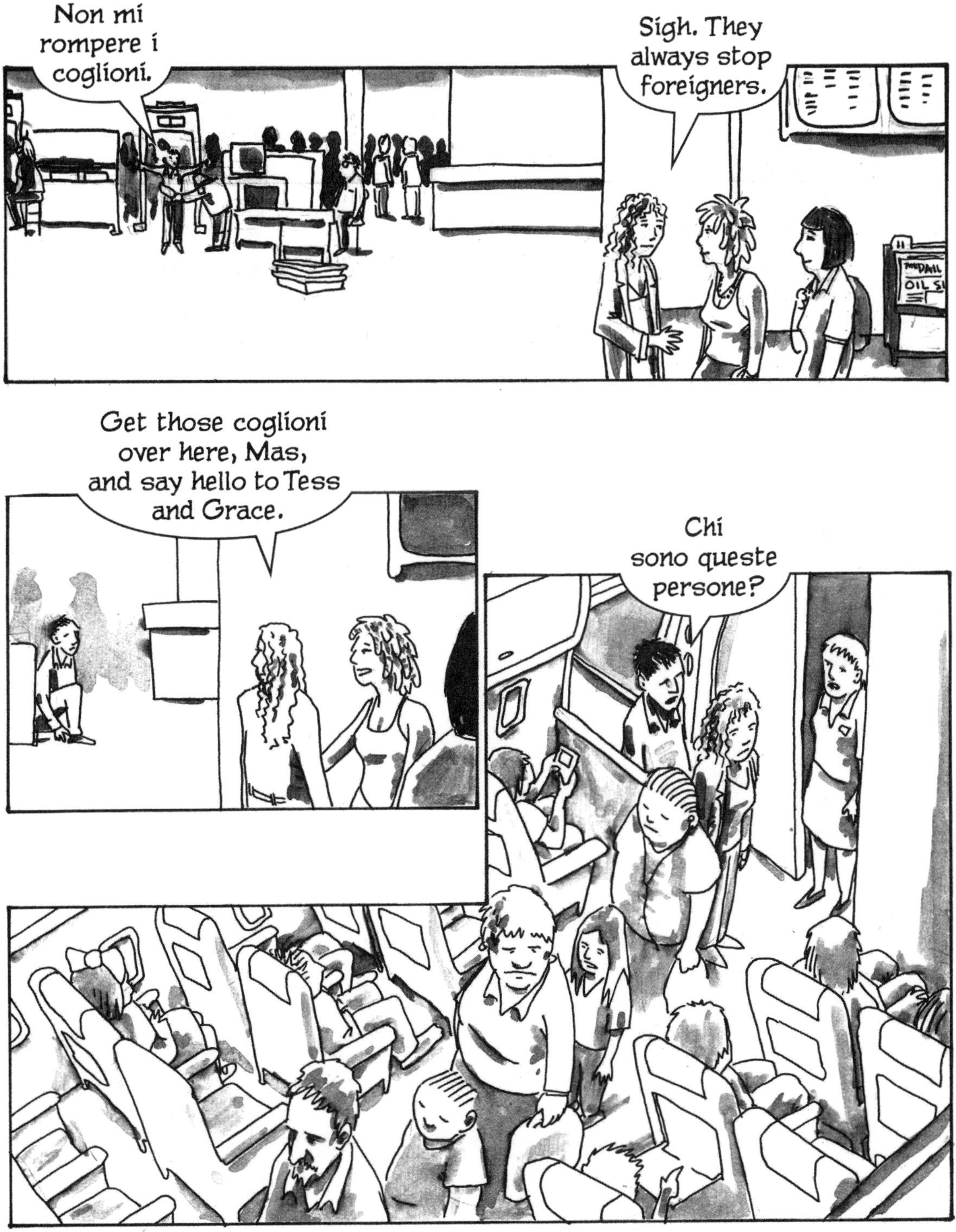
Non mi rompere i coglioni.
Sigh. They always stop foreigners.
Get those coglioni over here, Mas, and say hello to Tess and Grace.
Chi sono queste persone?

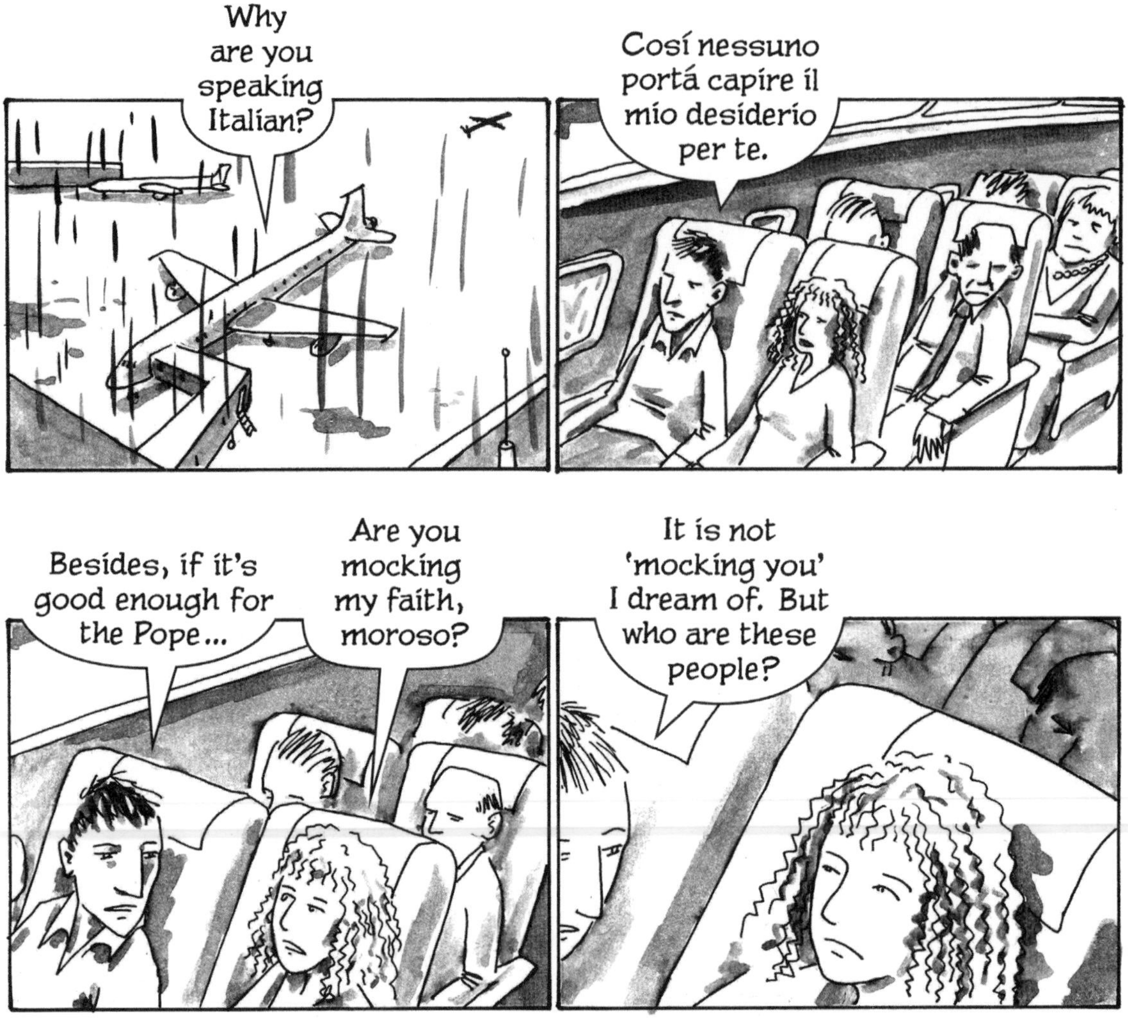
Why are you speaking Italian?
Cosí nessuno portá capire il mio desiderio per te.
Besides, if it's good enough for the Pope...
Are you mocking my faith, moroso?
It is not 'mocking you' I dream of. But who are these people?

Aaron Wolff, a biology teacher at Portland's Roosevelt High and the PDX 2 Gulf Coast group leader, and his son, Eben, Roosevelt's junior class president.

Jimmy Warren, conservation director for the Audubon Society.

Tiffany Garfield, a wind-energy lobbyist from Eugene, and her daughter, Laura, a senior at Catlin Gabel, a private school in Portland.

Max Hawk, anti-plastic activist and bird enthusiast.

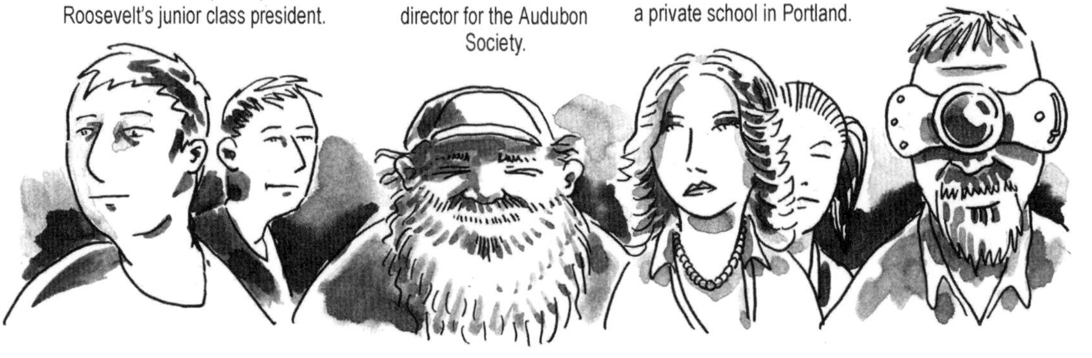

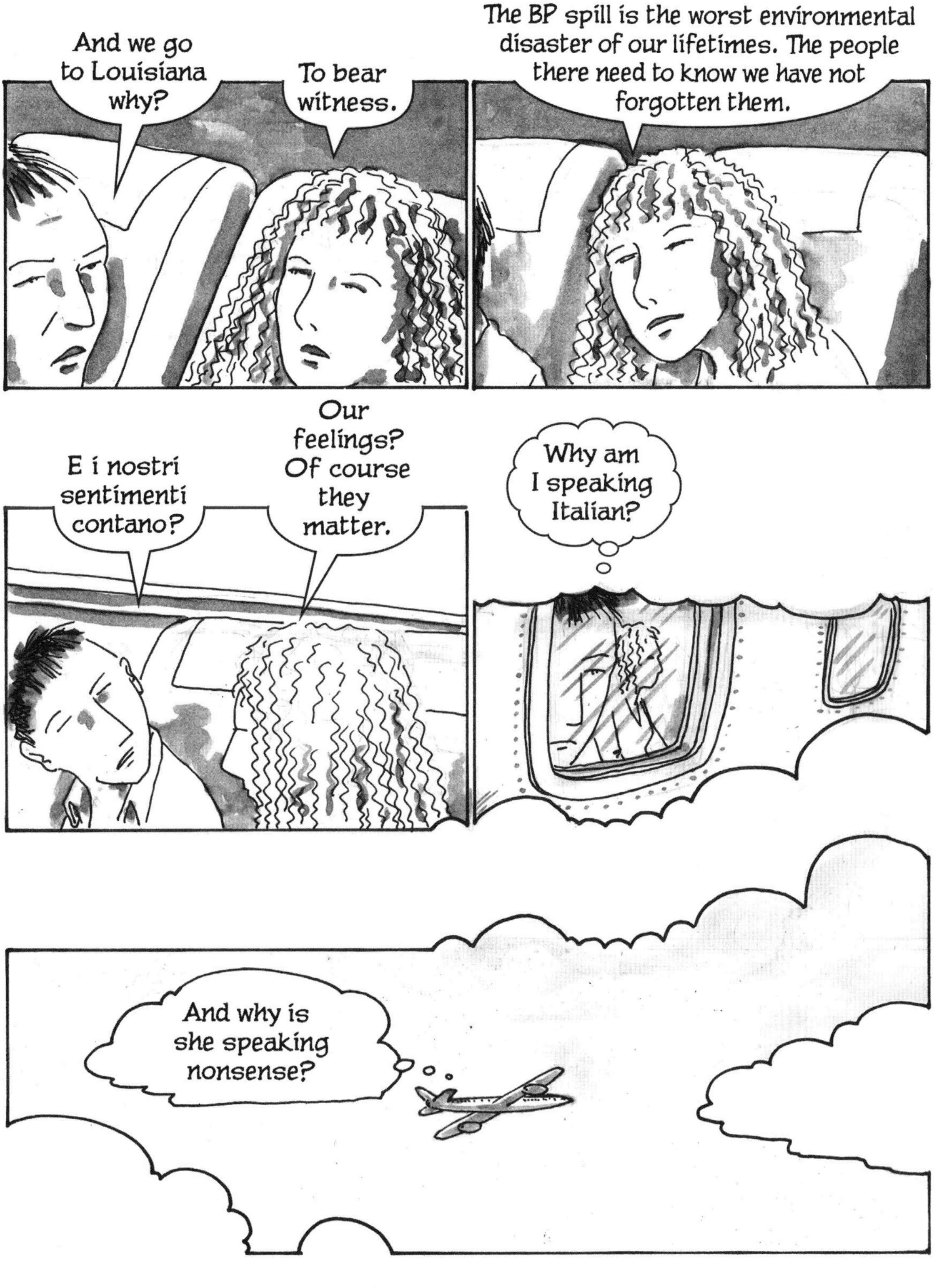
And we go to Louisiana why?
To bear witness.
The BP spill is the worst environmental disaster of our lifetimes. The people there need to know we have not forgotten them.
E i nostri sentimenti contano?
Our feelings? Of course they matter.
Why am I speaking Italian?
And why is she speaking nonsense?

Oil and Water

Deep Water Horizon Rig, Gulf of Mexico

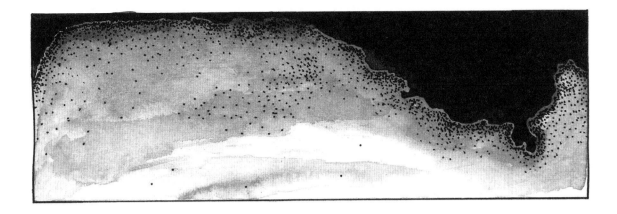

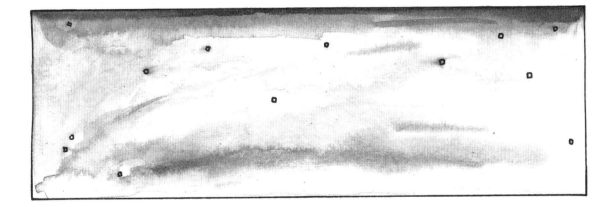

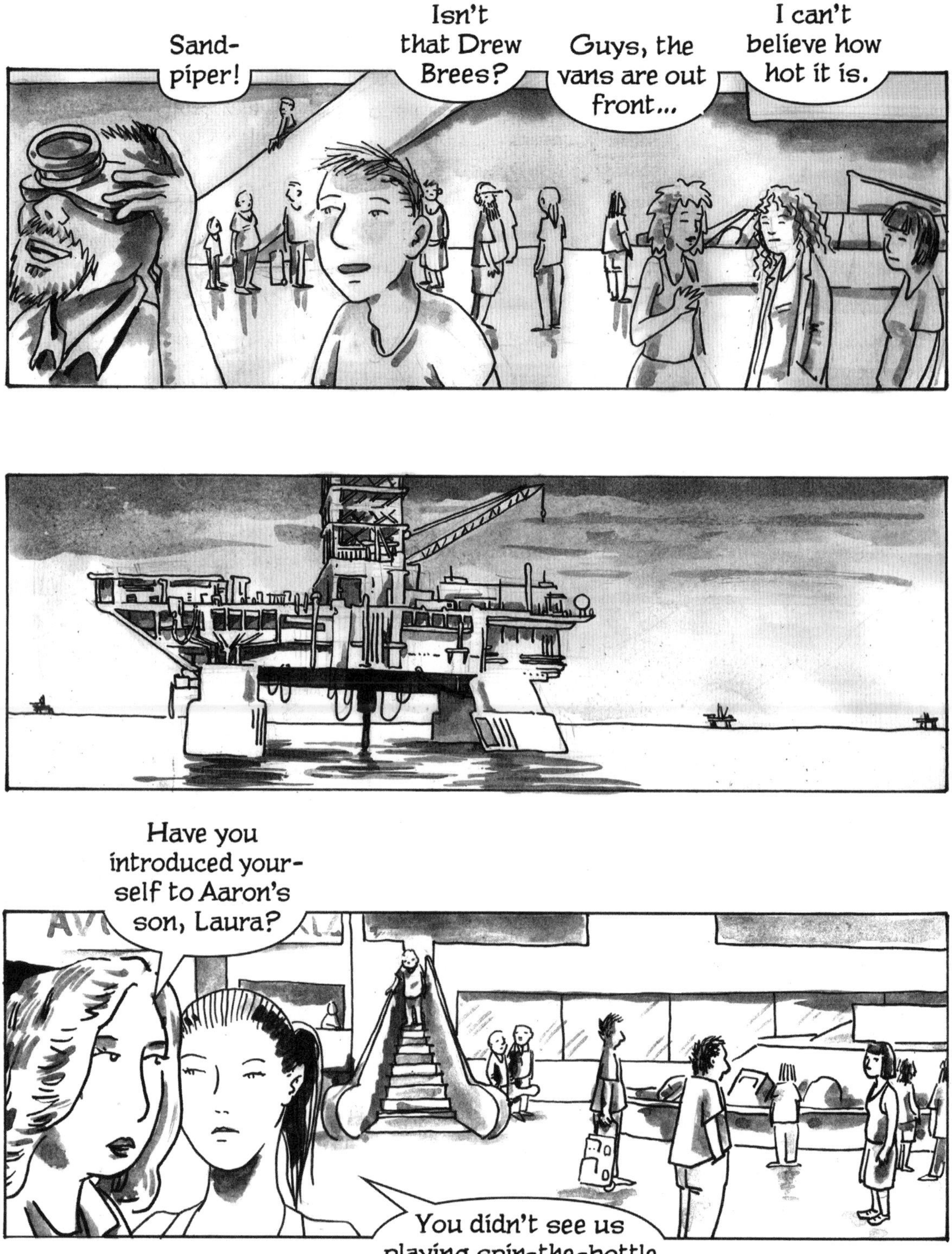
Sand-piper!
Isn't that Drew Brees?
Guys, the vans are out front...
I can't believe how hot it is.
Have you introduced your-self to Aaron's son, Laura?
You didn't see us playing spin-the-bottle in coach, Mom?

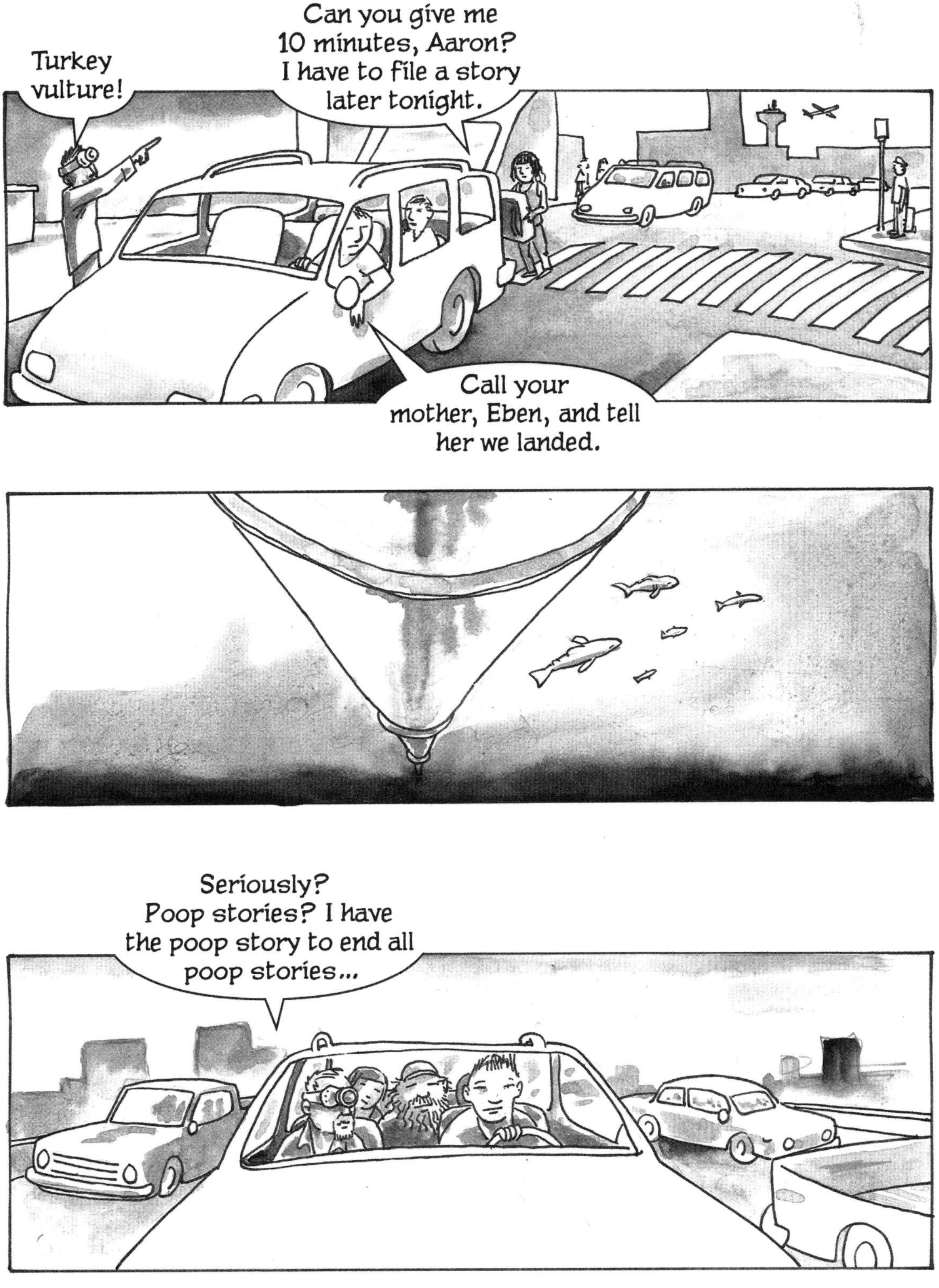
Turkey vulture!
Can you give me 10 minutes, Aaron? I have to file a story later tonight.
Call your mother, Eben, and tell her we landed.
Seriously? Poop stories? I have the poop story to end all poop stories...

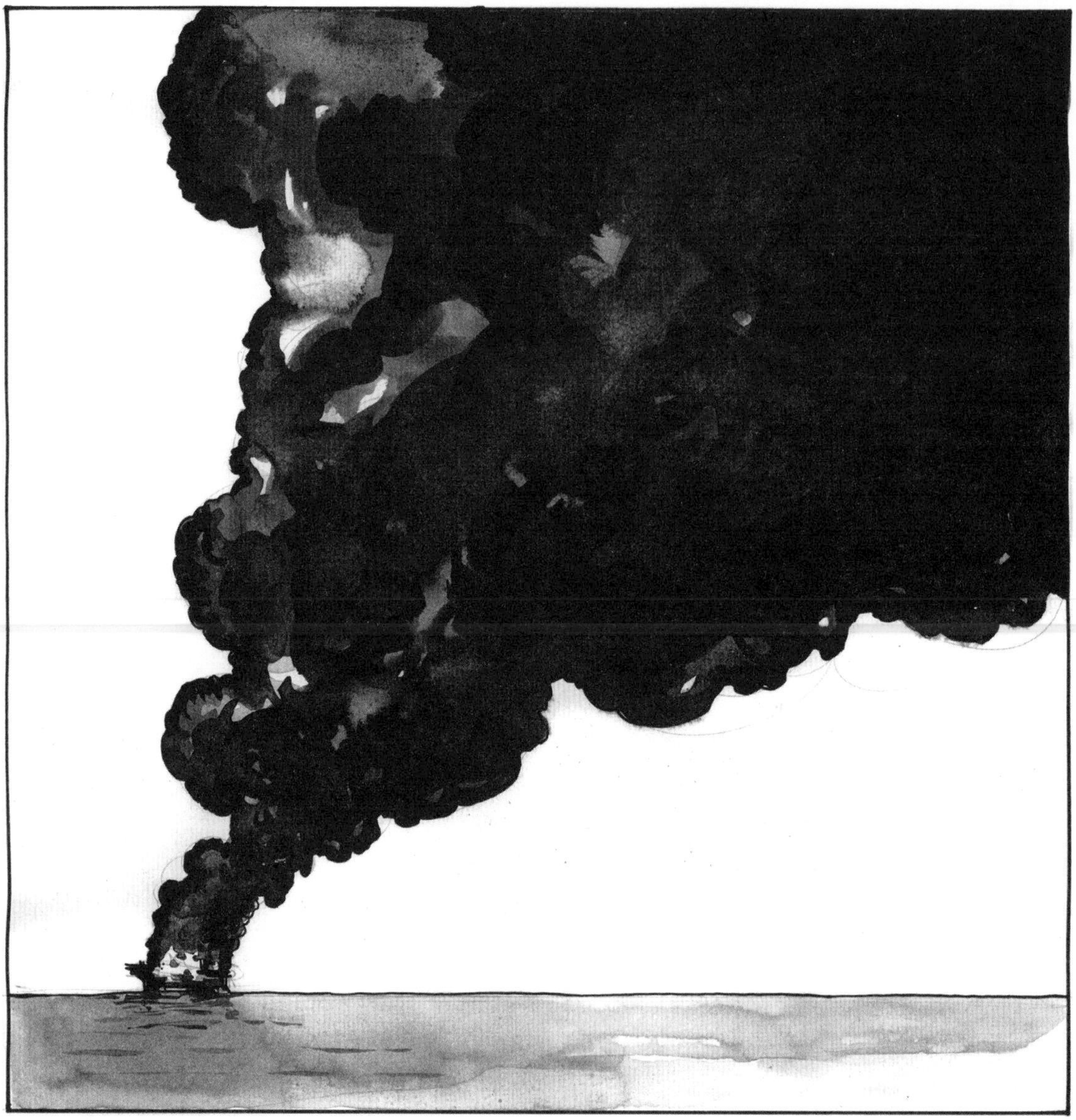

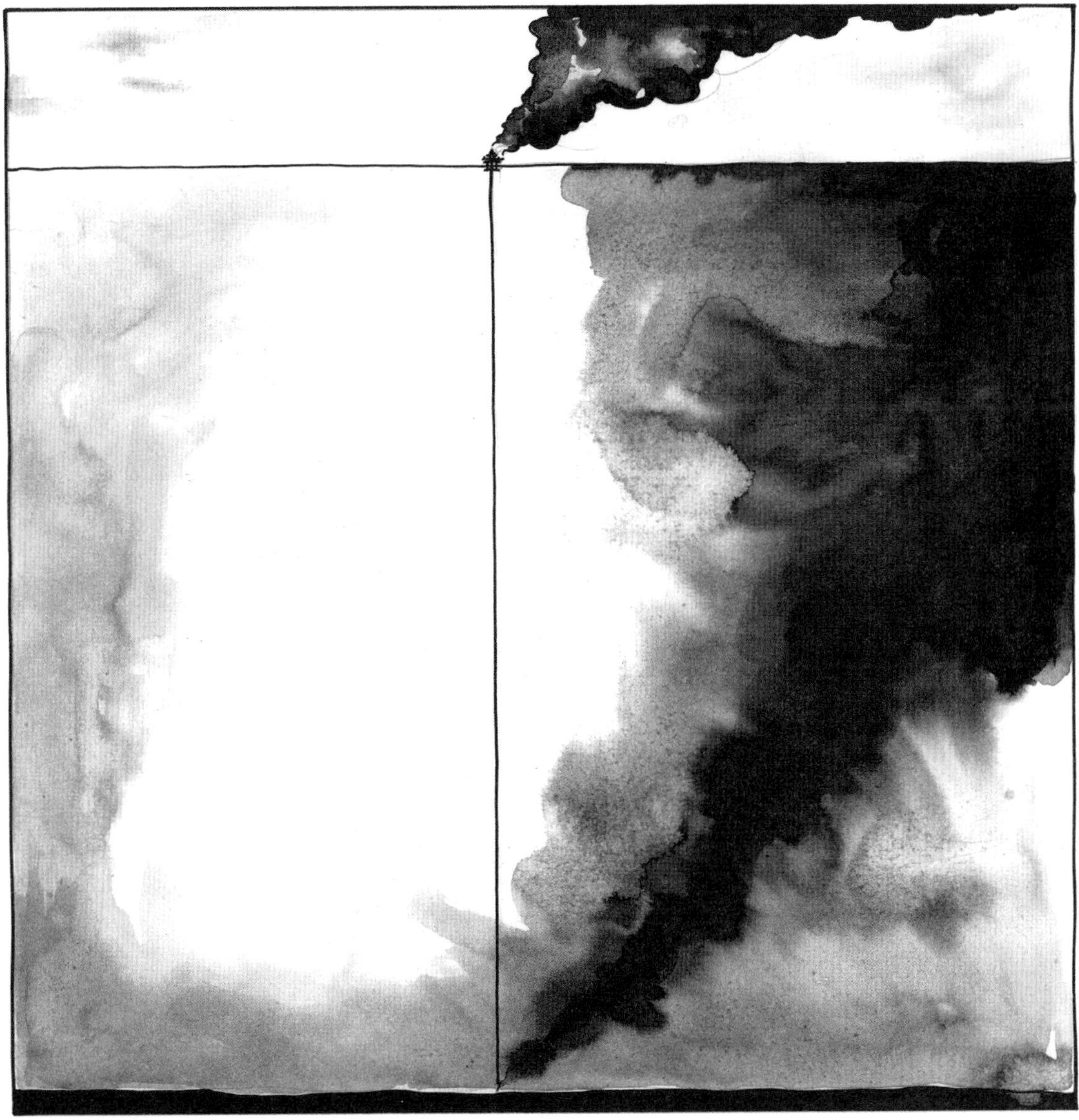

The Butterfly Effect

On the Deepwater Horizon — which cost $365 million to build — "BP had strict guidelines barring employees from carrying a cup of coffee without a lid," CNN/Money.com notes, "but no standard procedure for how to conduct a 'negative-pressure test,' a critical last step in avoiding a well blowout."

Penny wise, pound-foolish.

In the spring of 2010, BP's drilling costs on the rig were soaring toward $150 million. The lease on the rig alone cost $500,000 per day, so the company was cutting corners to cut costs.

By going with a long-string well design, which eliminated barriers to escaping gas, BP saved $7-10 million.

Haliburton recommended 21 pipe centralizers to position the carbon-steel lining inside the drill hole. BP settled for using six... and saved 10 hours on their drilling schedule, or $210,000.

By not using weighted mud to secure the well casing, BP saved $128,000 in mud and another 12 hours of labor, a total savings of $380,000.

While the American Petroleum Institute recommends circulating heavy drilling mud around the well casing as its installed, BP settled for sea water at the well's bottom... and saved another $252,000.

And when the well blew and the smoke cleared?

Eleven deaths. Eighty-seven days of oil pouring into the Gulf of Mexico. Thousands of lawsuits. An estimated $40 billion in clean-up costs.

And a brutal new case study in penny wise, pound foolish.

Miracles

New Orleans, LA

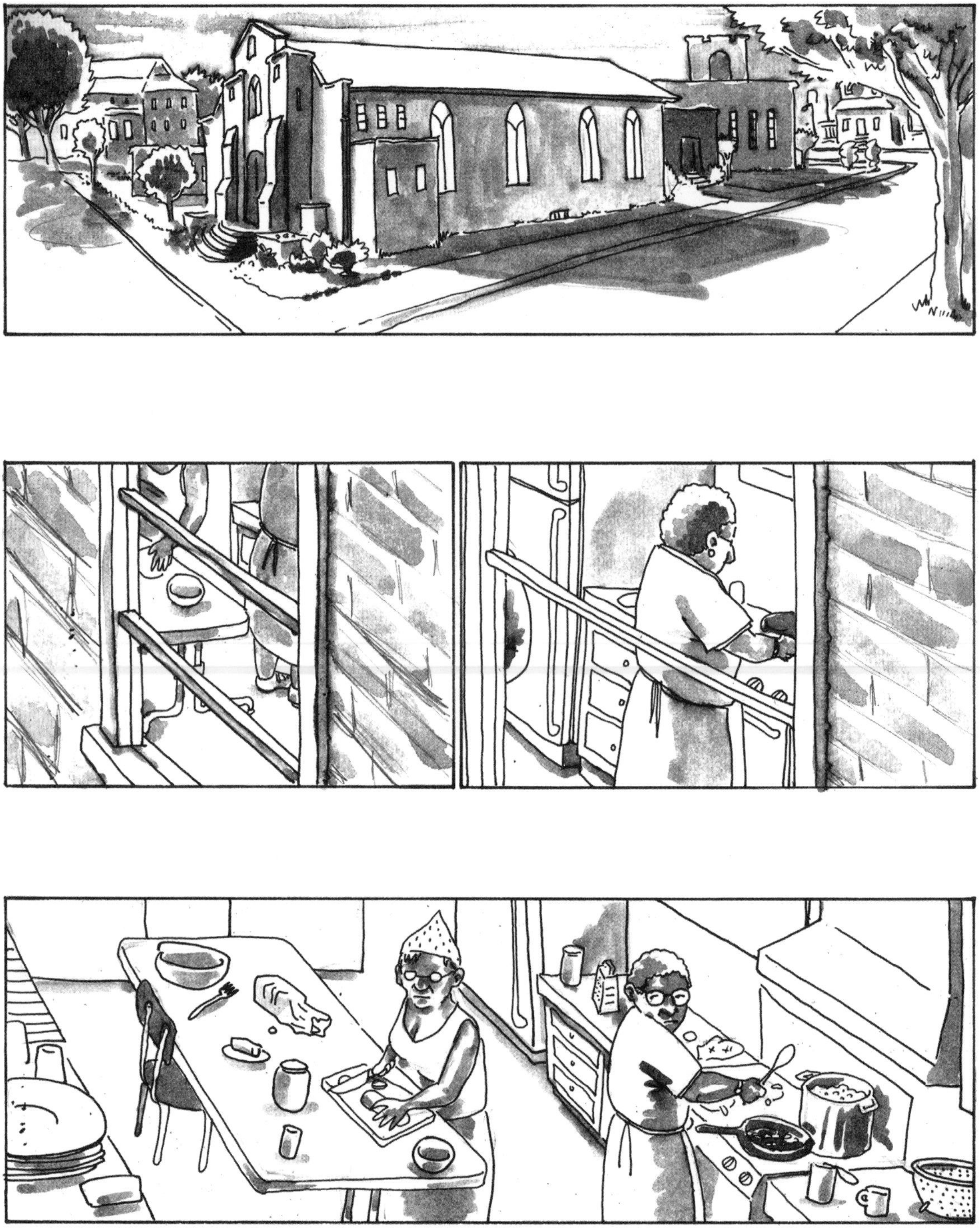

Jazzercise tonight?
Nope. Do-gooders from Orygun.
Doin' what?
Got no earthly idea. Get the door?

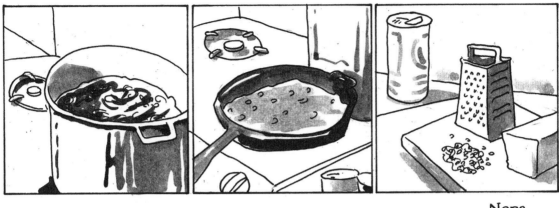

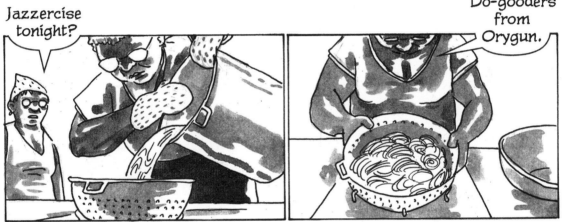

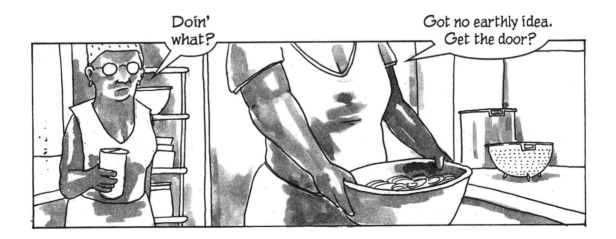

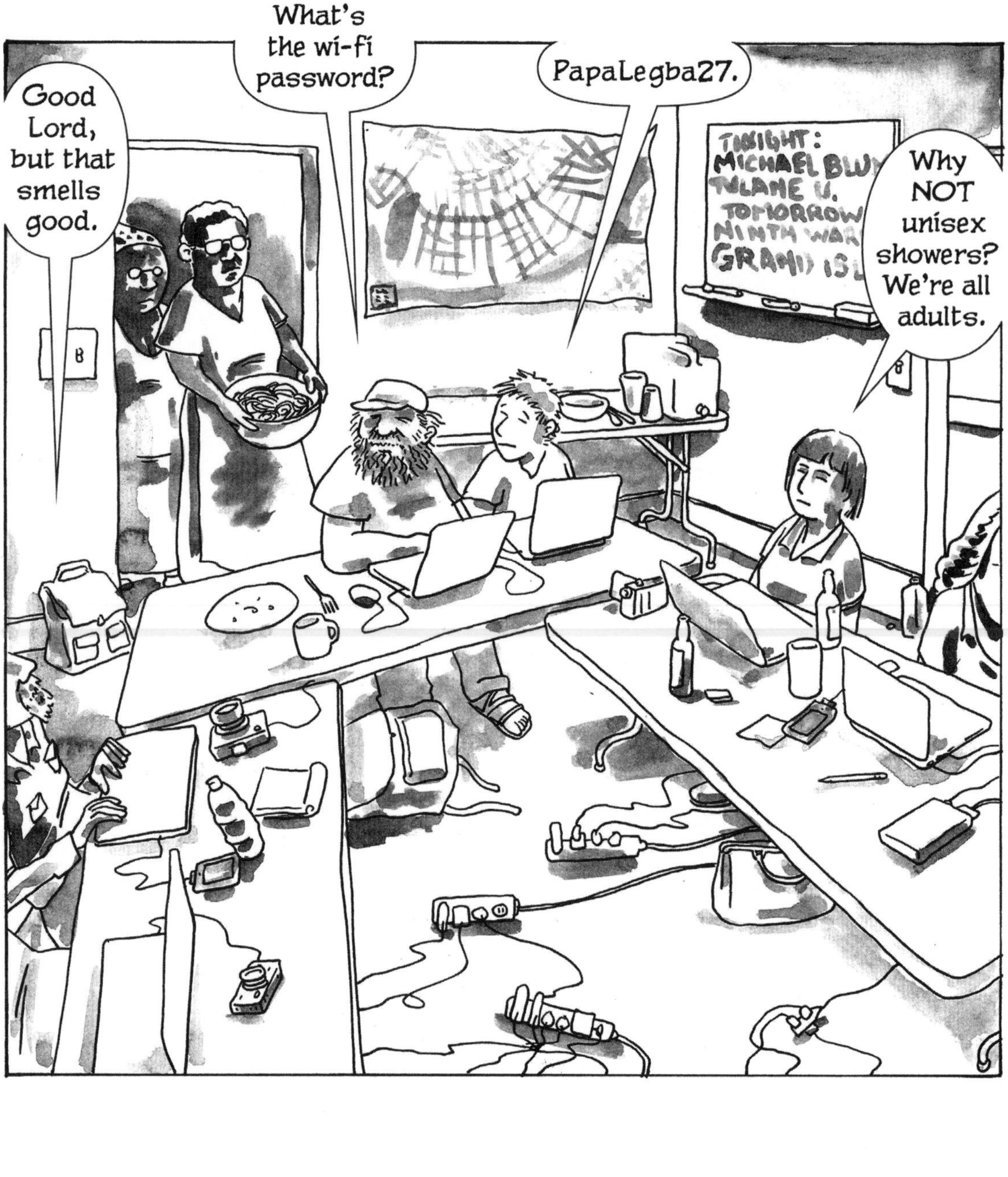
Good Lord, but that smells good.
What's the wi-fi password?
PapaLegba27.
TONIGHT:
TULANE U.
TOMORROW
Why NOT unisex showers? We're all adults.

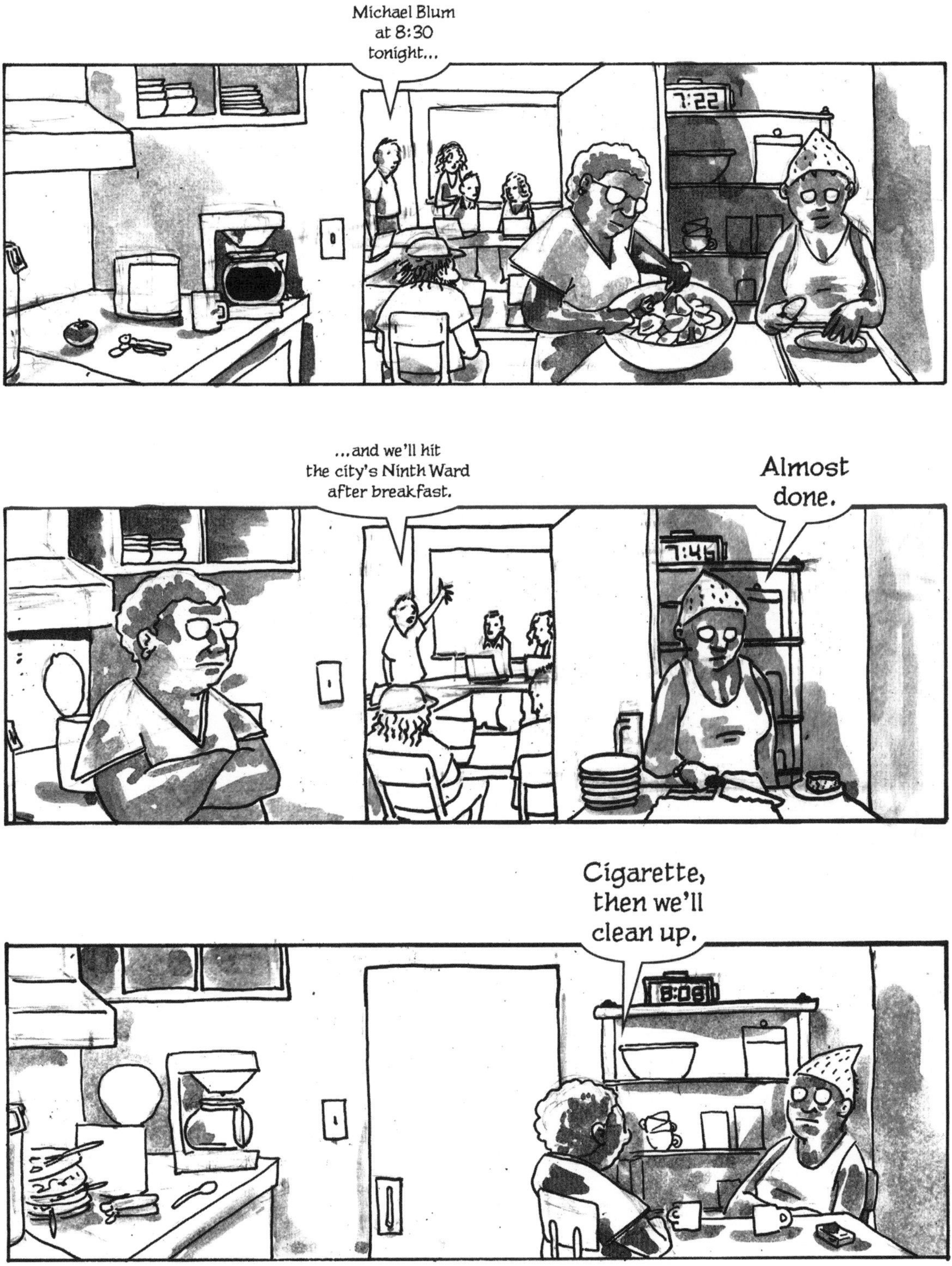
Michael Blum at 8:30 tonight...
...and we'll hit the city's Ninth Ward after breakfast.
Almost done.
Cigarette, then we'll clean up.

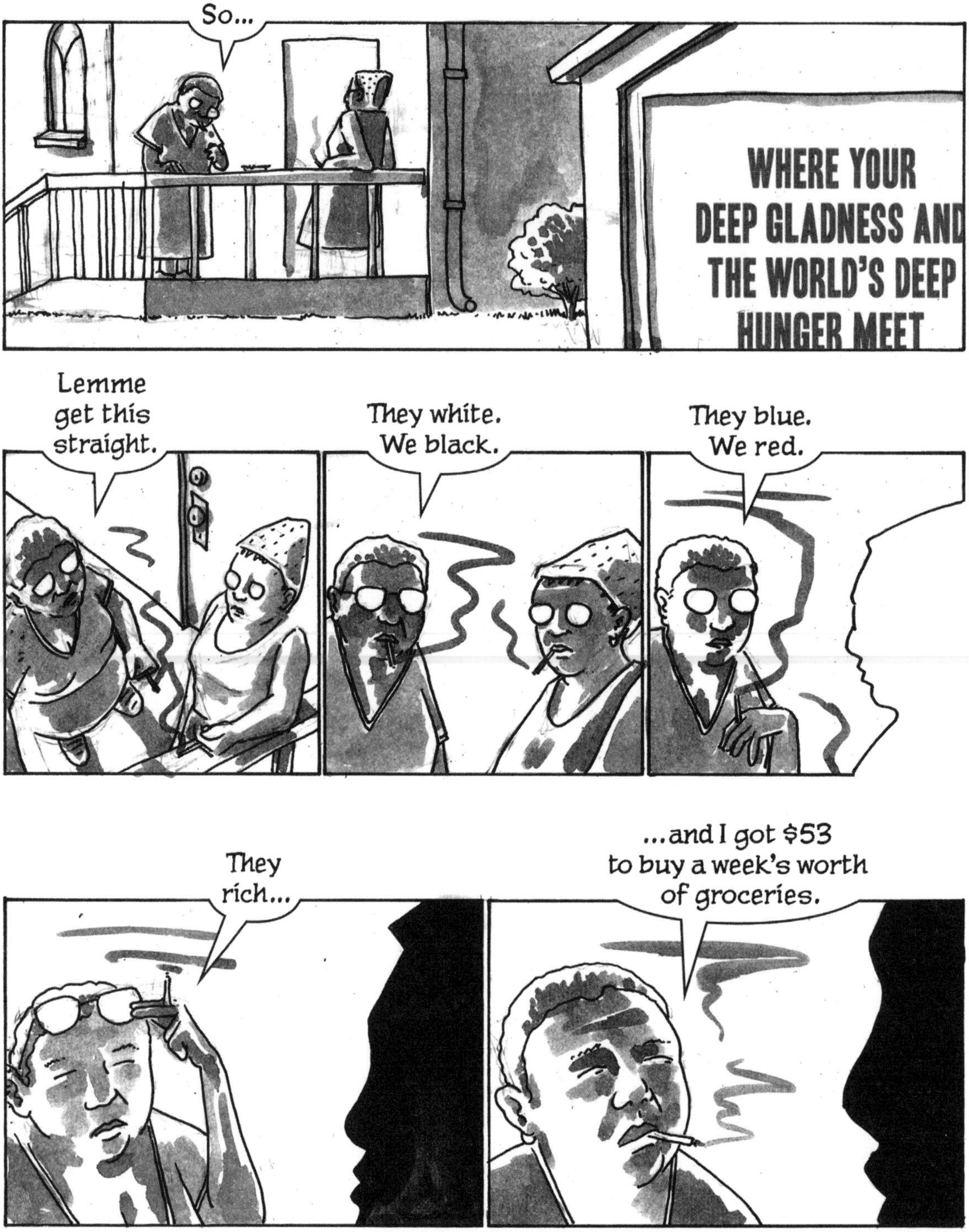
So...
WHERE YOUR DEEP GLADNESS AND THE WORLD'S DEEP HUNGER MEET
Lemme get this straight.
They white. We black.
They blue. We red.
They rich...
...and I got $53 to buy a week's worth of groceries.

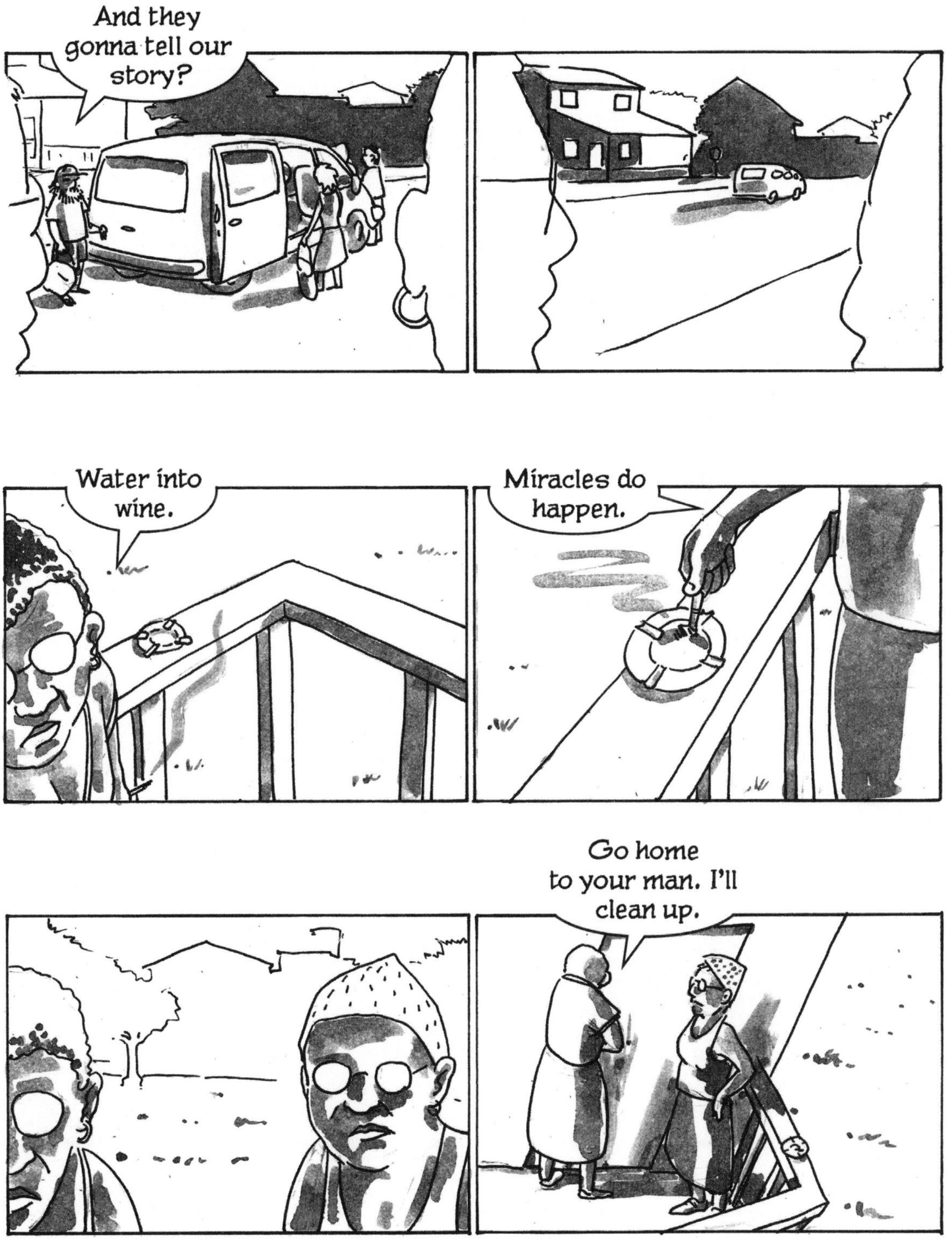
And they gonna tell our story?
Water into wine.
Miracles do happen.
Go home to your man. I'll clean up.

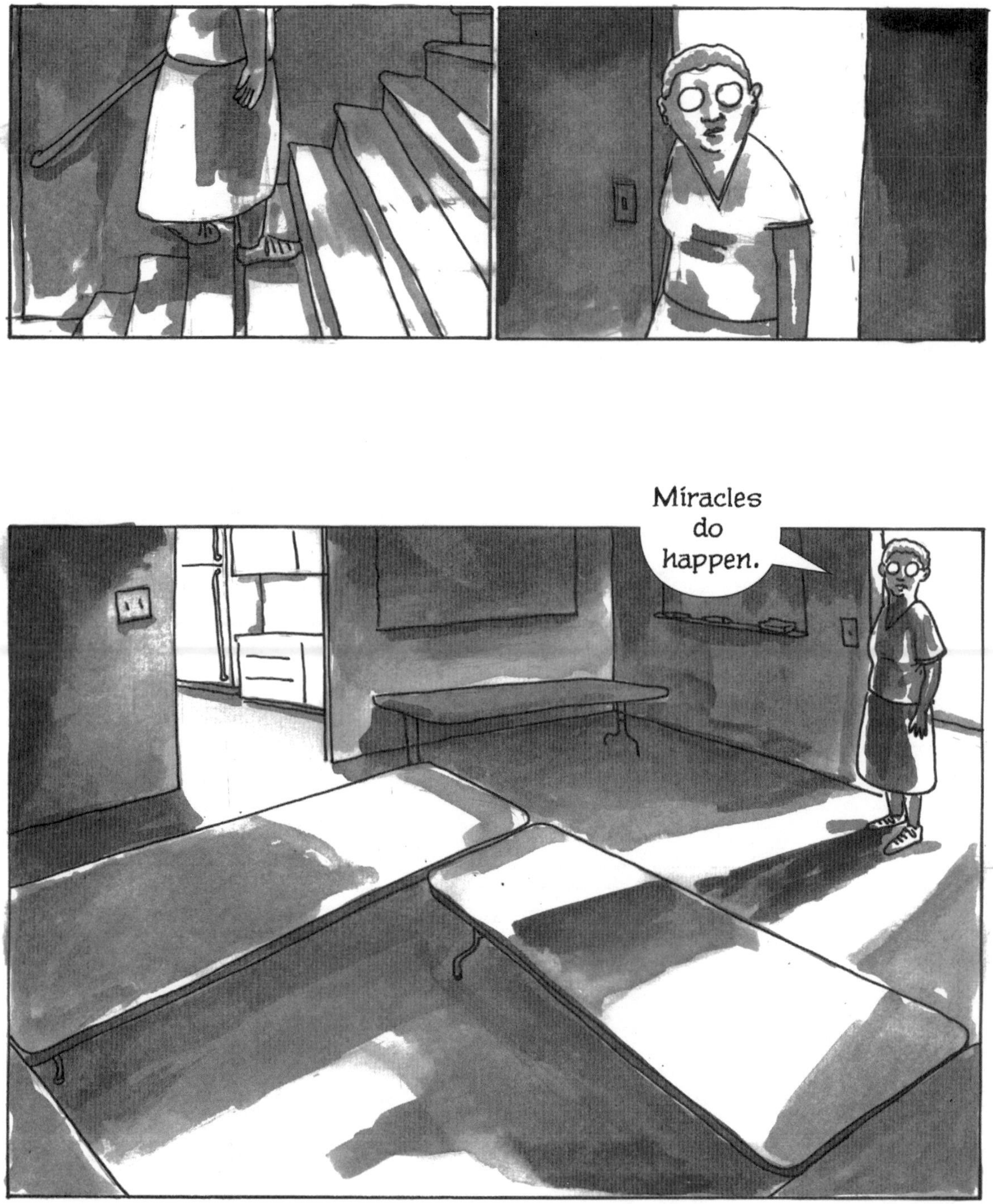
Miracles do happen.

Ninth Ward

New Orleans, LA

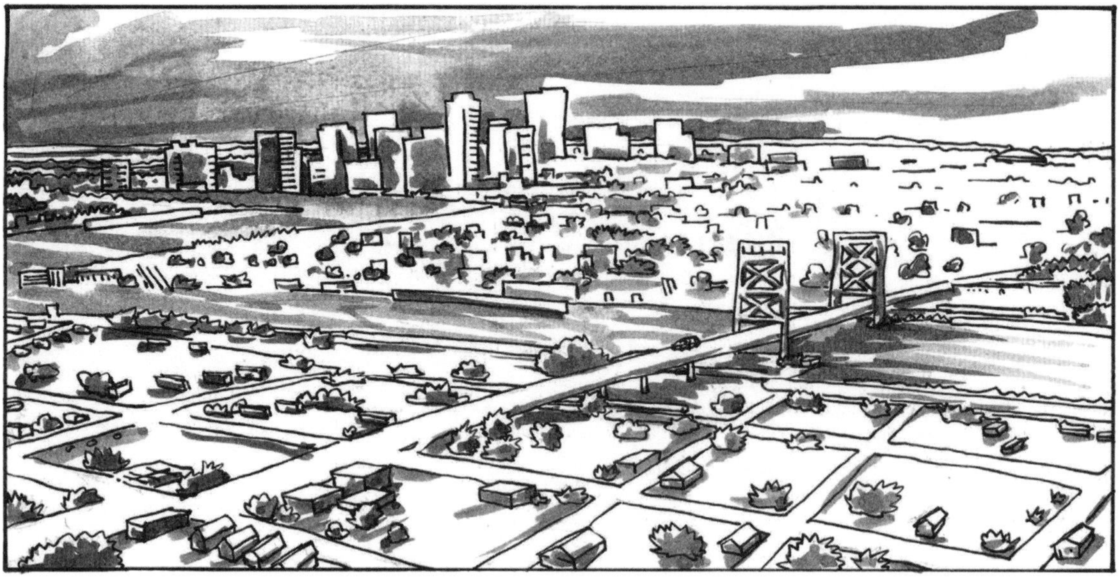

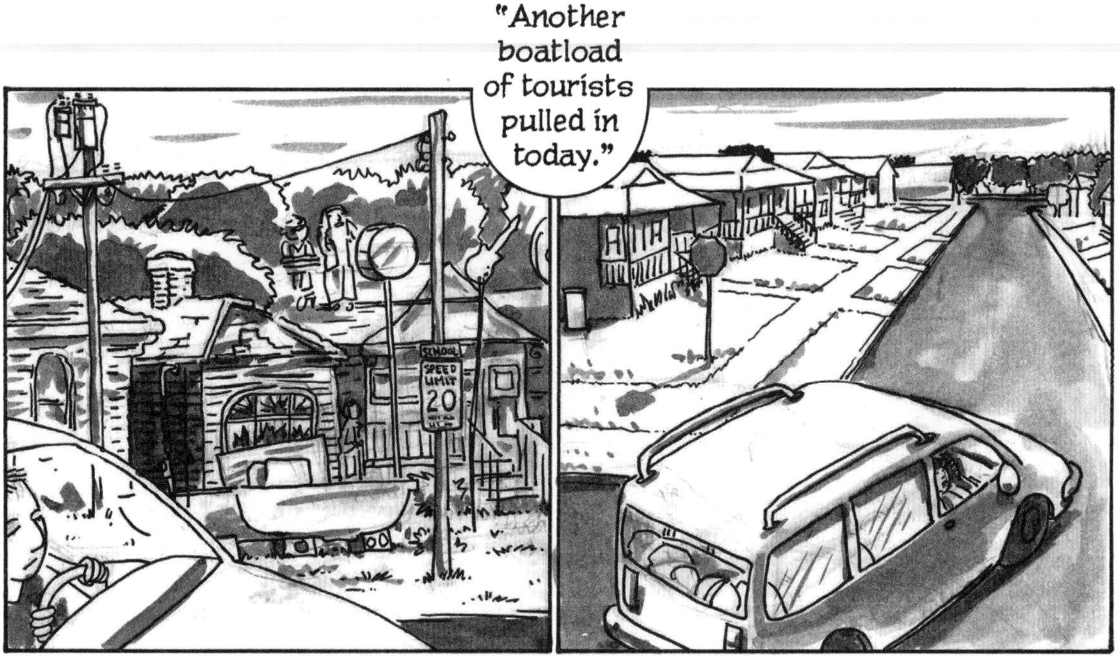
"Another boatload of tourists pulled in today."
SCHOOL
SPEED LIMIT
20

"They floated up and down the street like fat and happy bumblebees, plastered on the pollen of the Ward."

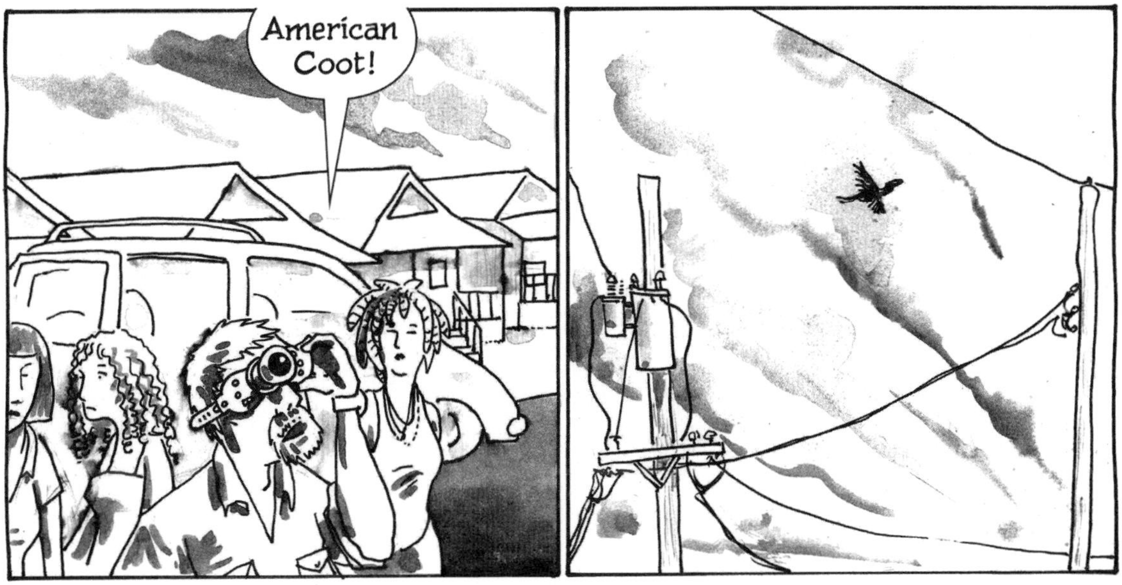
American Coot!

"Dude with the map finally puffs himself up and gives a speech."

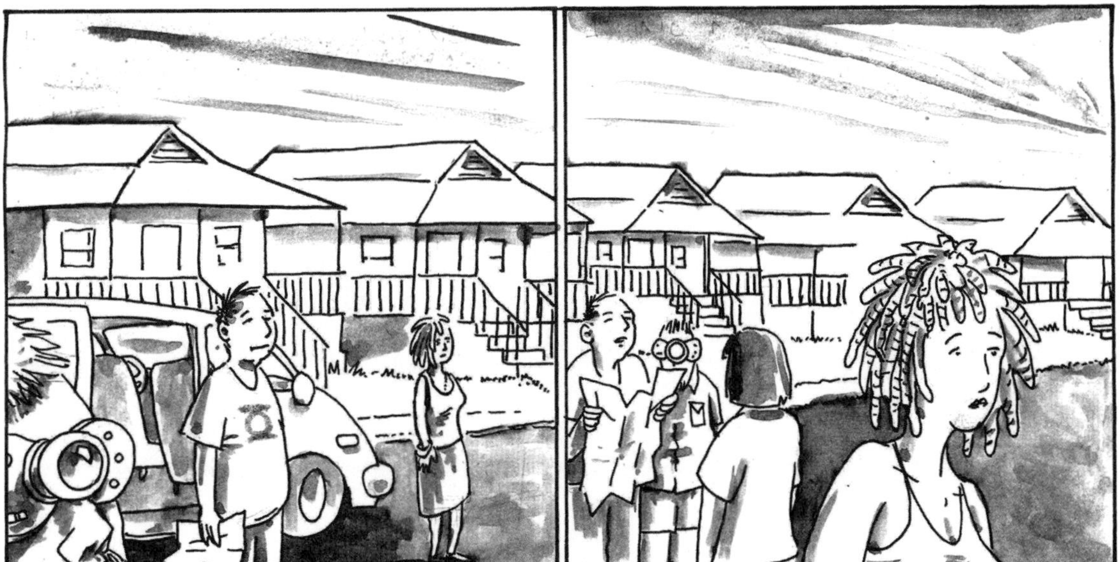

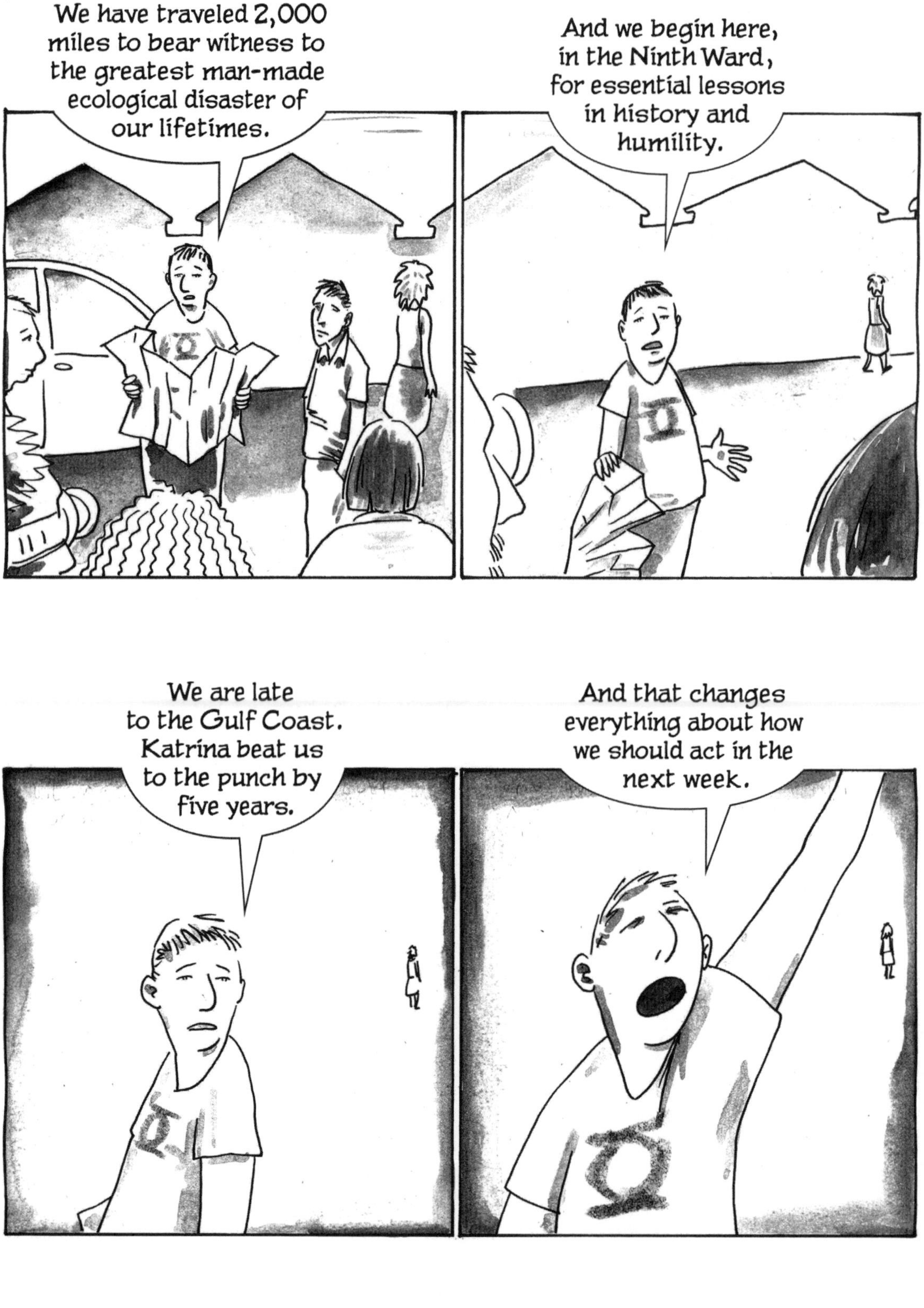
We have traveled 2,000 miles to bear witness to the greatest man-made ecological disaster of our lifetimes.
And we begin here, in the Ninth Ward, for essential lessons in history and humility.
We are late to the Gulf Coast. Katrina beat us to the punch by five years.
And that changes everything about how we should act in the next week.

"Me, I'm watchin' the girl."

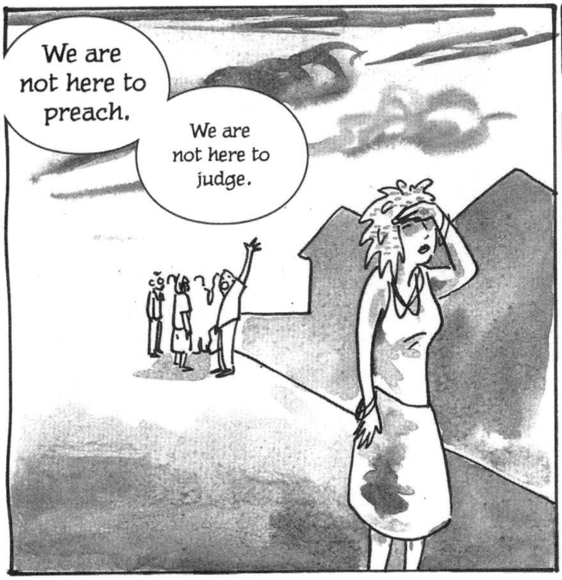
We are not here to preach.
We are not here to judge.

"White chick. Gangsta hair. Dreadlock diva."

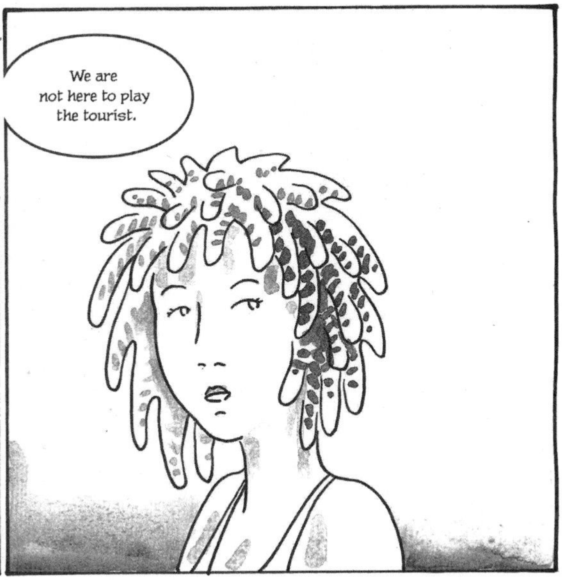
We are not here to play the tourist.

"Fearless, too. Like she'd already come to terms with strange men and dark places. Walked smack up to me. Asked to take a picture."

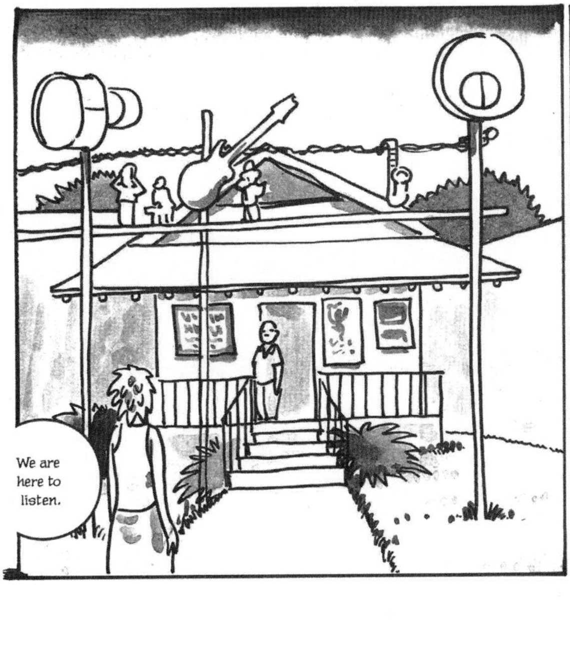
We are here to listen.

"So I invite her inside."

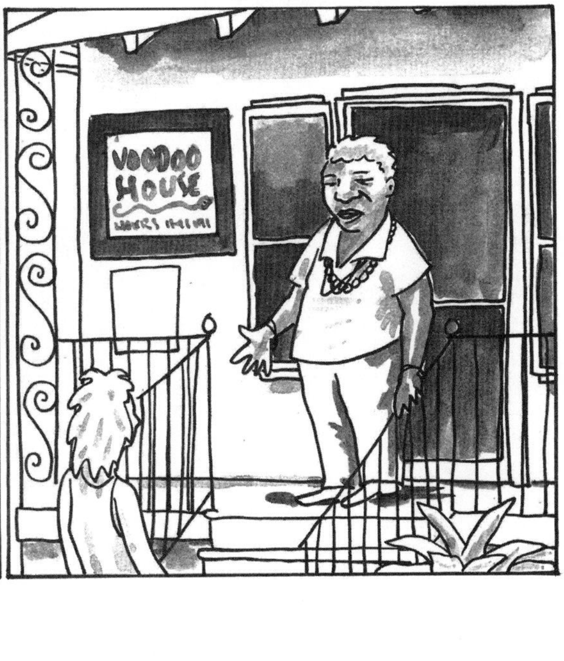
VOODOO HOUSE

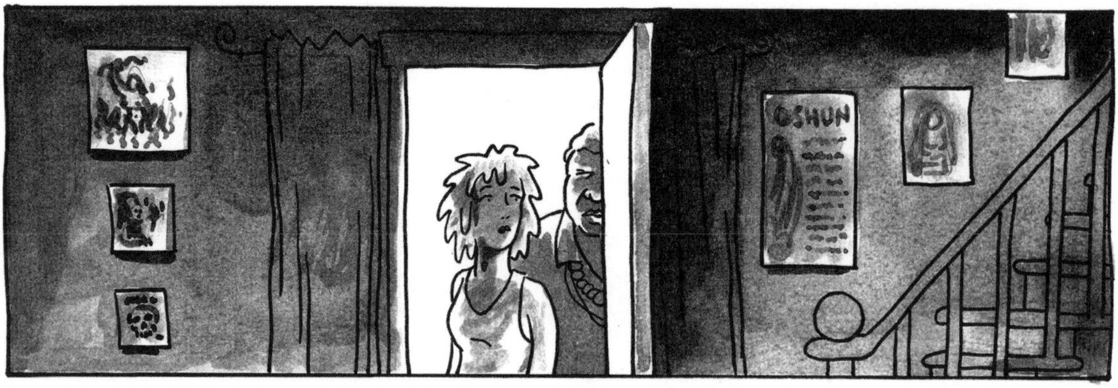
OSHUN

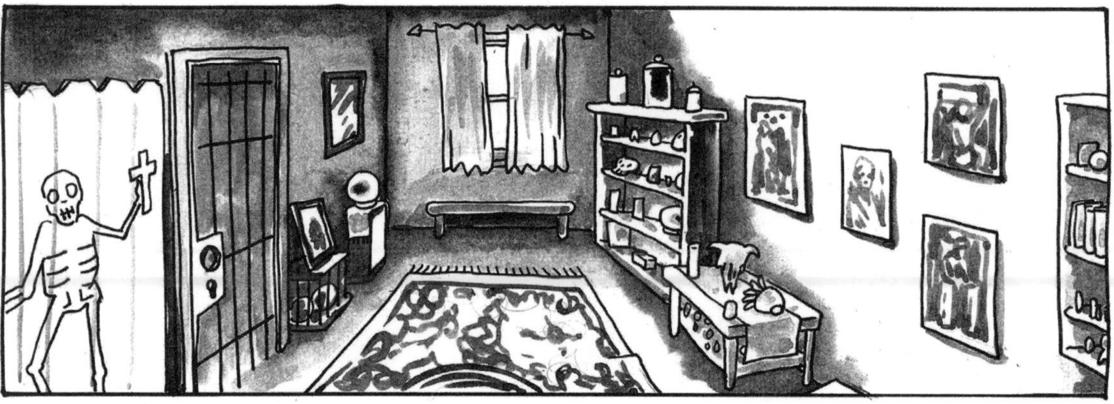

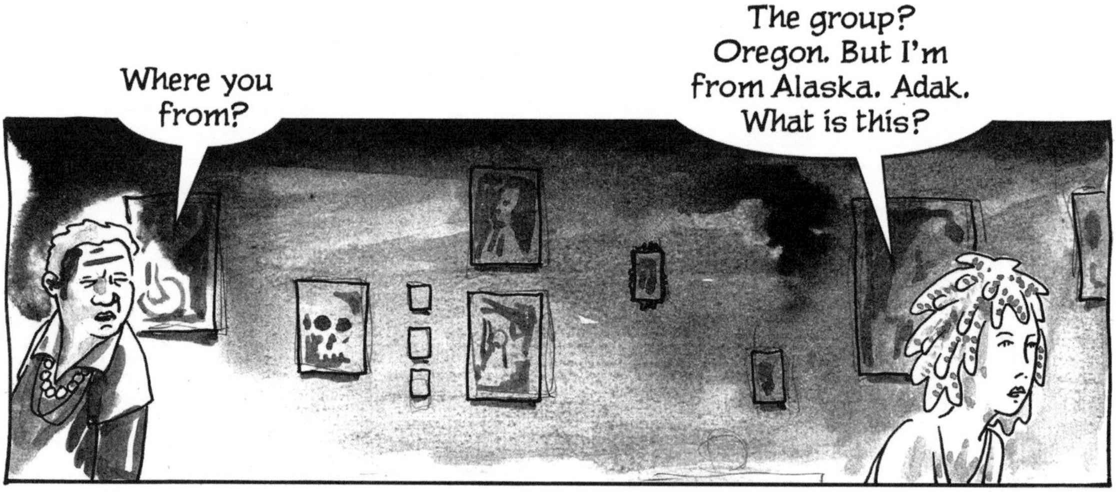
Where you from?
The group? Oregon. But I'm from Alaska. Adak. What is this?

Hurricane prevention ritual altar.
And what's this?
Katrina. The high-water mark.
Bitch ran over us. Hurdled the levees. Flooded the ward. Shut down the refineries. Spanked the marshes. Unleashed the cops.
Stole the magic.
Well, that sucks...
Oh, shit...

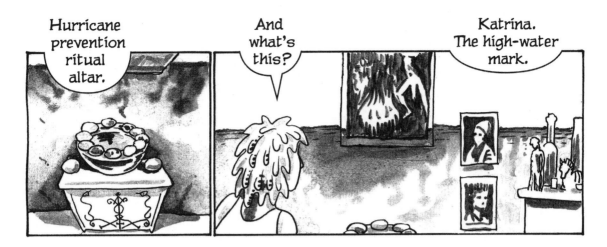

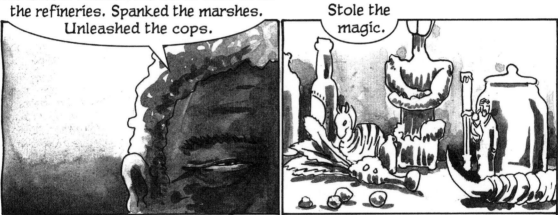

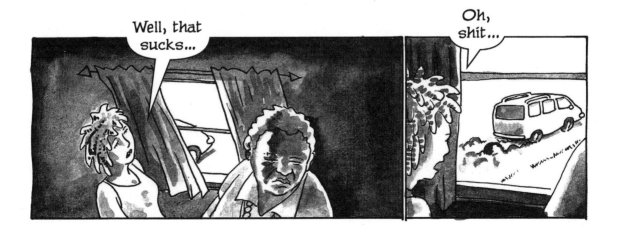

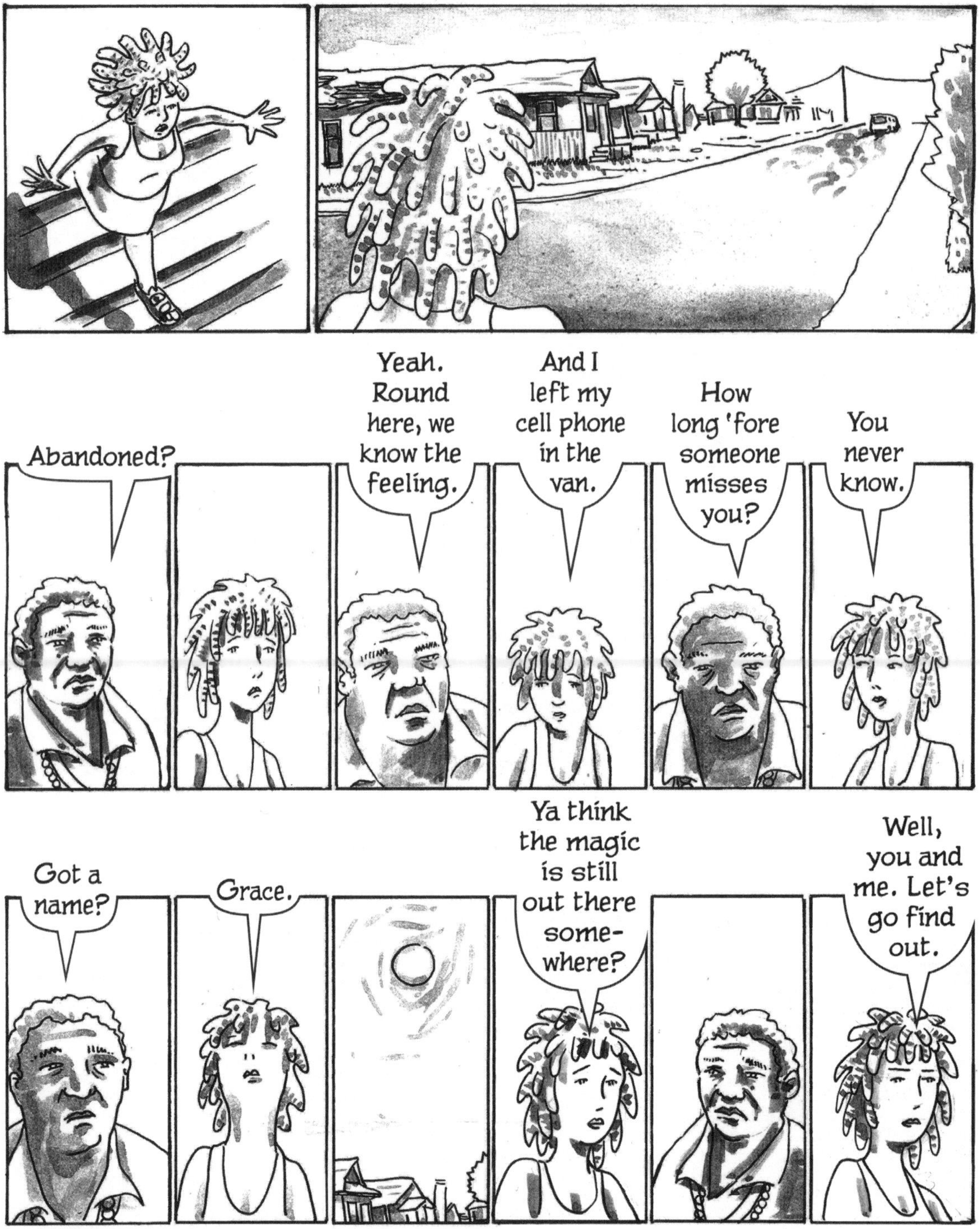
Abandoned?
Yeah. Round here, we know the feeling.
And I left my cell phone in the van.
How long 'fore someone misses you?
You never know.
Got a name?
Grace.
Ya think the magic is still out there some-where?
Well, you and me. Let's go find out.

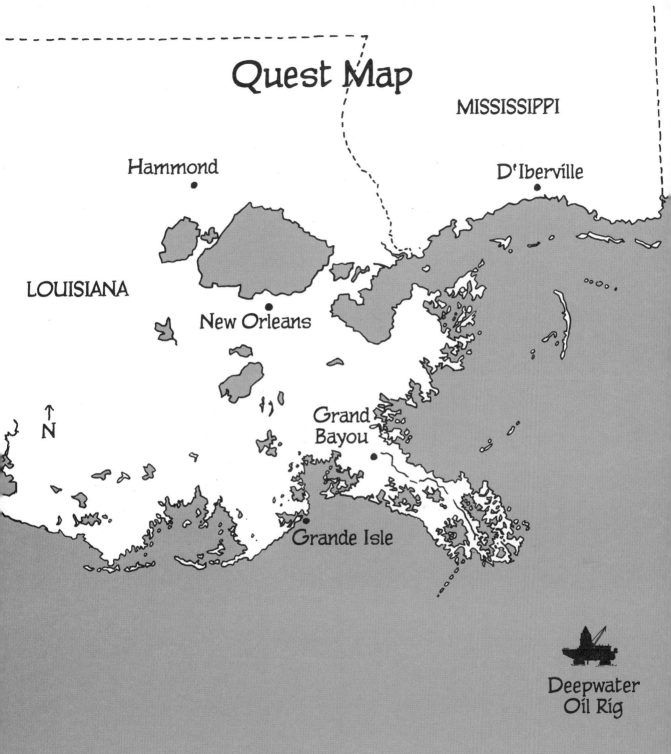

Quest Map

MISSISSIPPI

Hammond

D'Iberville

LOUISIANA

New Orleans

↑
N

Grand
Bayou

Grande Isle

Deepwater
Oil Rig

20 mi

Shark

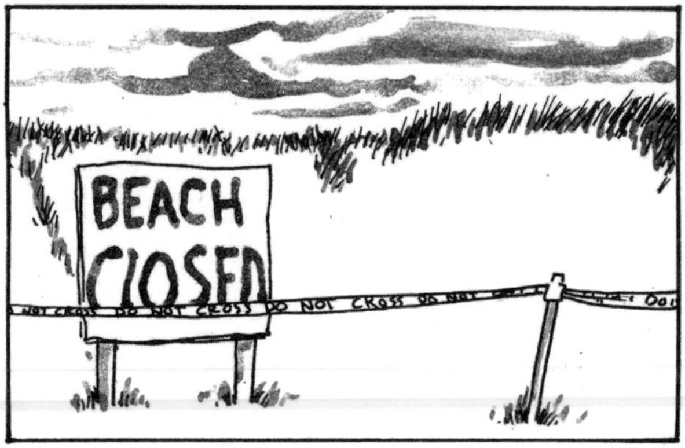
BEACH
CLOSED
DO NOT CROSS DO NOT CROSS DO NOT CROSS

Grand Isle, LA

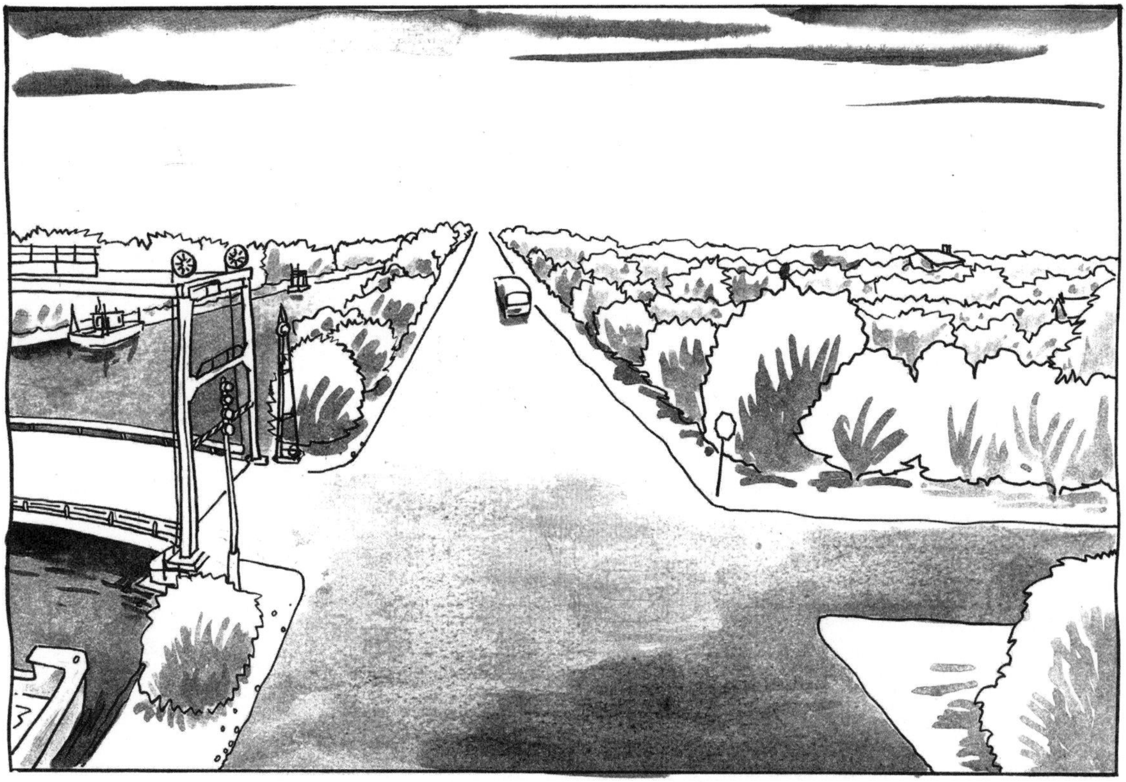

We went, that
first night...

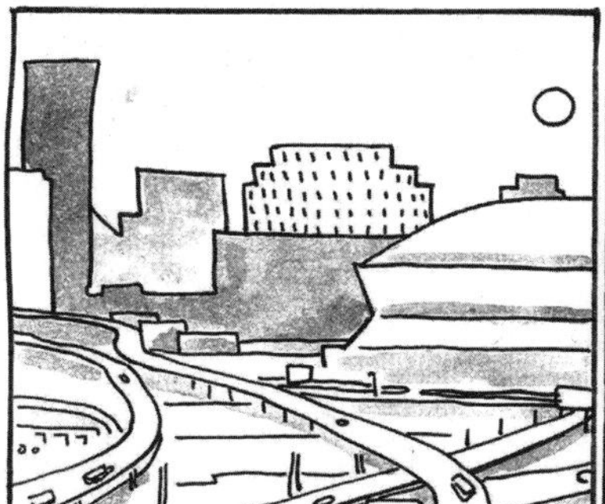

...to Tulane University,
the St. Charles
Campus...

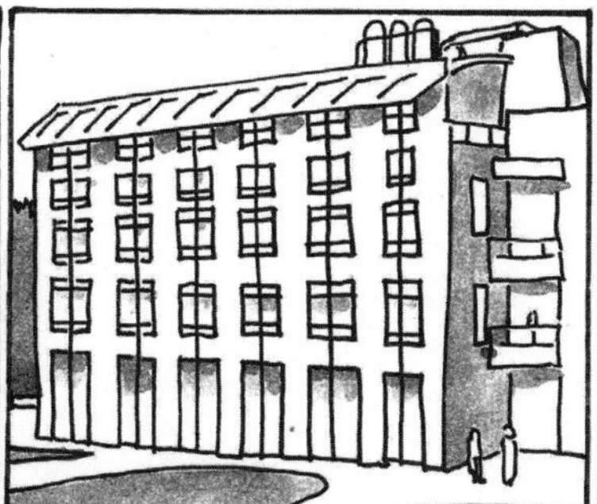

...to meet Michael Blum,
Stephen Colbert's favorite
coastal ecologist.

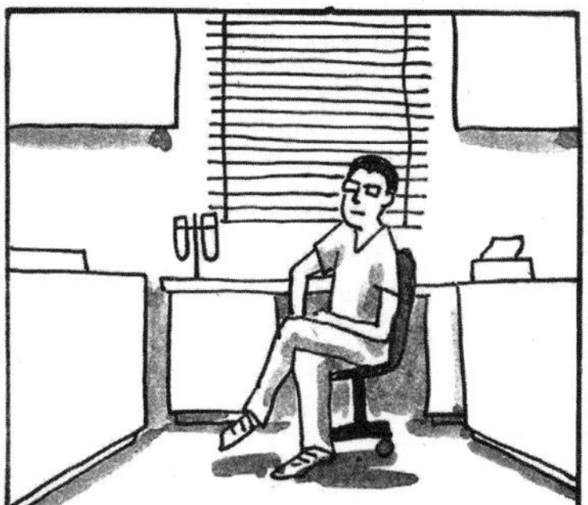

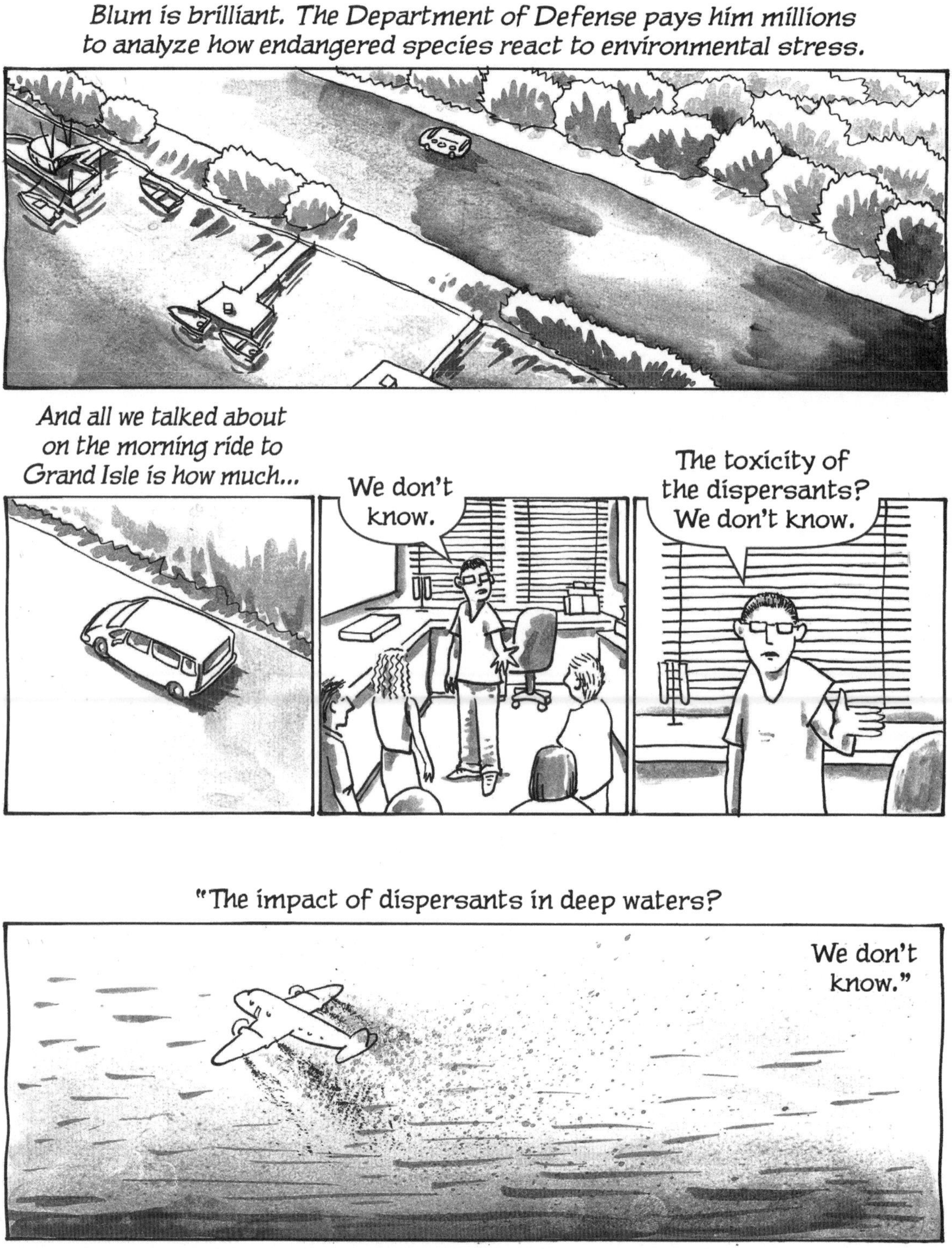
Blum is brilliant. The Department of Defense pays him millions to analyze how endangered species react to environmental stress.
And all we talked about on the morning ride to Grand Isle is how much...
We don't know.
The toxicity of the dispersants? We don't know.
"The impact of dispersants in deep waters?
We don't know."

It doesn't help, Blum said, that most of the local scientists were already locked up in contracts with British Petroleum.

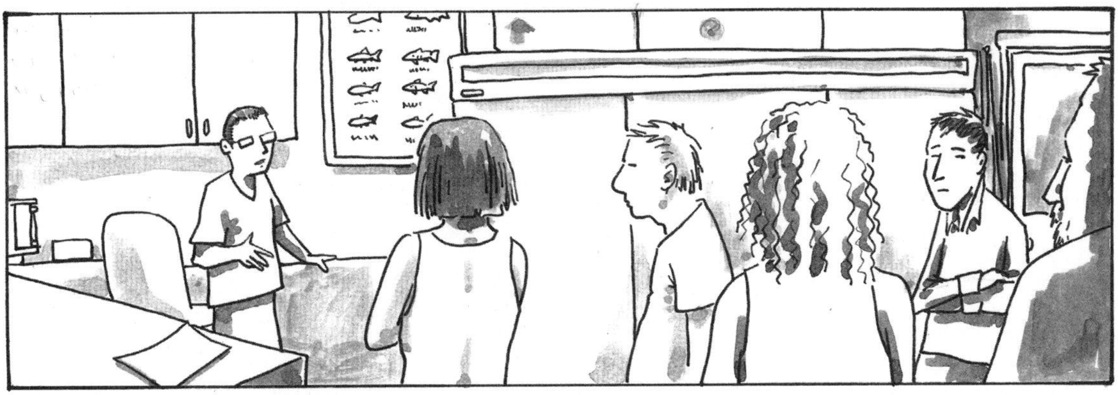

"Twenty-five percent of the oil has dissolved, much like sugar dissolves in water.

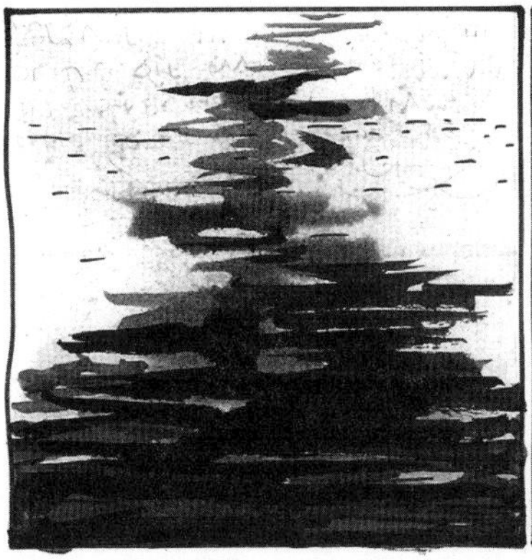

"But you'd drink sugar water.

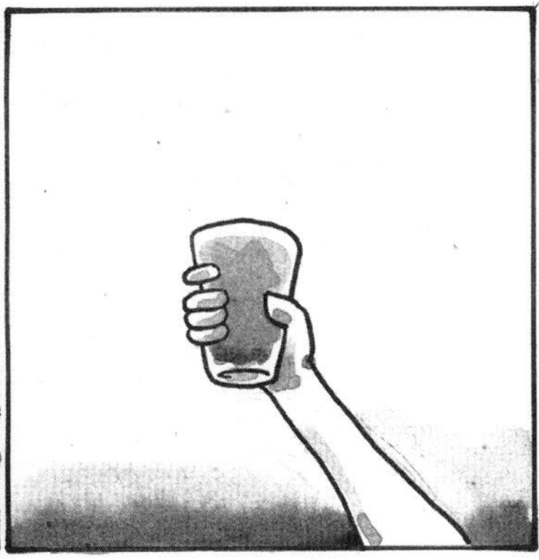

"Would you drink oil water?"

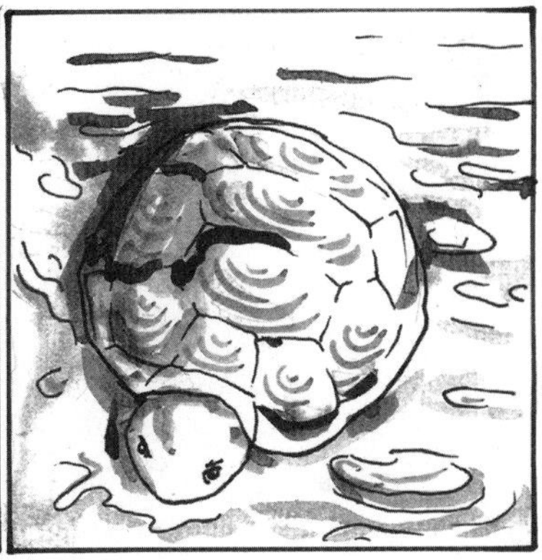

Halfway to Grand Isle, we had Louisiana's answer.

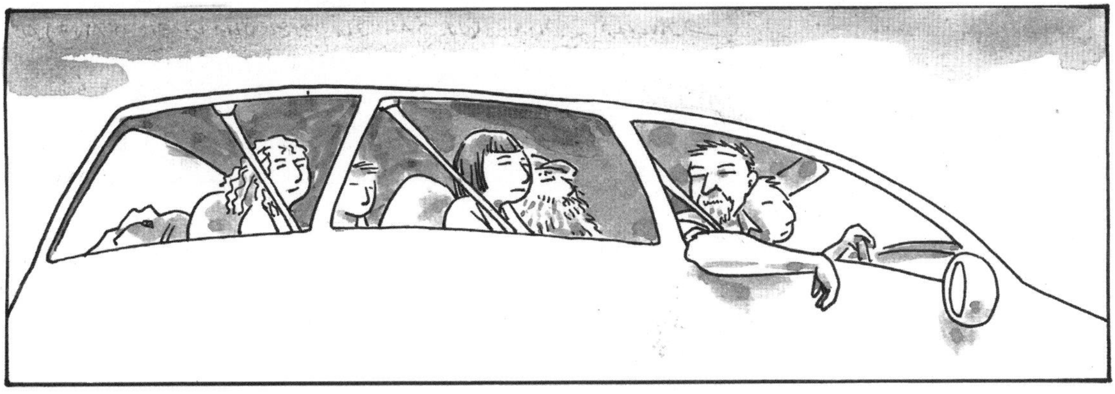

We piled out of the van, convinced we'd finally crossed

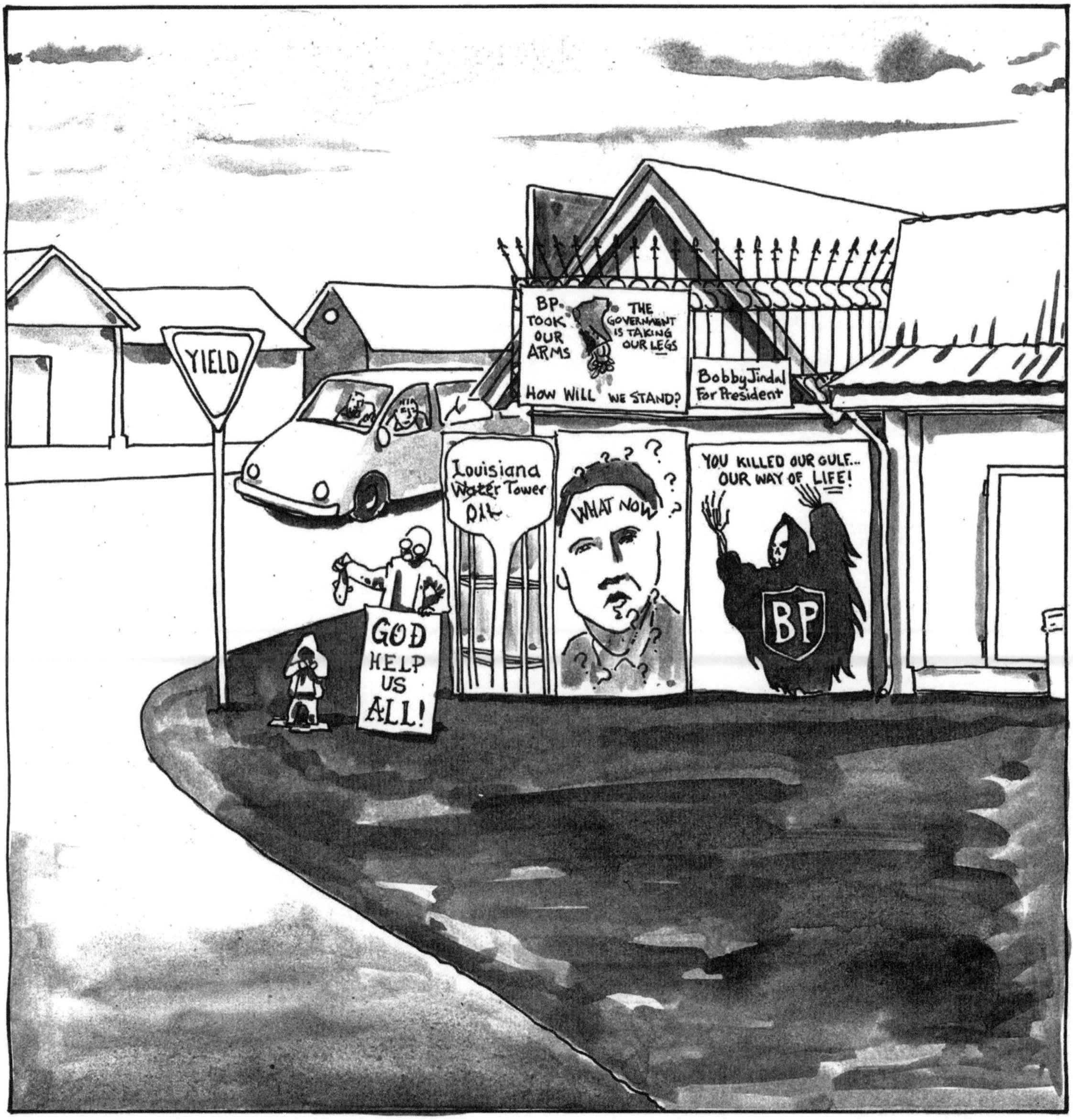
YIELD
BP TOOK OUR ARMS
THE GOVERNMENT IS TAKING OUR LEGS
HOW WILL WE STAND?
Bobby Jindal For President
Louisiana Water Tower
WHAT NOW
YOU KILLED OUR GULF... OUR WAY OF LIFE!
BP
GOD HELP US ALL!

into a Louisiana you couldn't read about back in Portland.

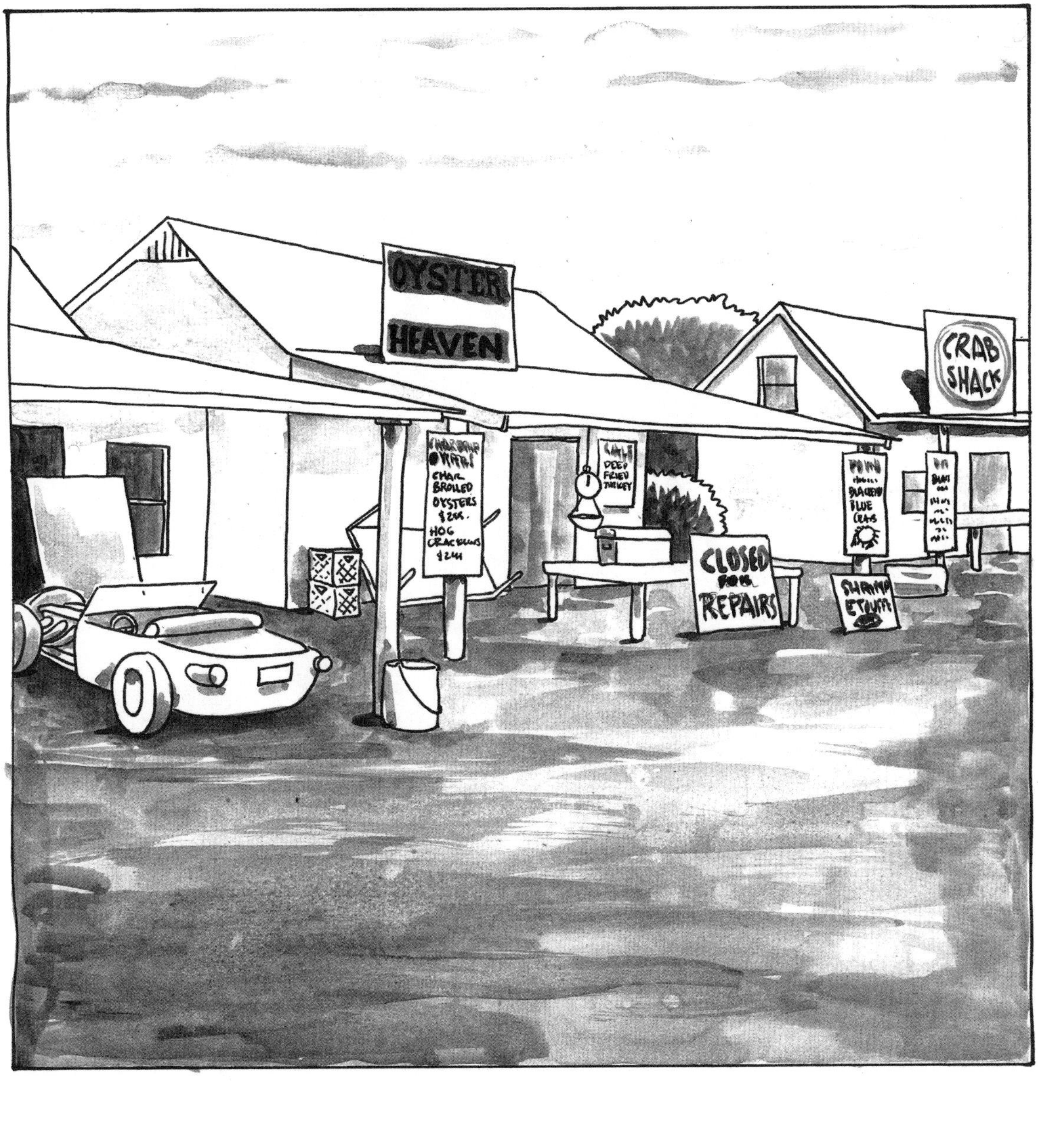
OYSTER HEAVEN
CHAR BROILED OYSTERS
HOG
DEEP FRIED TURKEY
CLOSED
REPAIRS
BLUE
CRAB SHACK

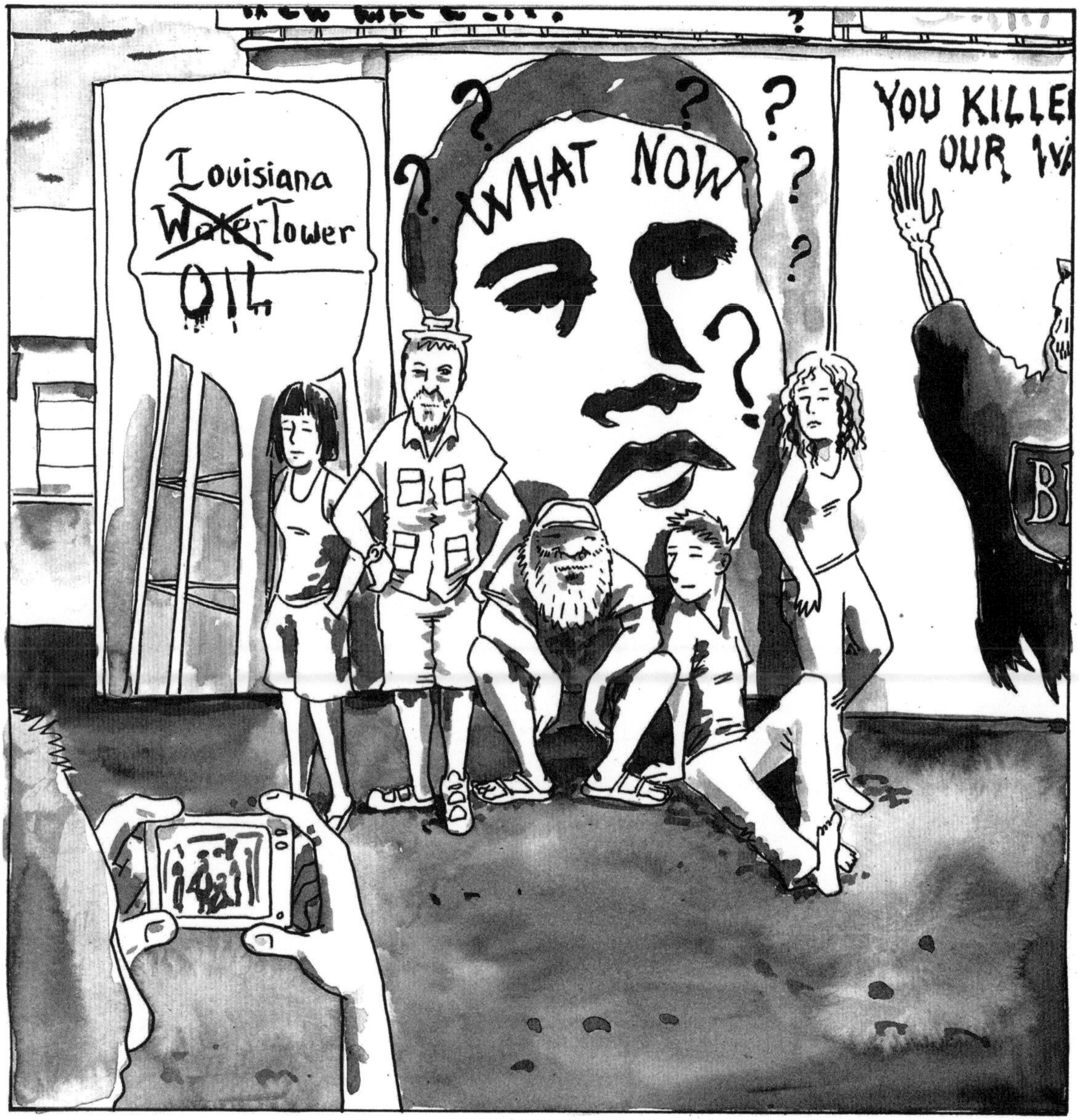
Louisiana
Water Tower
OIL
WHAT NOW?
YOU KILLE
OUR WA

We were due in Grand Isle, two hours south of New Orleans, at 9 a.m. for a tour of the brown-pelican colonies in the salt marshes abutting the peninsula.

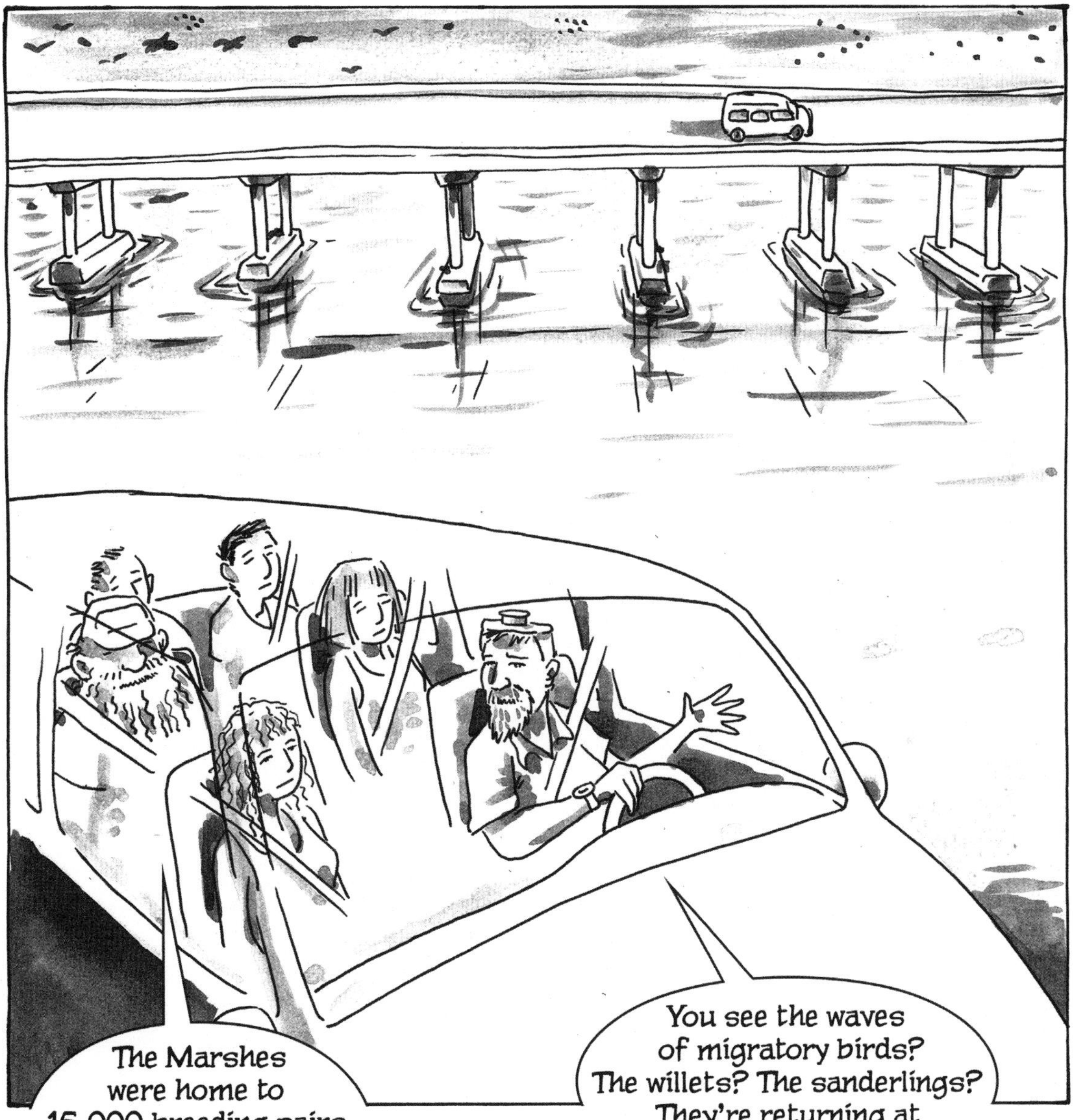

The Marshes were home to 15,000 breeding pairs before Katrina and Rita rolled through in 2006.
You see the waves of migratory birds? The willets? The sanderlings? They're returning at the worst time.

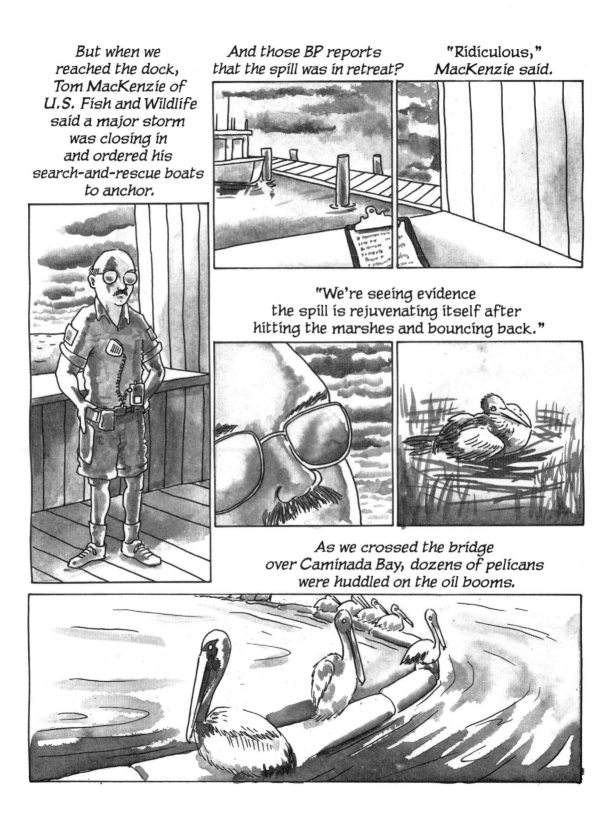

But when we reached the dock, Tom MacKenzie of U.S. Fish and Wildlife said a major storm was closing in and ordered his search-and-rescue boats to anchor.

And those BP reports that the spill was in retreat?

"Ridiculous," MacKenzie said.

"We're seeing evidence the spill is rejuvenating itself after hitting the marshes and bouncing back."

As we crossed the bridge over Caminada Bay, dozens of pelicans were huddled on the oil booms.

Few other summer regulars had returned to the barrier island.
The beachcombers had fled to Myrtle or Daytona.

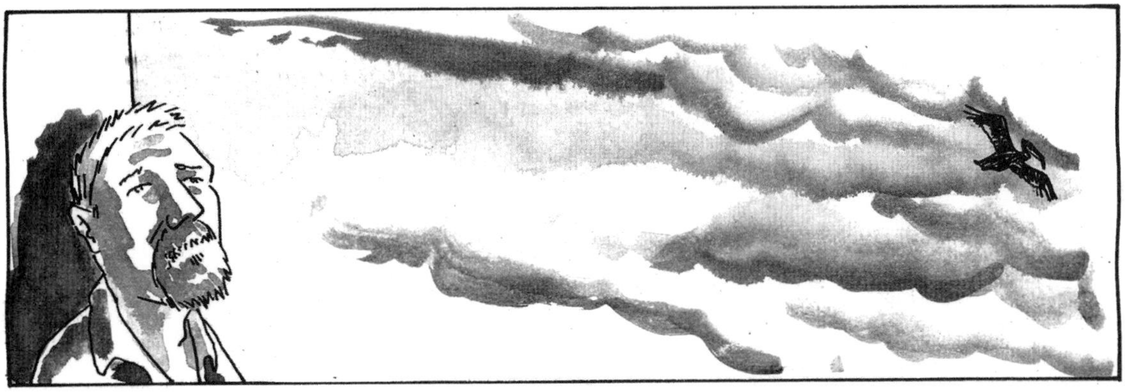

The locals adjust.

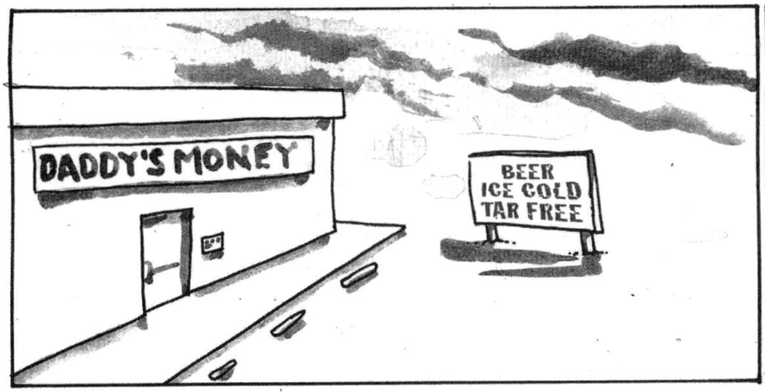
DADDY'S MONEY
BEER
ICE COLD
TAR FREE

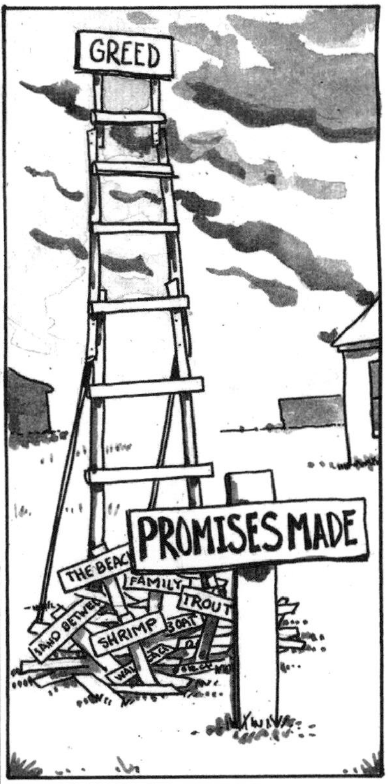
GREED
PROMISES MADE
FAMILY
TROUT
SHRIMP
BOAT

The main drag
through town
was littered with
gallows' humor.

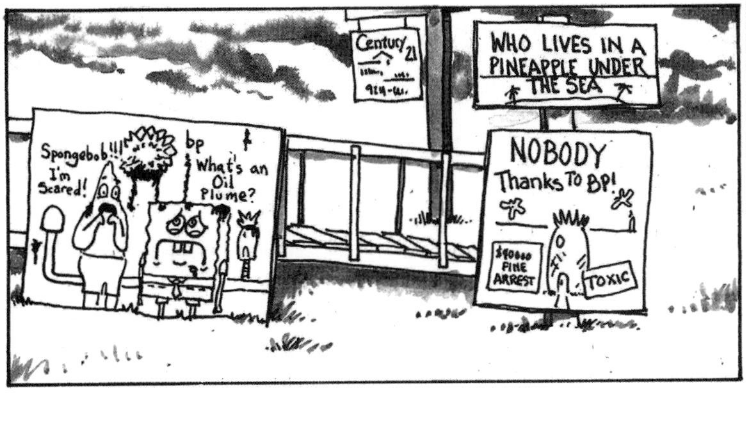
Spongebob!!!
I'm Scared!
bp
What's an Oil Plume?
Century 21
WHO LIVES IN A PINEAPPLE UNDER THE SEA
NOBODY
Thanks To BP!
$90000 FINE ARREST
TOXIC

At 3 p.m., we went out with the tide.

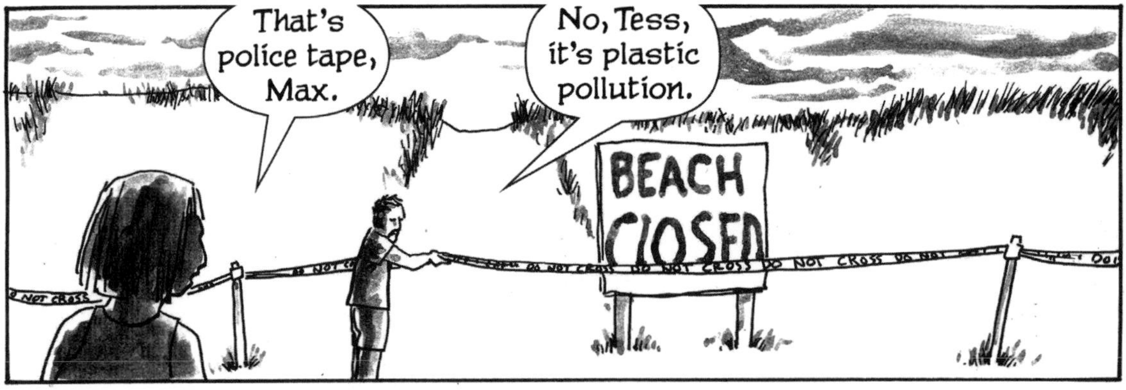
That's police tape, Max.
No, Tess, it's plastic pollution.
BEACH CLOSED

The beach was stripped clean, virtually sterilized, courtesy of BP's version of an ice-rink Zamboni.

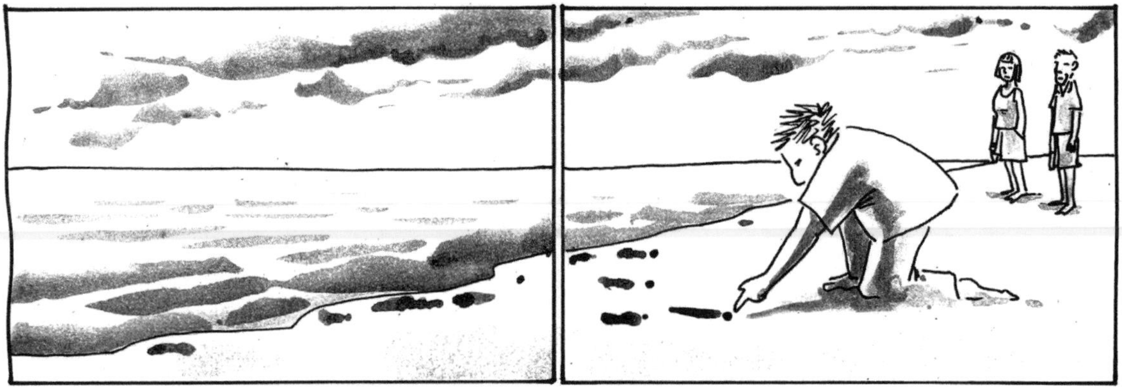

There were few waves, few birds, no boats offshore, only a half-dozen oil rigs on the listless, monotone horizon.

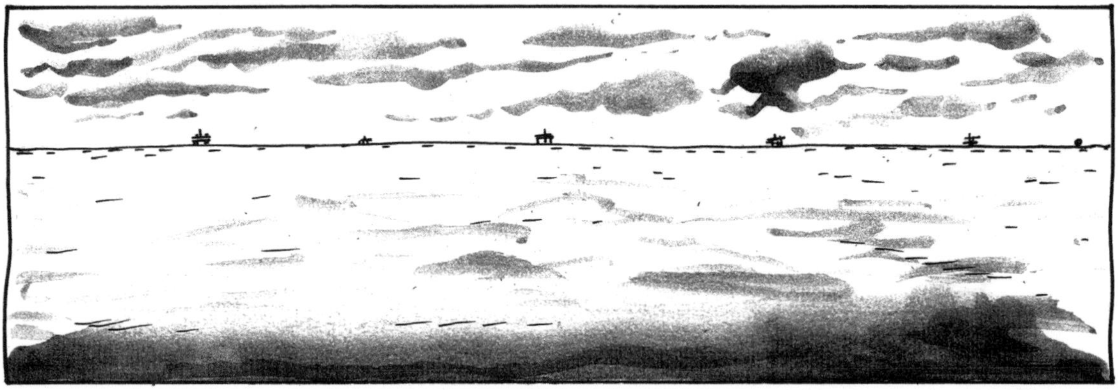

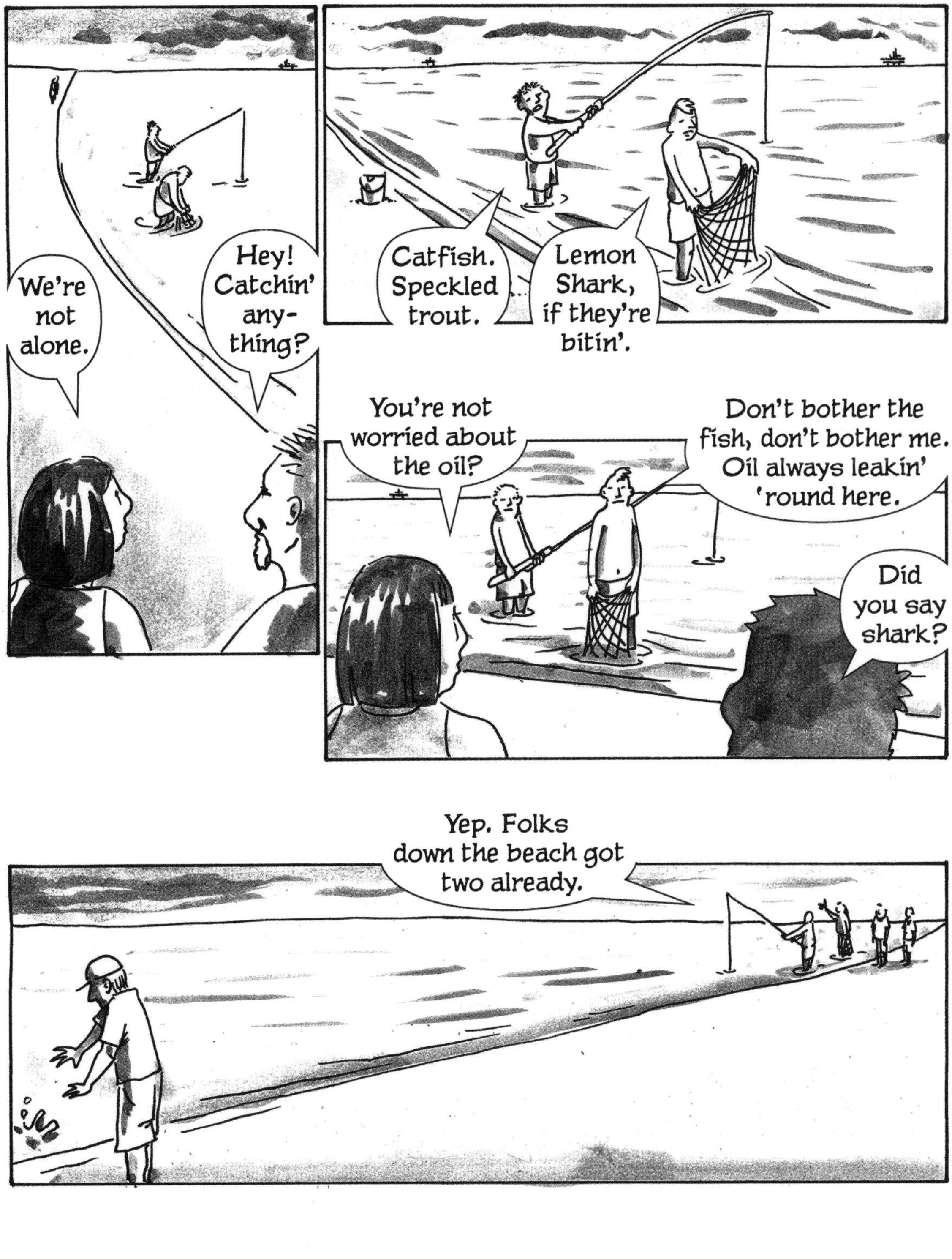

We're not alone.
Hey! Catchin' any-thing?
Catfish. Speckled trout.
Lemon Shark, if they're bitin'.
You're not worried about the oil?
Don't bother the fish, don't bother me. Oil always leakin' 'round here.
Did you say shark?
Yep. Folks down the beach got two already.

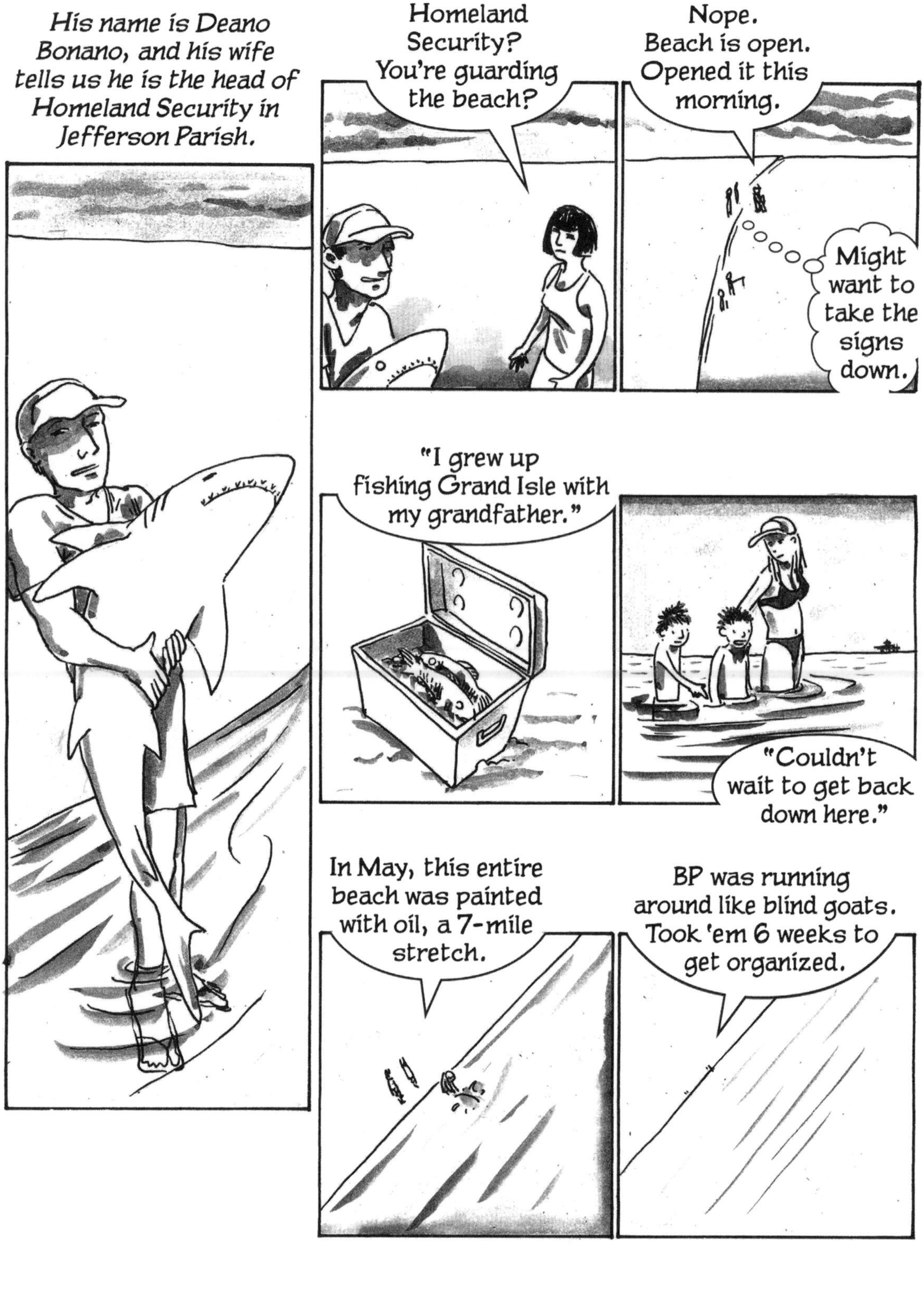
His name is Deano Bonano, and his wife tells us he is the head of Homeland Security in Jefferson Parish.
Homeland Security? You're guarding the beach?
Nope. Beach is open. Opened it this morning.
Might want to take the signs down.
"I grew up fishing Grand Isle with my grandfather."
"Couldn't wait to get back down here."
In May, this entire beach was painted with oil, a 7-mile stretch.
BP was running around like blind goats. Took 'em 6 weeks to get organized.

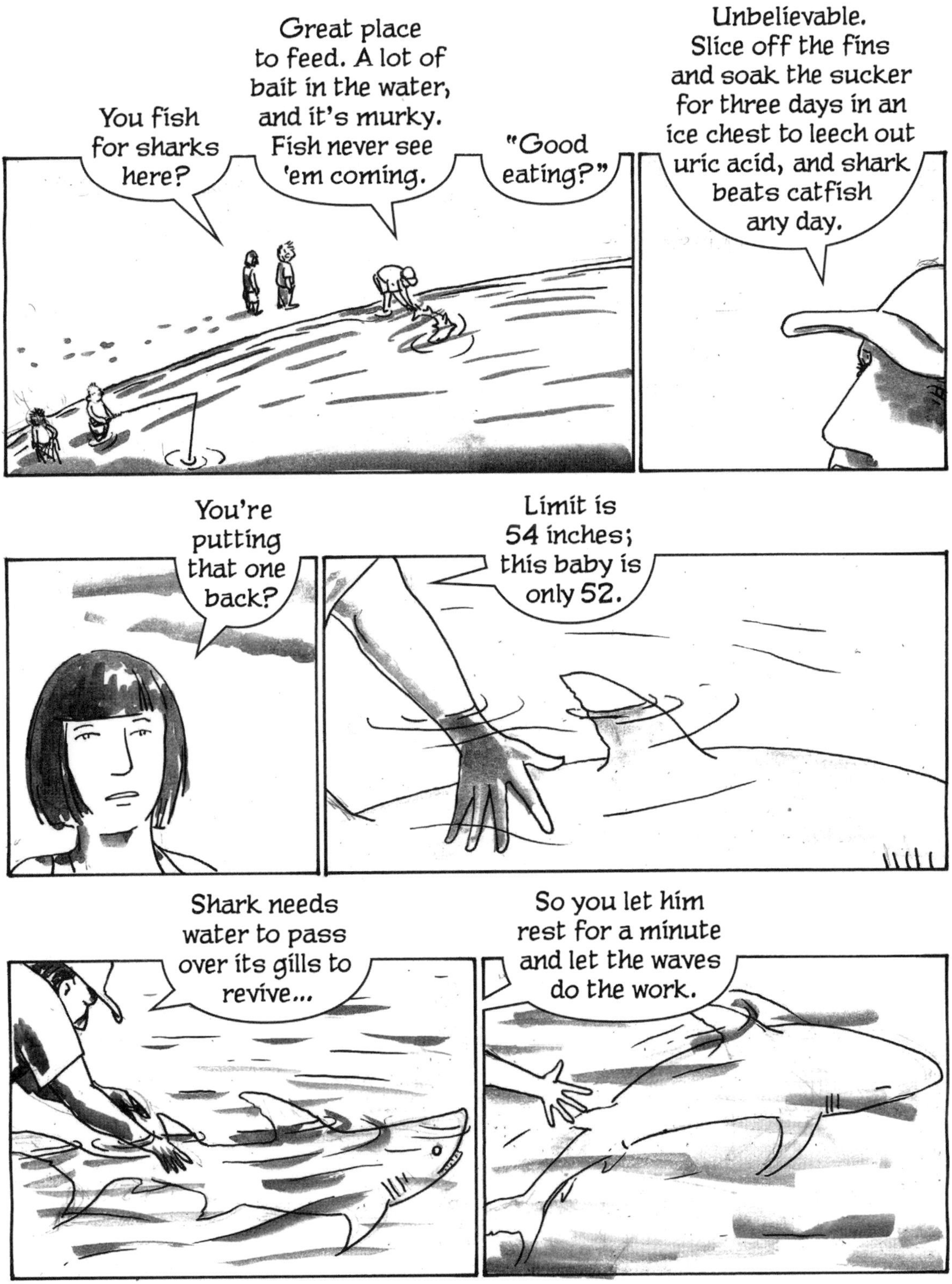
You fish for sharks here?
Great place to feed. A lot of bait in the water, and it's murky. Fish never see 'em coming.
"Good eating?"
Unbelievable. Slice off the fins and soak the sucker for three days in an ice chest to leech out uric acid, and shark beats catfish any day.
You're putting that one back?
Limit is 54 inches; this baby is only 52.
Shark needs water to pass over its gills to revive...
So you let him rest for a minute and let the waves do the work.

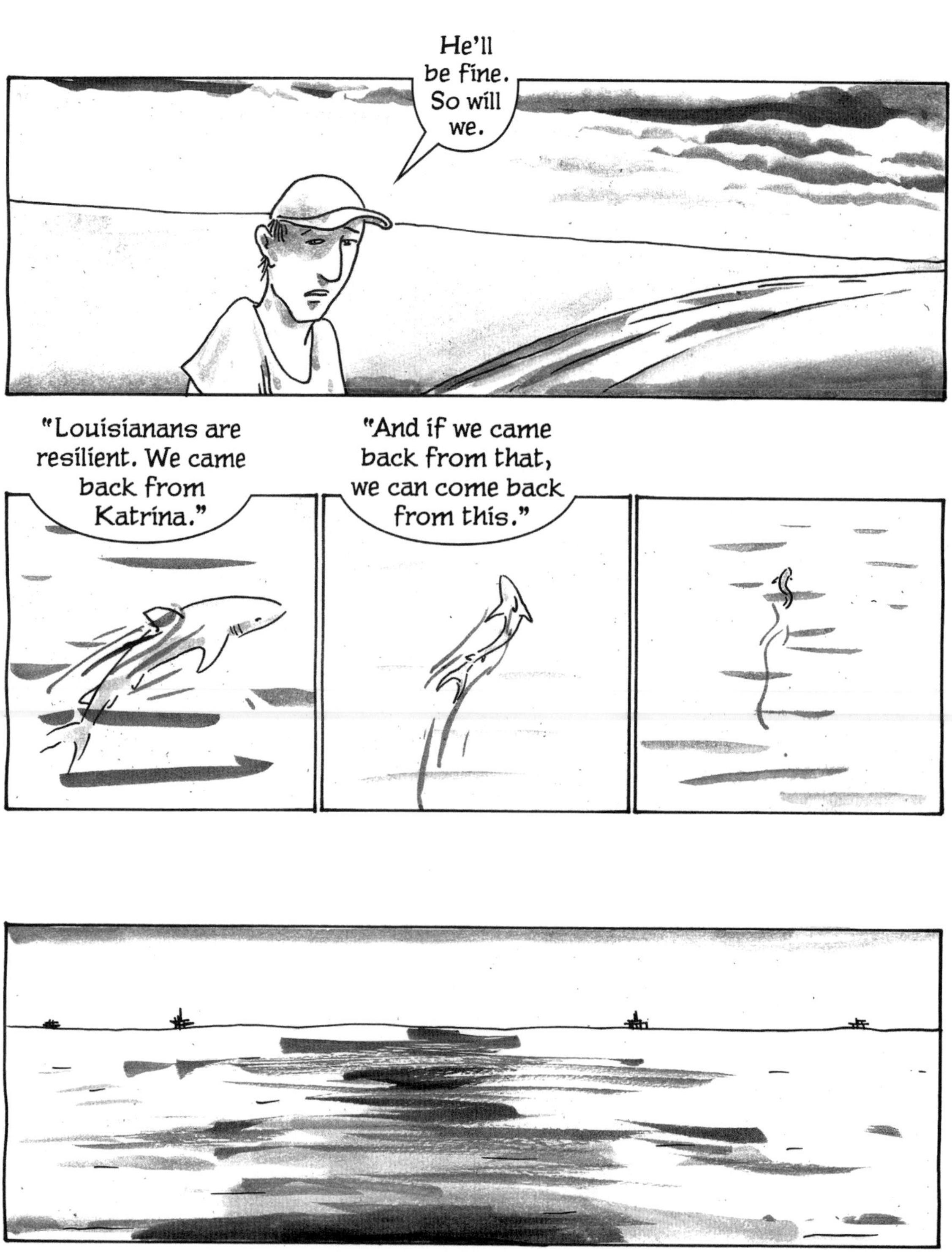
He'll be fine. So will we.
"Louisianans are resilient. We came back from Katrina."
"And if we came back from that, we can come back from this."

Drill, Baby, Drill

Thirteen months after the BP Oil Spill, Jack Gerard, president of the American Petroleum Institute proudly noted that more than 42,000 wells had been drilled in the Gulf of Mexico since the 1940s.

Why did off-shore drilling not encounter the resistance in Louisiana that it would eventually face off the coasts of California and Florida?

- Louisiana is dominated by coastal marshes, not beaches. Almost no one lives within sight of the rigs; there are almost no beaches on which to walk and stumble upon an oil-choked pelican.

- Off-shore drilling developed in the Gulf *before* the commercial fishing industry realized that shrimp thrived in the open Gulf waters, not just in the estuaries.

- Certain species of fish are drawn to "hard substrate," such as reefs, rocks and hard ocean bottoms. Oil rigs provide one-quarter of all such hard substrate in the Gulf, endearing them to fishermen.

- In St. Mary Parish, scene of the initial Outer Continental Shelf drilling, only 12.2 percent of the local population had graduated from high school in 1940. A degree wasn't necessary to go to work on the rigs.

Southern Chaos

Grand Bayou, LA

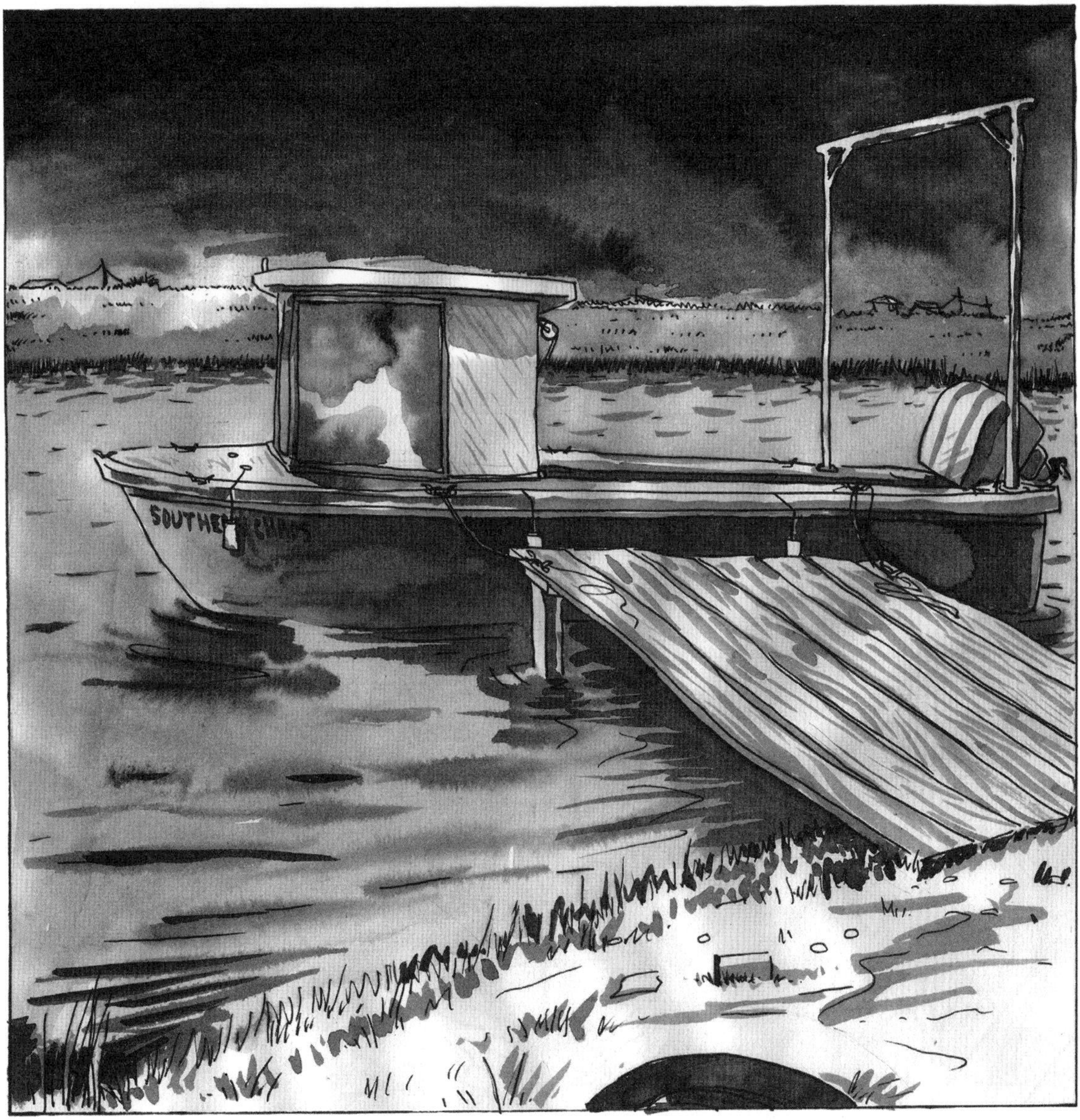

Alarm's set for 4 a.m.

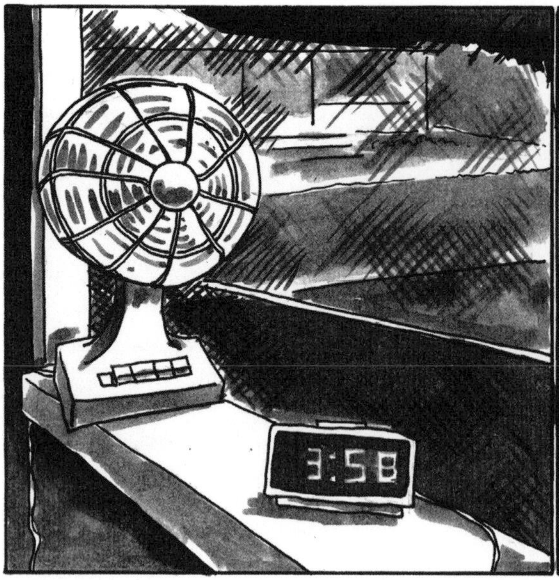
3:58

I pick Carol up
20 minutes later...

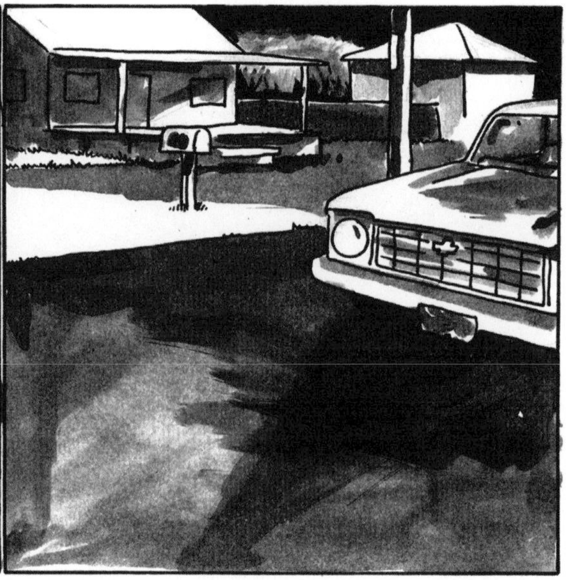

...and the
seven flats of pogy
at 5.

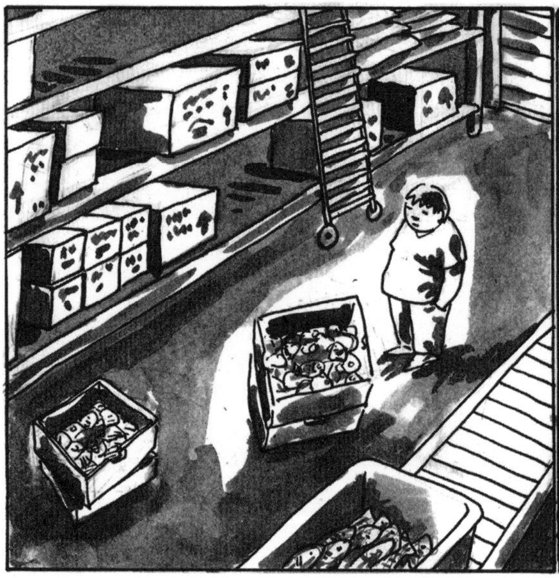

Stink'll hold off
for four hours, maybe,
two in the sun.

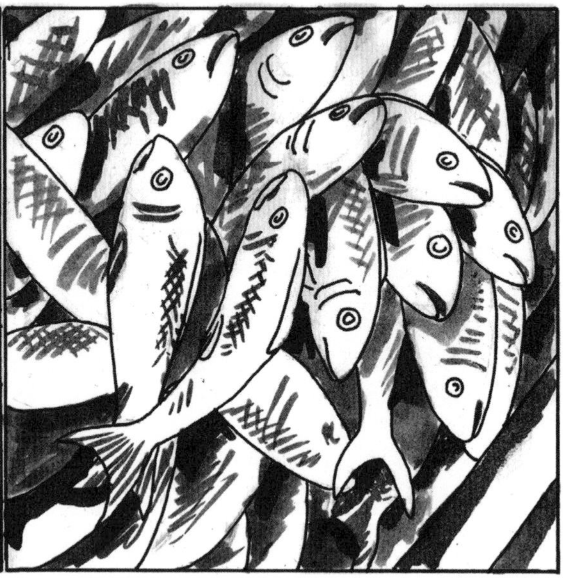

We take the Five Nine into Nawlins,
then 23 to Grand Bayou.

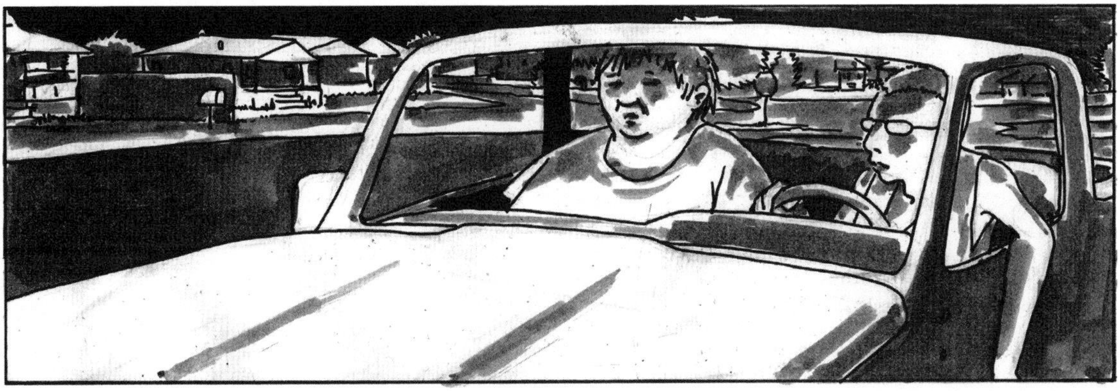

Drive takes two-and-a-half hours
if we don't spike a deer.

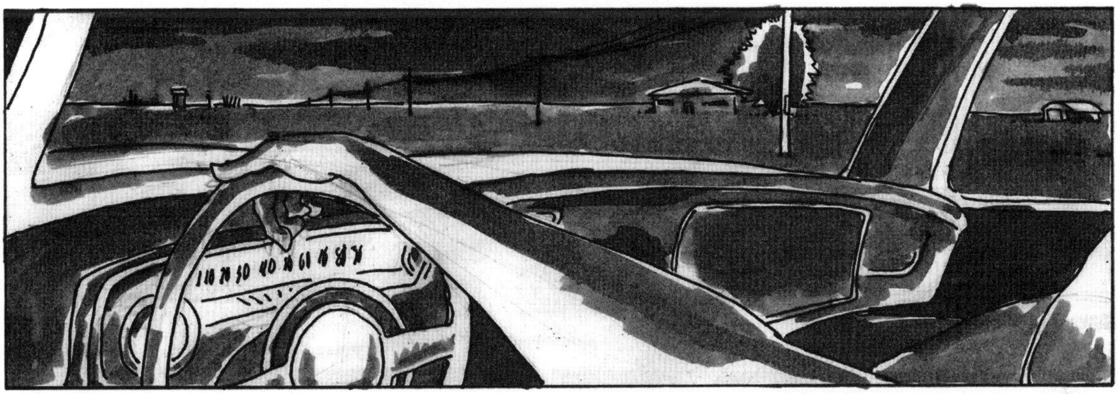

Got no clue how the damn deer flies
get in the truck.

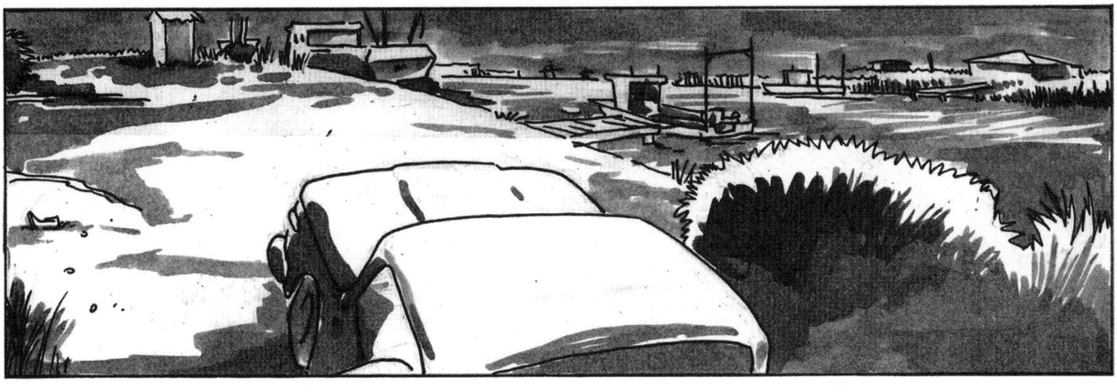

Waters from
Grand Bayou to Bay Jimmy
been in the family
for 50 years.

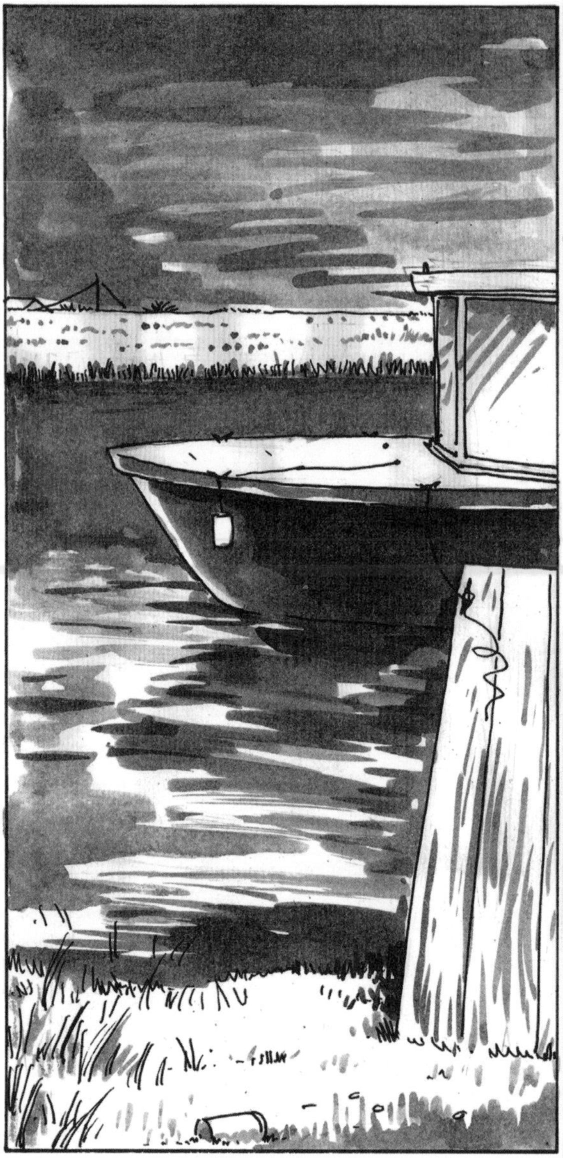

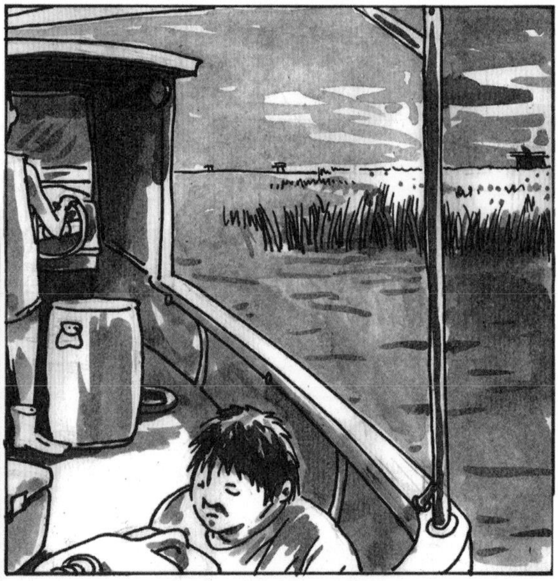

Rules are simple.
When shrimp season closes,
you oyster.

Oyster season closes, you shrimp.

When both seasons close,
you crab.

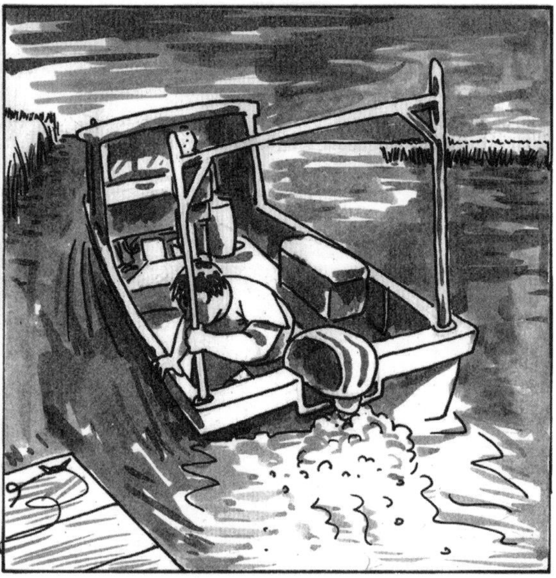

Like crab still pencils out.

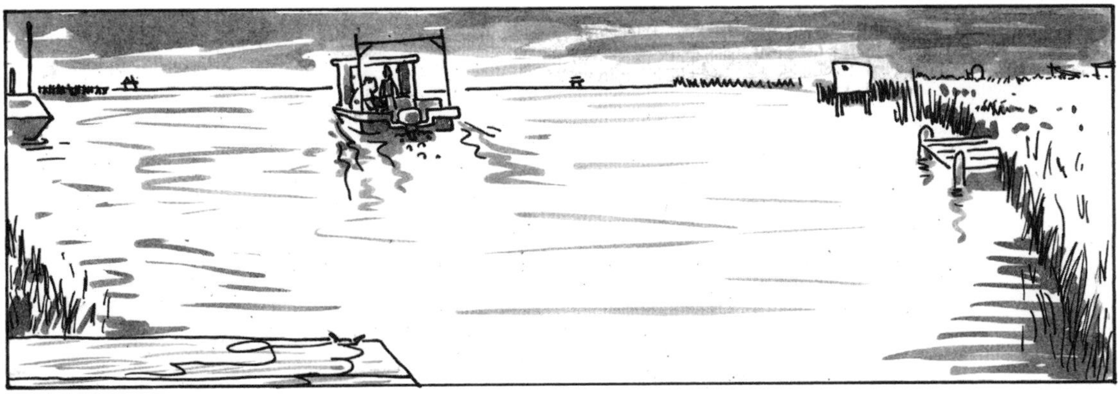

Nine hours on the water.
500 pots.

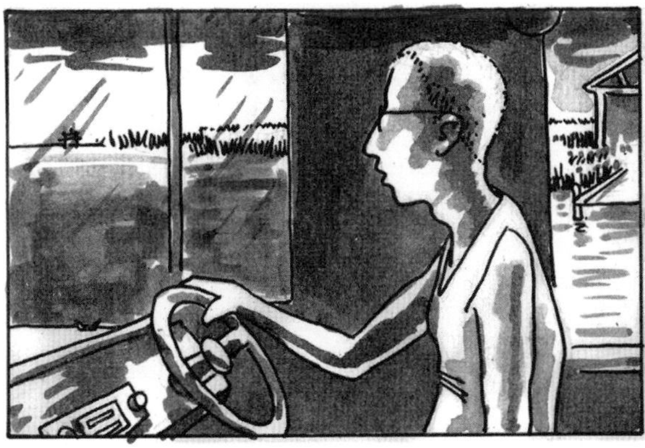

Got more than that
but there ain't enough hours
in the day.

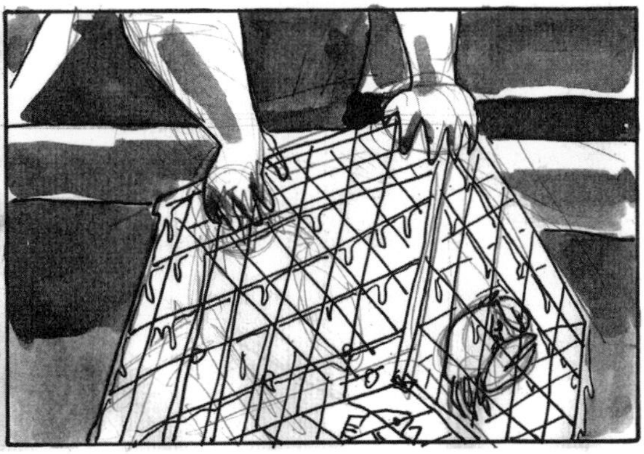

Before BP, we'd clear 2,000 pounds.

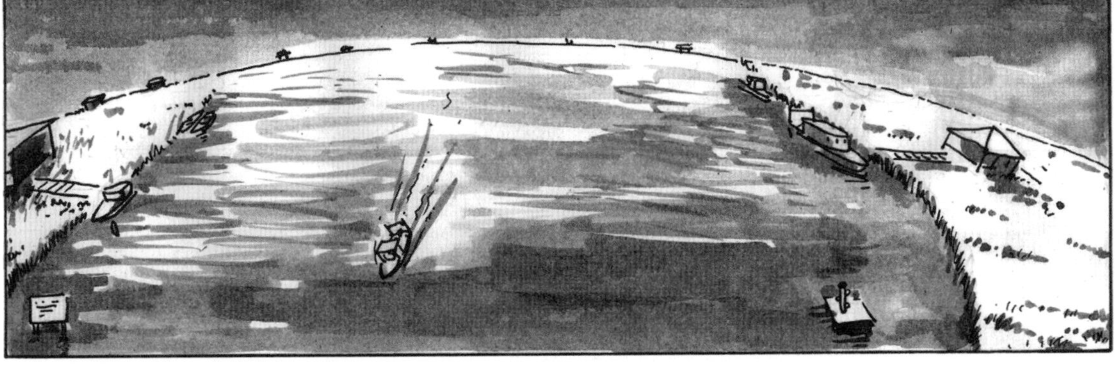

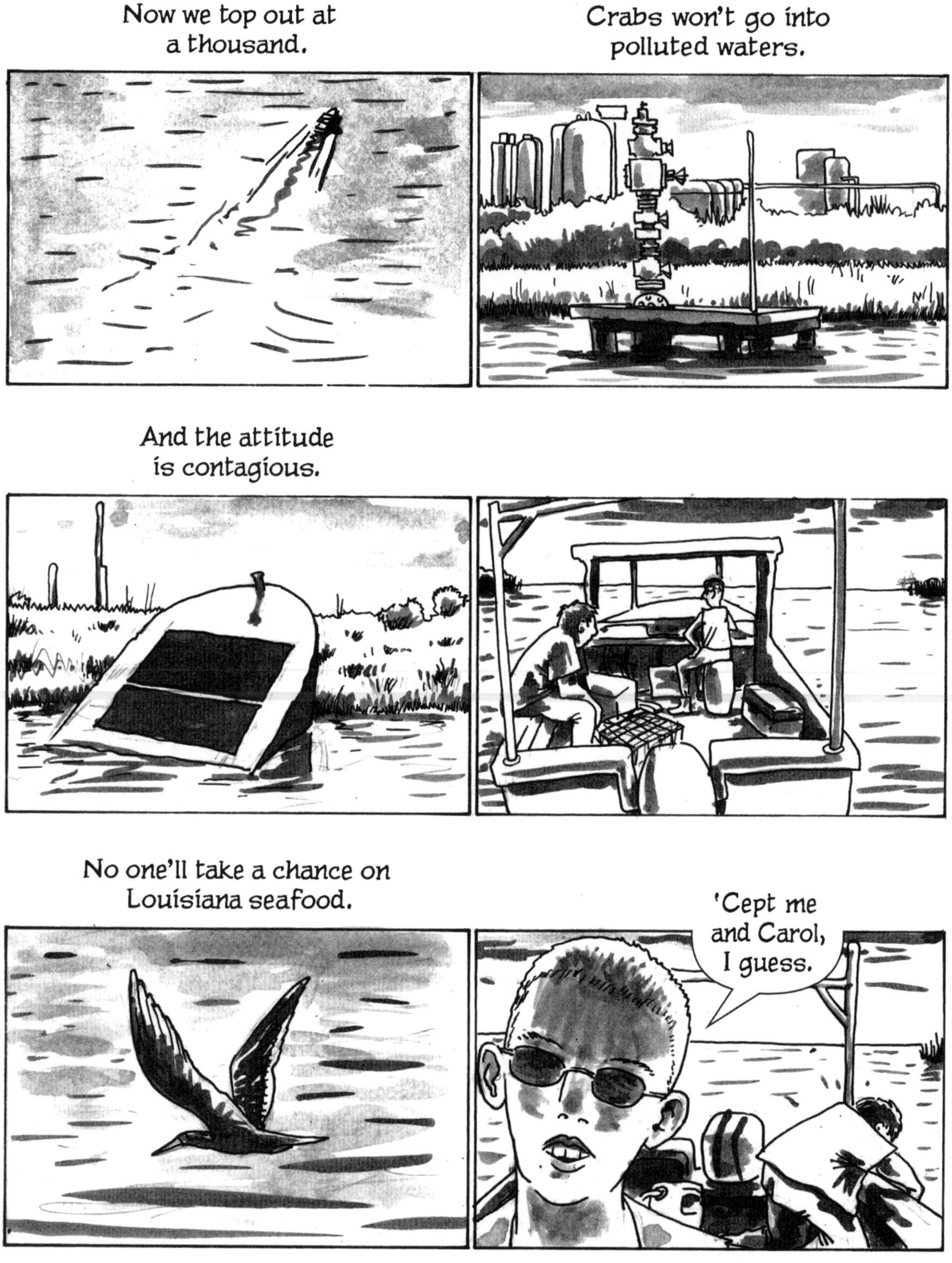
Now we top out at a thousand.
Crabs won't go into polluted waters.
And the attitude is contagious.
No one'll take a chance on Louisiana seafood.
'Cept me and Carol, I guess.

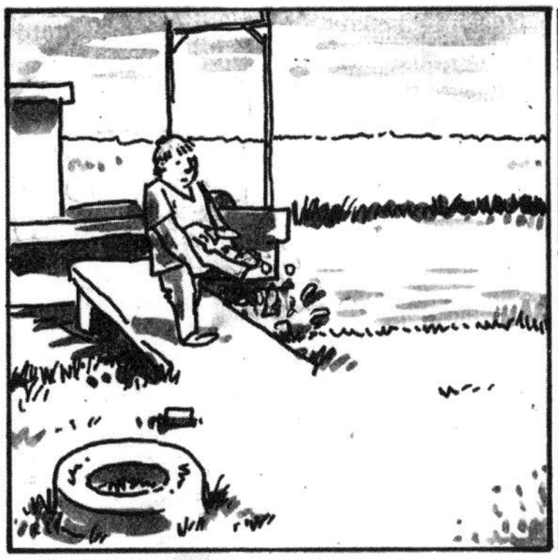

We'll be back on the road at 5,
home by 8.

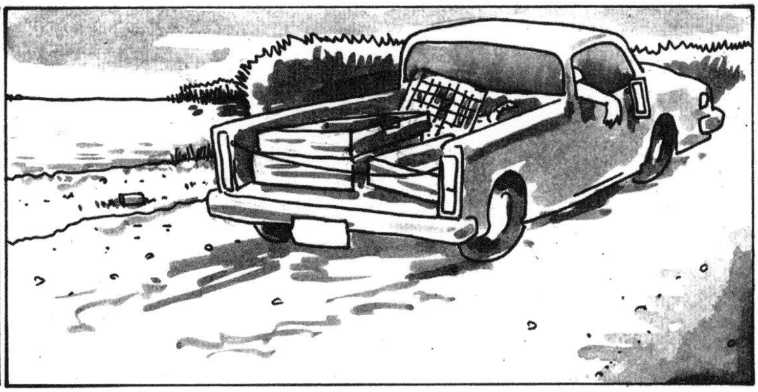

Don't bother with dinner.

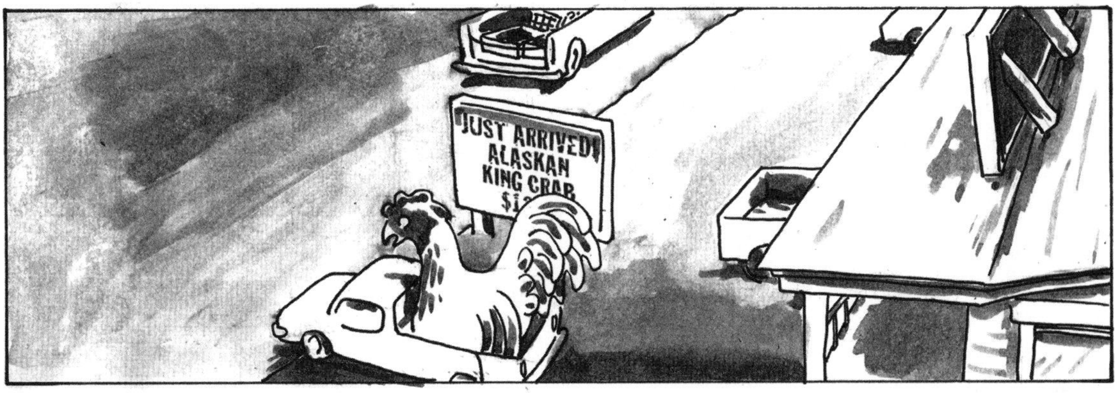
JUST ARRIVED!
ALASKAN
KING CRAB

Damn alarm's still set for 4.

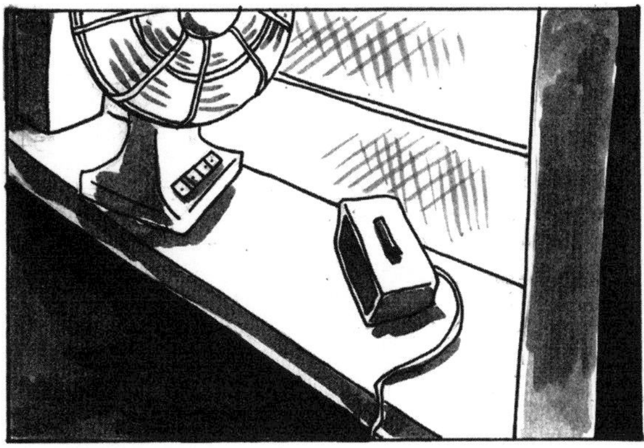

The pogy?
Pogy don't make the trip.

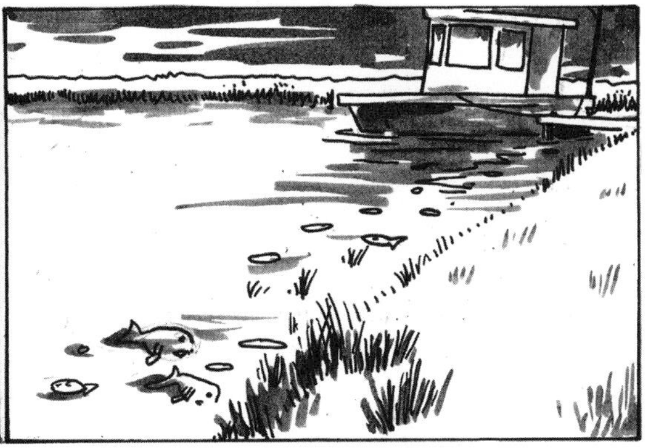

Lost

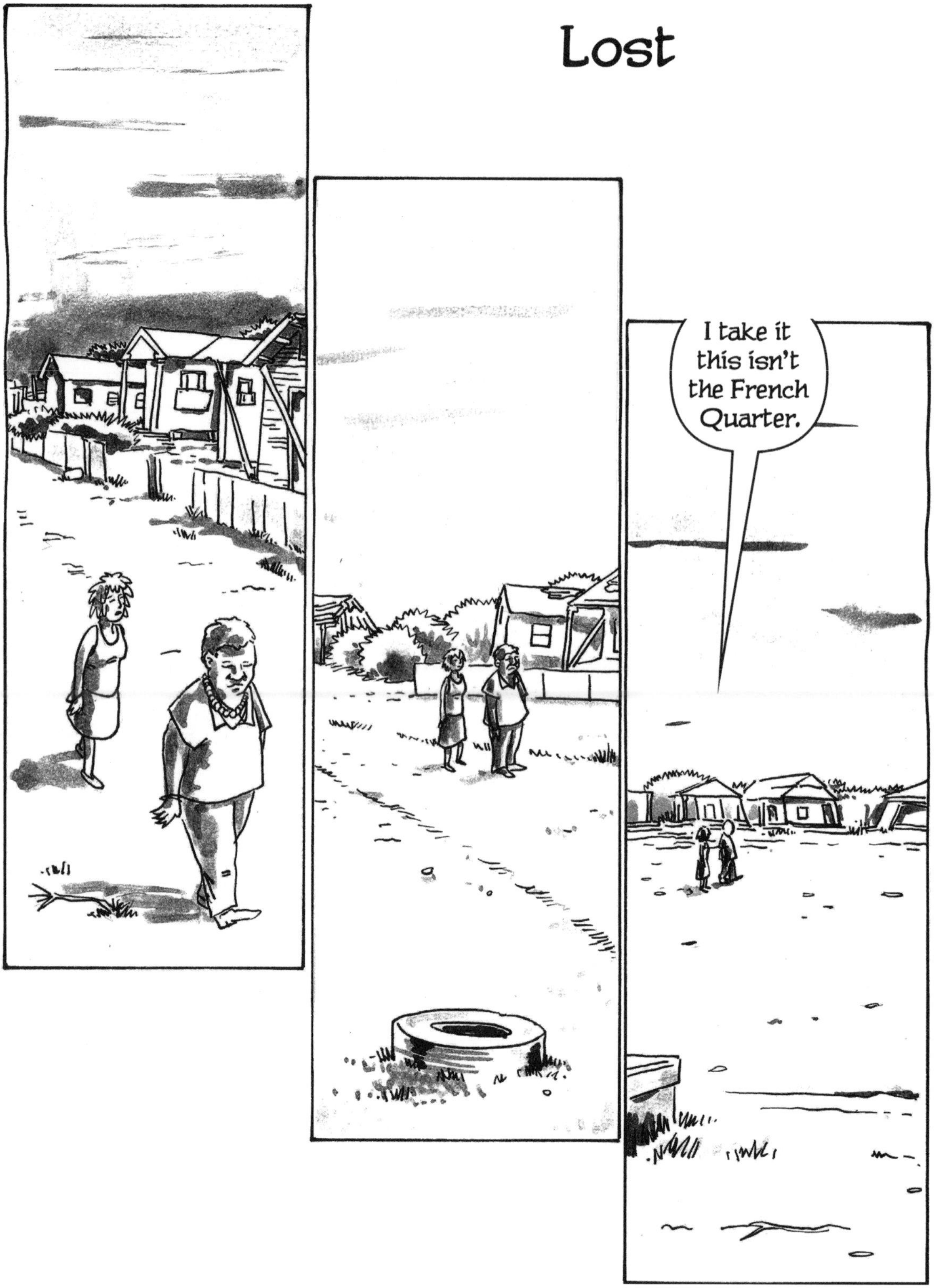
I take it this isn't the French Quarter.

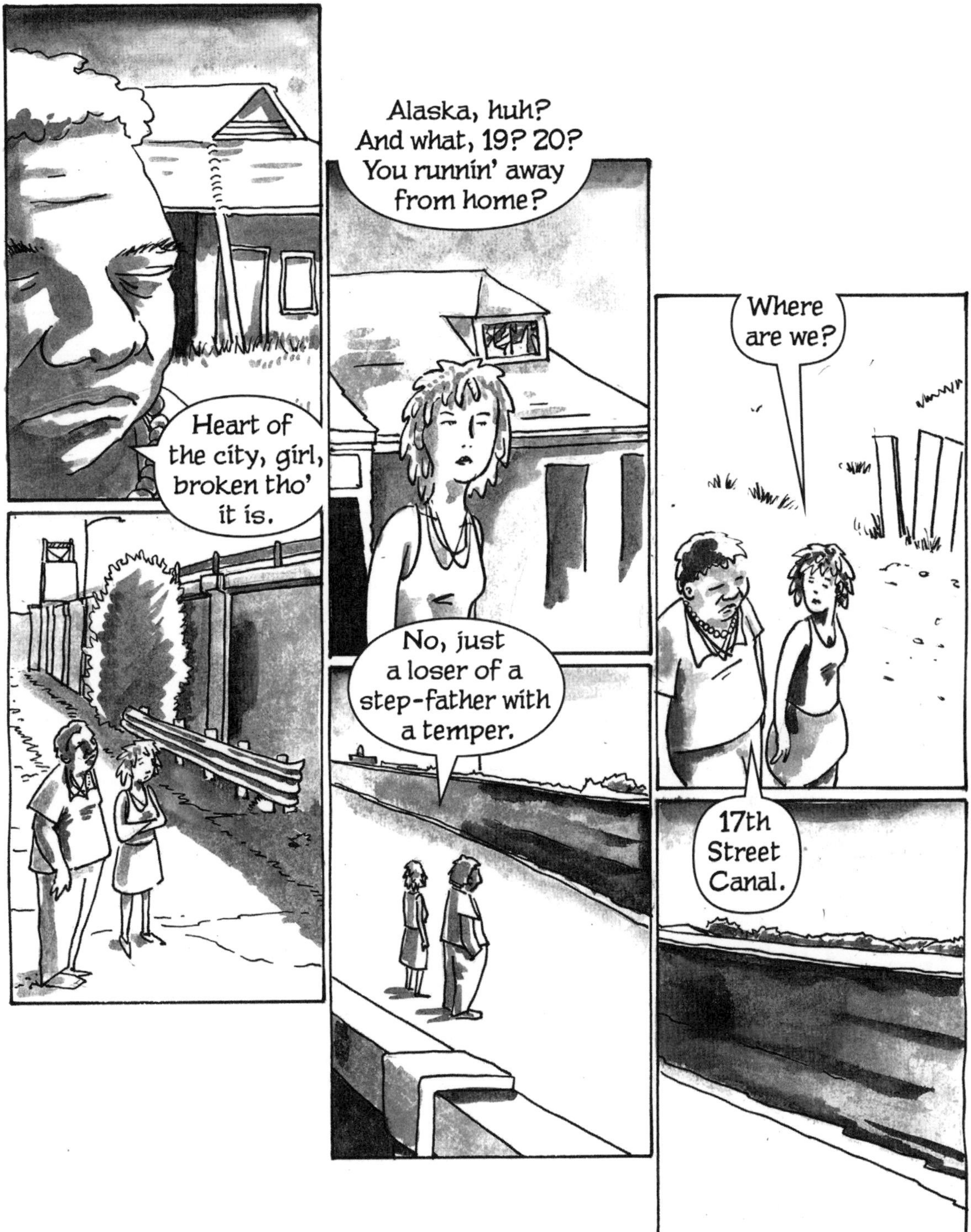
Heart of the city, girl, broken tho' it is.
Alaska, huh? And what, 19? 20? You runnin' away from home?
No, just a loser of a step-father with a temper.
Where are we?
17th Street Canal.

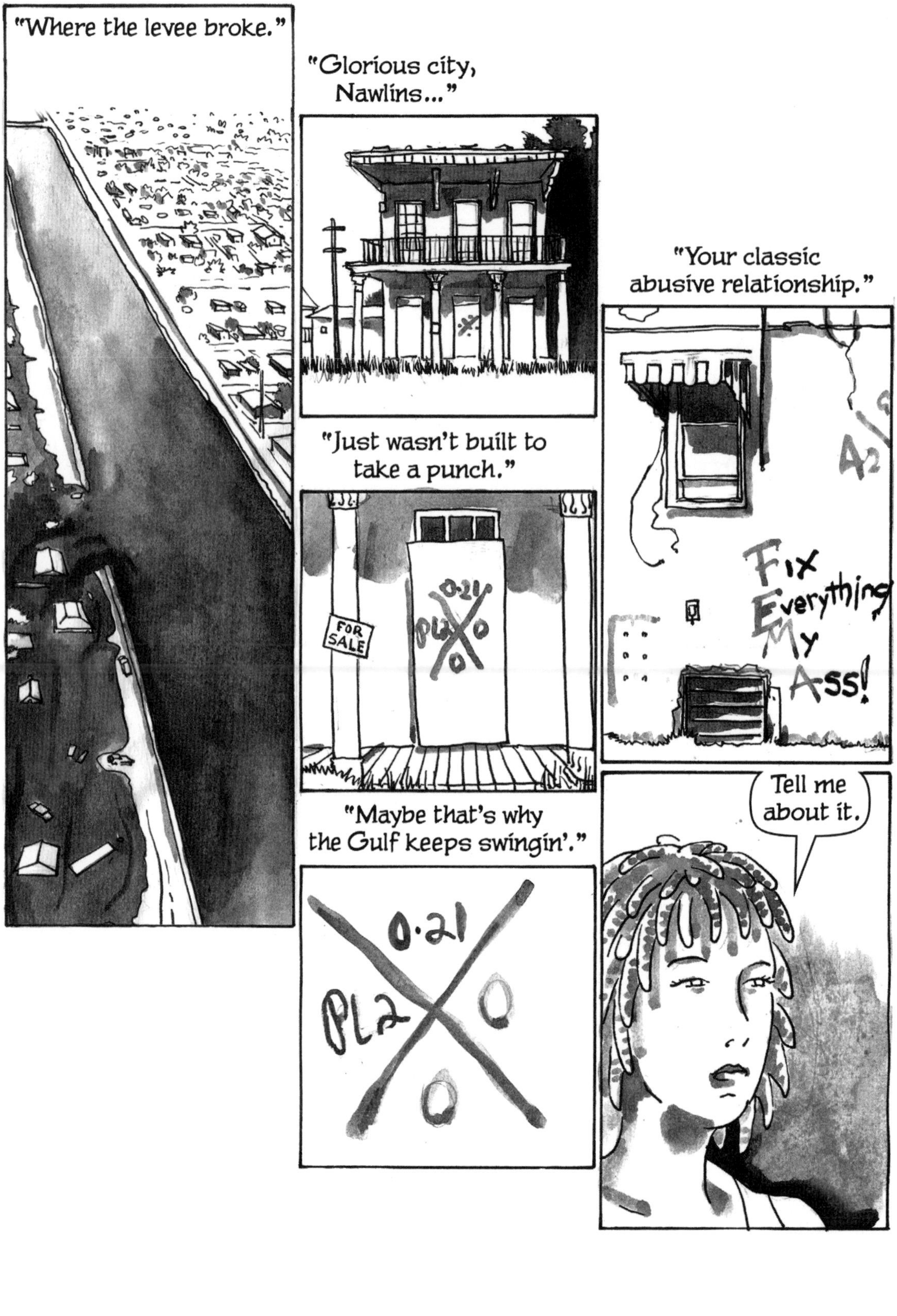
"Where the levee broke."
"Glorious city, Nawlins..."
"Just wasn't built to take a punch."
FOR SALE
0.21
PL2
0
0
"Maybe that's why the Gulf keeps swingin'."
0.21
PL2
0
0
"Your classic abusive relationship."
42
Fix Everything My Ass!
Tell me about it.

An Open Wound

When the waters rose and the levees crumbled in August 2005, more than 80 percent of the neighborhoods in New Orleans were flooded as Hurricane Katrina surged through the city, opening wounds that still hadn't closed when the Deepwater Horizon exploded.

According to the 2010 census, New Orleans is home to 44 percent fewer children than lived in the city in the year 2000.

In May 2010, 860 New Orleans families were still parked in FEMA trailers, down from the 45,000 families who were living in those rat holes in 2007, two years *after* Katrina.

On the five-year anniversary of the hurricane, public-school enrollment in the city was 38,000, compared to the 65,000 students enrolled in 2005. Over 90 percent of those students are African-American.

Not a single one of the 217 square miles of Louisiana coastal land consumed by Katrina and Rita had been rescued from the waves.

But all the news wasn't bad. Although New Orleans per-capita murder rate remained the highest in the nation, it dropped from 65 to 52 per 100,000 people between 2005 and 2010.

FMK

Hammond, LA

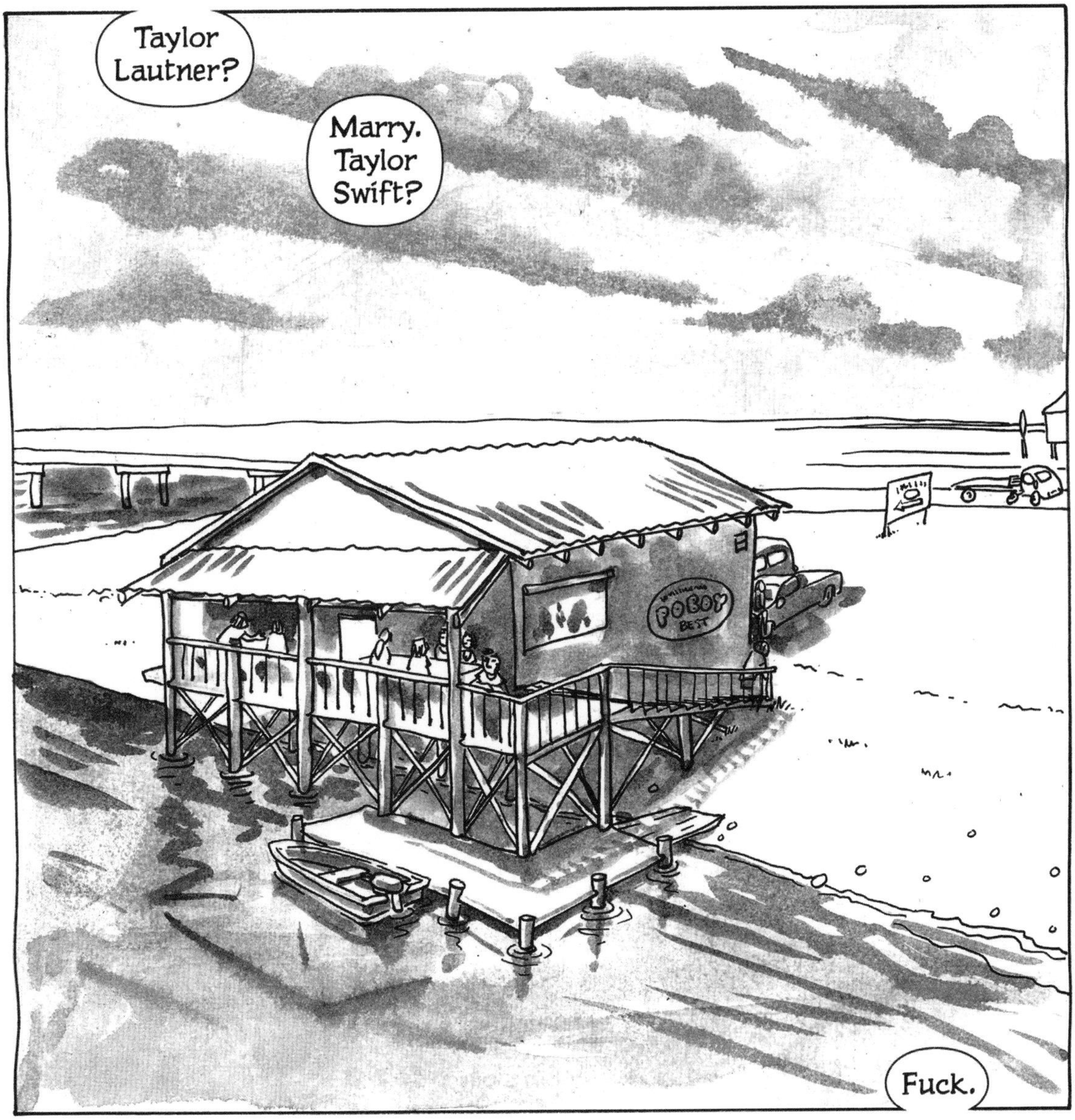
Taylor Lautner?
Marry. Taylor Swift?
Fuck.

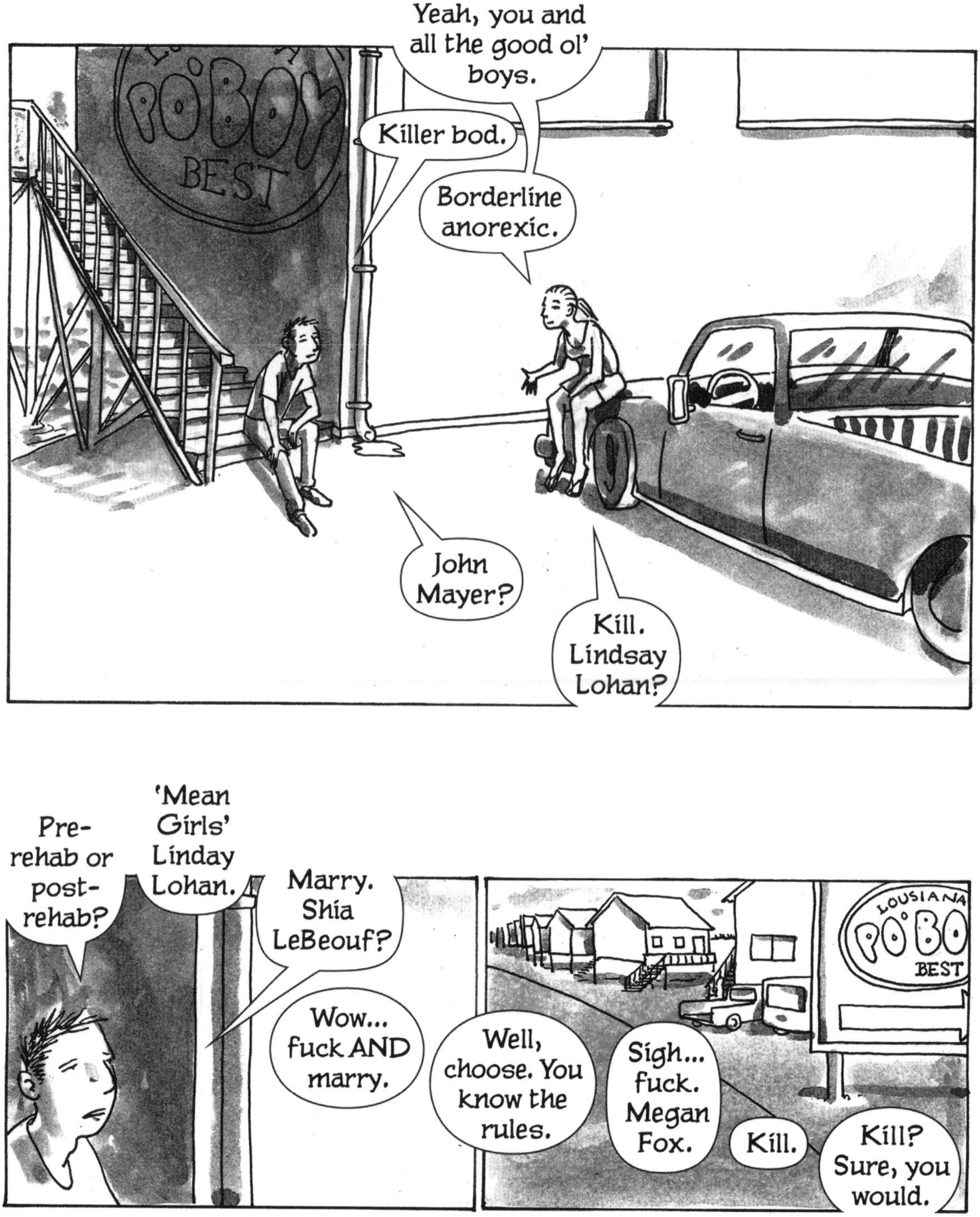
Yeah, you and all the good ol' boys.
Killer bod.
Borderline anorexic.
John Mayer?
Kill. Lindsay Lohan?
Pre-rehab or post-rehab?
'Mean Girls' Linday Lohan.
Marry. Shia LeBeouf?
Wow... fuck AND marry.
Well, choose. You know the rules.
Sigh... fuck. Megan Fox.
Kill.
Kill? Sure, you would.
LOUSIANA
BEST

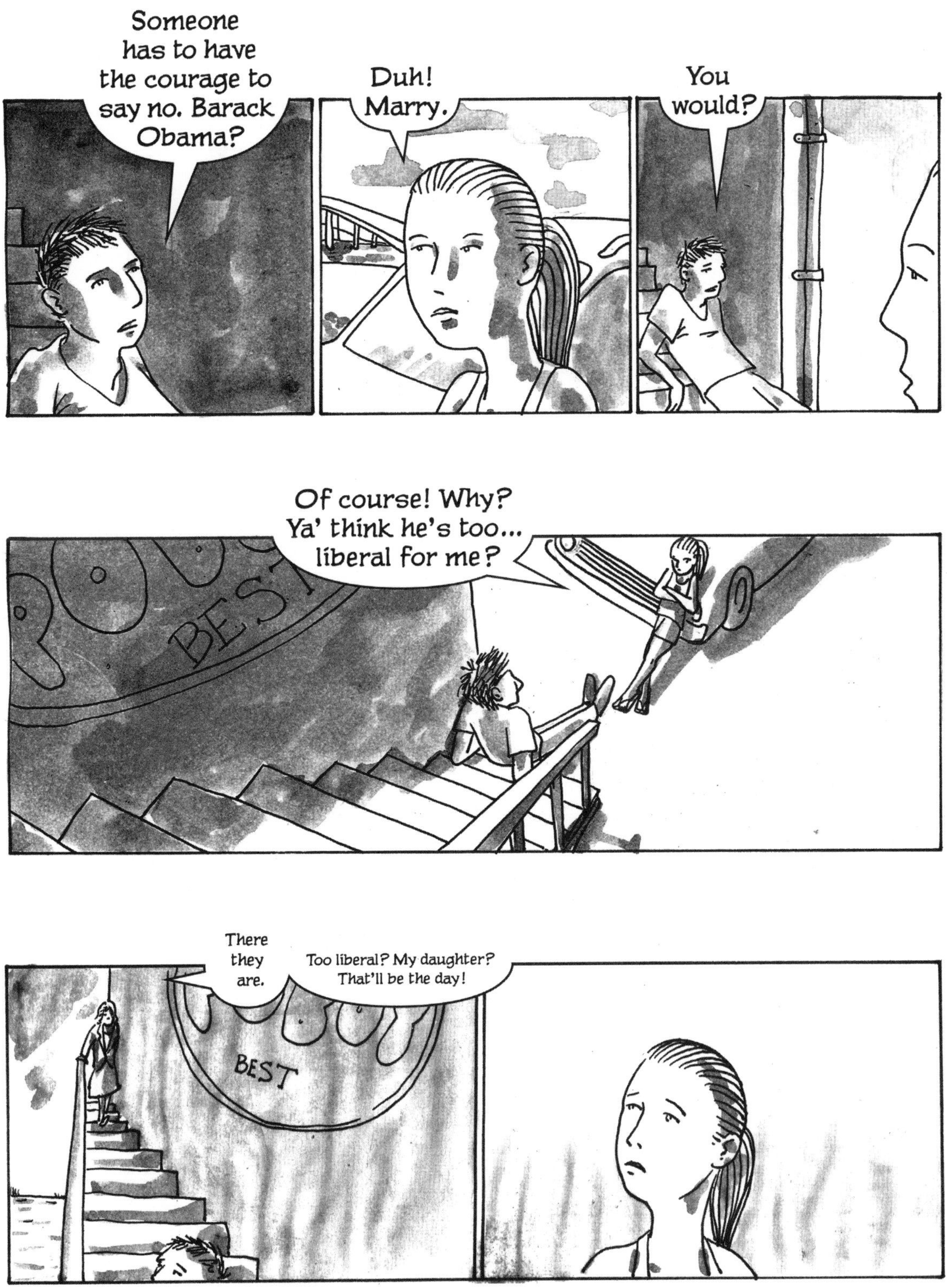
Someone has to have the courage to say no. Barack Obama?
Duh! Marry.
You would?
Of course! Why? Ya' think he's too... liberal for me?
BEST
There they are.
Too liberal? My daughter? That'll be the day!
BEST

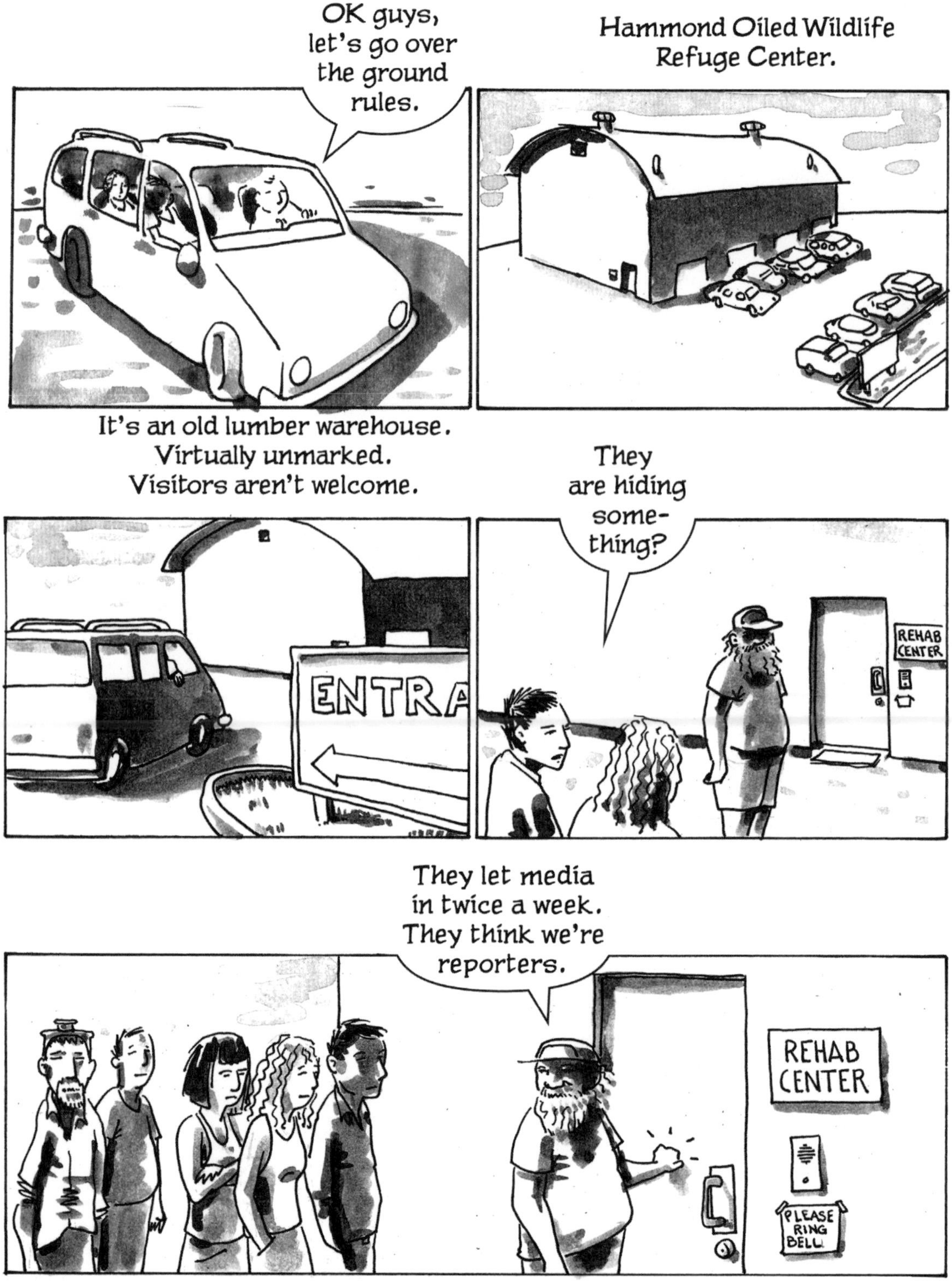
OK guys, let's go over the ground rules.
Hammond Oiled Wildlife Refuge Center.
It's an old lumber warehouse. Virtually unmarked. Visitors aren't welcome.
ENTRA
They are hiding some-thing?
REHAB CENTER
They let media in twice a week. They think we're reporters.
REHAB CENTER
PLEASE RING BELL

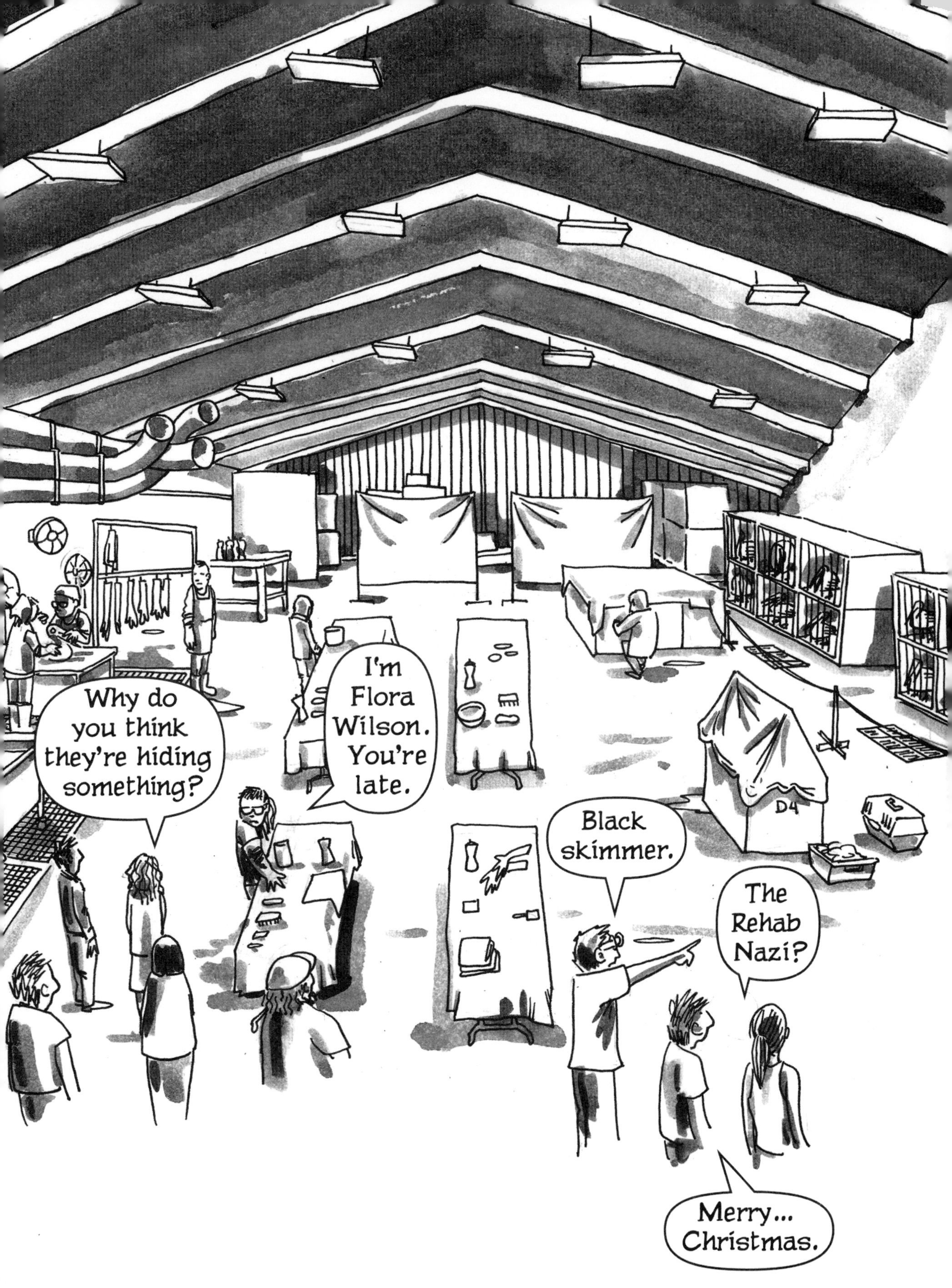
Why do you think they're hiding something?
I'm Flora Wilson. You're late.
Black skimmer.
The Rehab Nazi?
Merry... Christmas.
D4

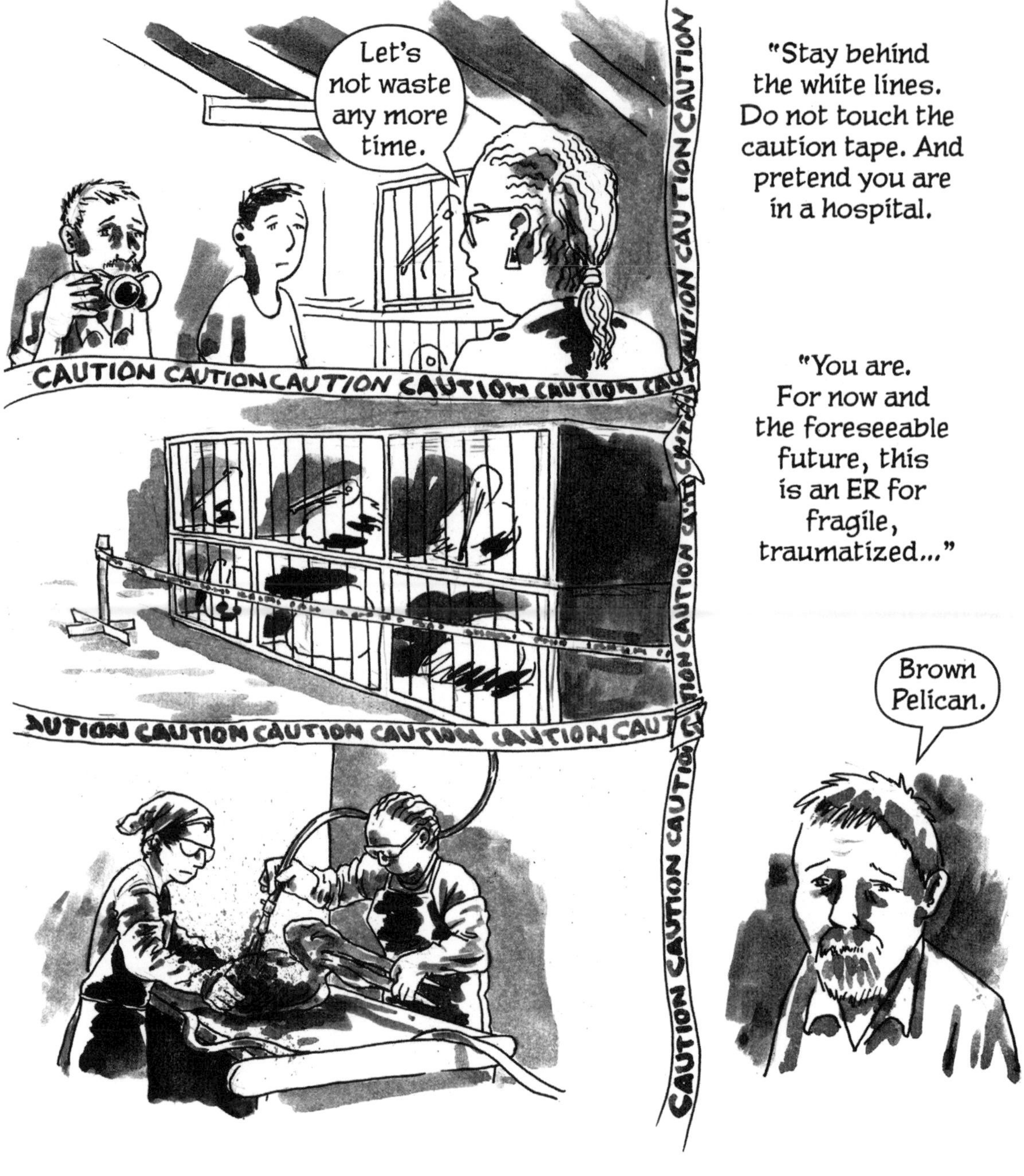
Let's not waste any more time.
"Stay behind the white lines. Do not touch the caution tape. And pretend you are in a hospital.
"You are. For now and the foreseeable future, this is an ER for fragile, traumatized..."
Brown Pelican.

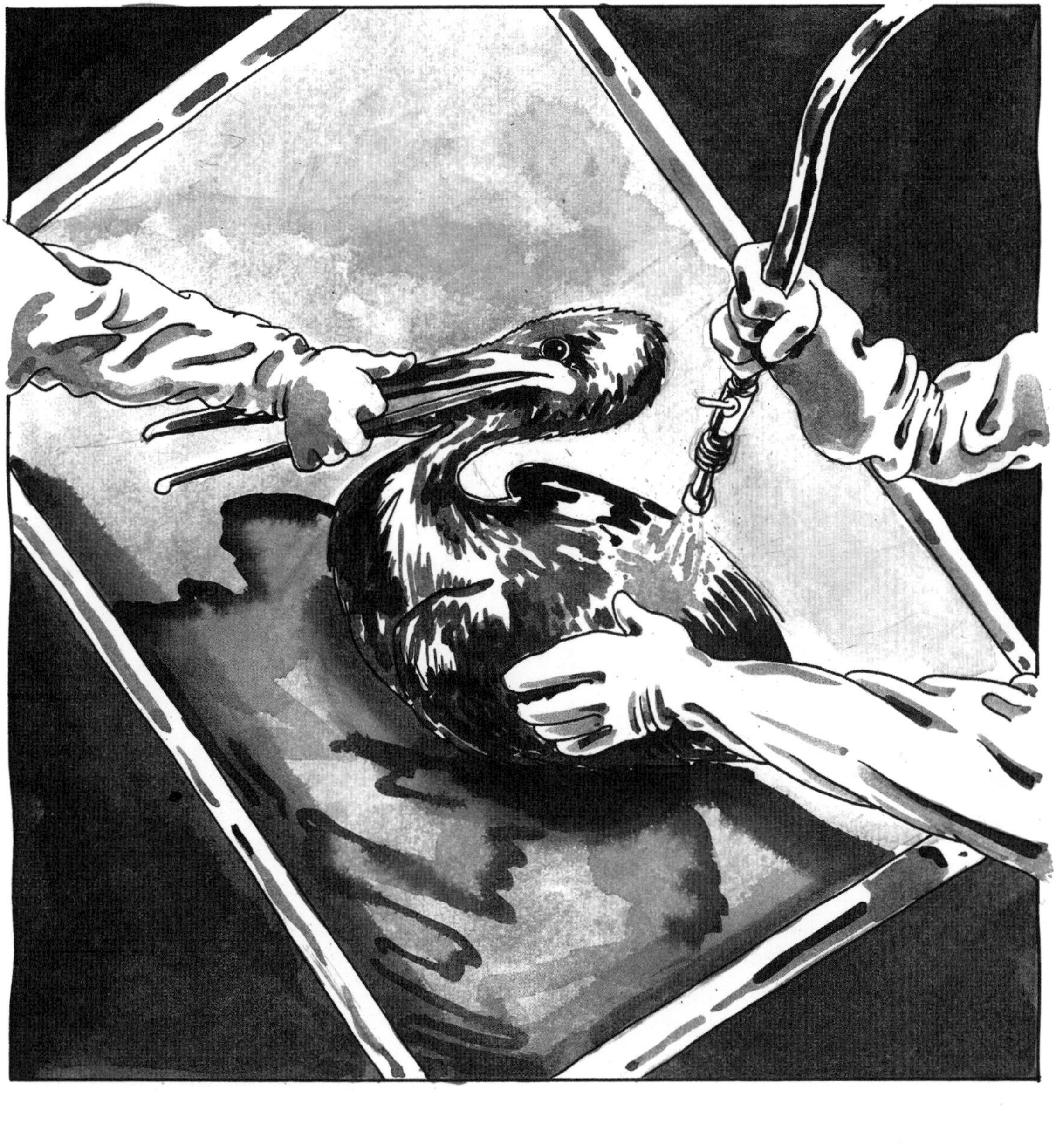

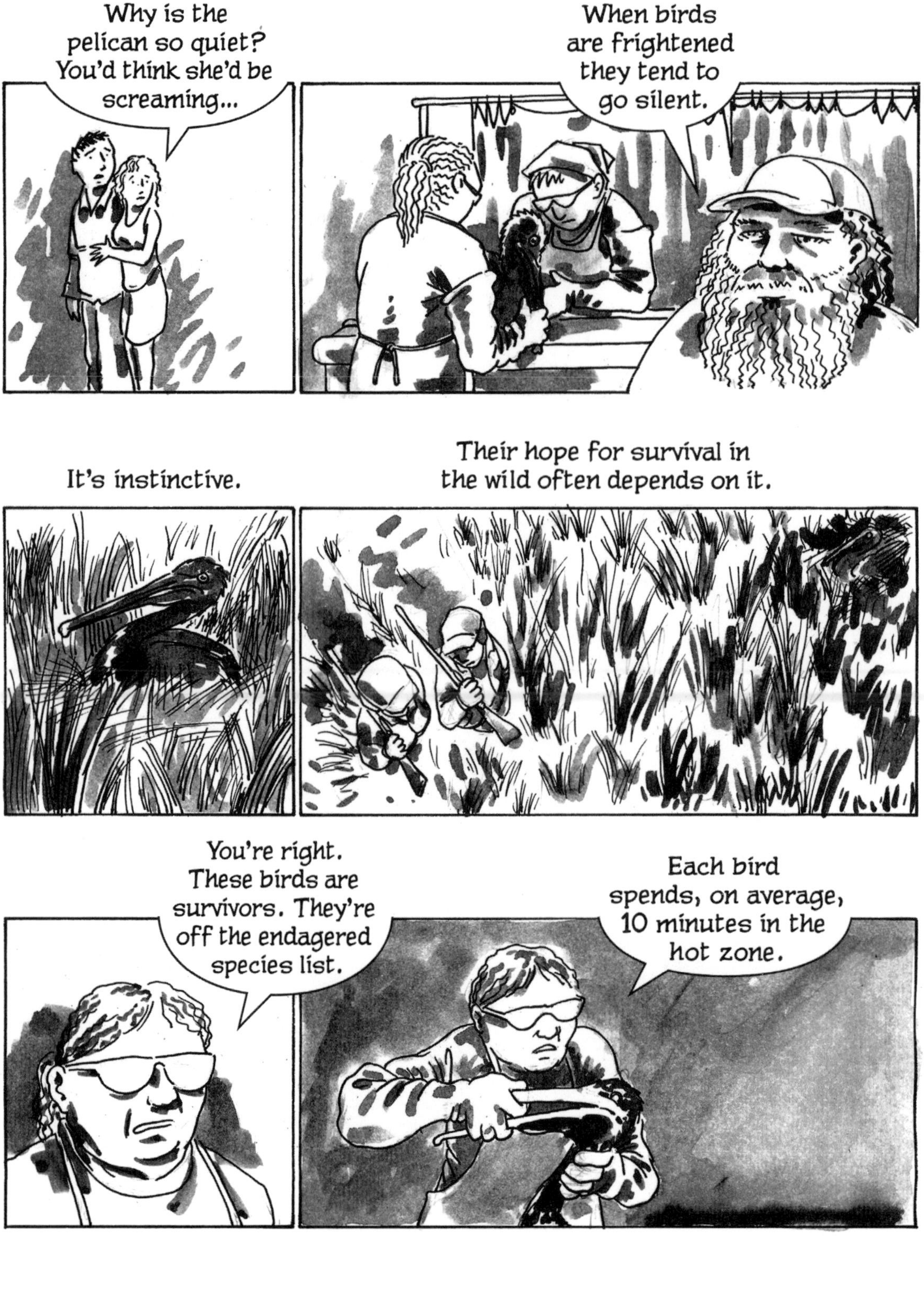
Why is the pelican so quiet? You'd think she'd be screaming...
When birds are frightened they tend to go silent.
It's instinctive.
Their hope for survival in the wild often depends on it.
You're right. These birds are survivors. They're off the endagered species list.
Each bird spends, on average, 10 minutes in the hot zone.

When the birds arrive, they must first be stabilized.
Invariably, they're in shock.
Because their instinct is to preen...
Should we be taking notes?
...they have ingested toxic amounts of oil.
The birds are warmed and given fluids.
JOINT INCIDENT COMMAND
Once the bird is stabilized, the washing begins.
Several rinses are required.

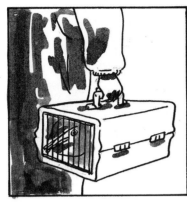

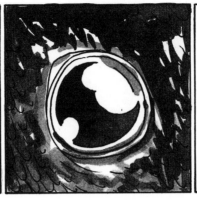

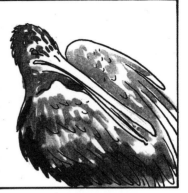

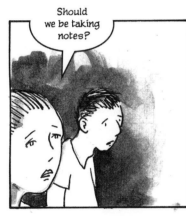

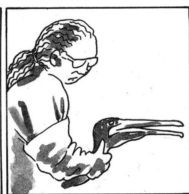

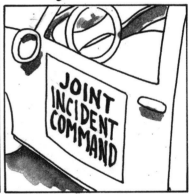

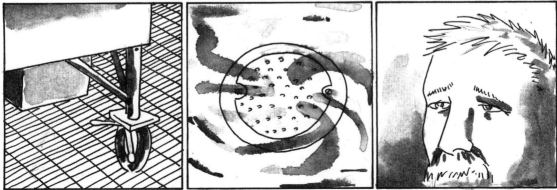

Saline solution for the eyes, dishwasher detergent for the feathers.

On average, three volunteers are required to restrain the bird.

To date 1,415 birds-- including 600 pelicans-- have been treated here and released to the wild.

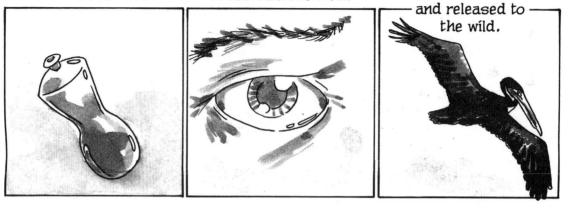

Ma'am...

...energy tax credits.

Ma'am... Ma'am...

...cell calls are not allowed. They frighten the birds.

Why all the fans?

The fumes off the birds are very toxic.

I have another group waiting. Please make your way to the exit.

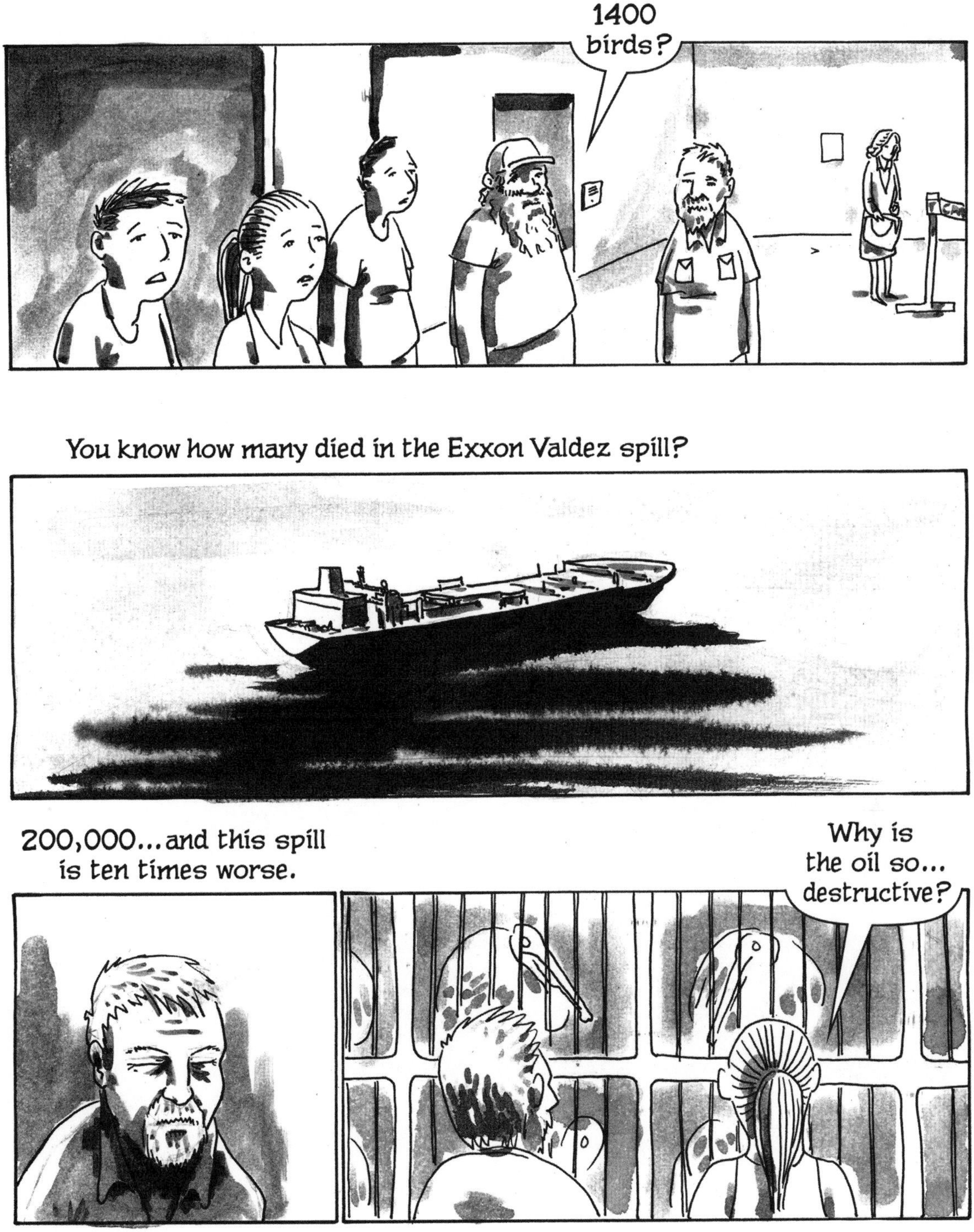
1400 birds?
You know how many died in the Exxon Valdez spill?
200,000...and this spill is ten times worse.
Why is the oil so... destructive?

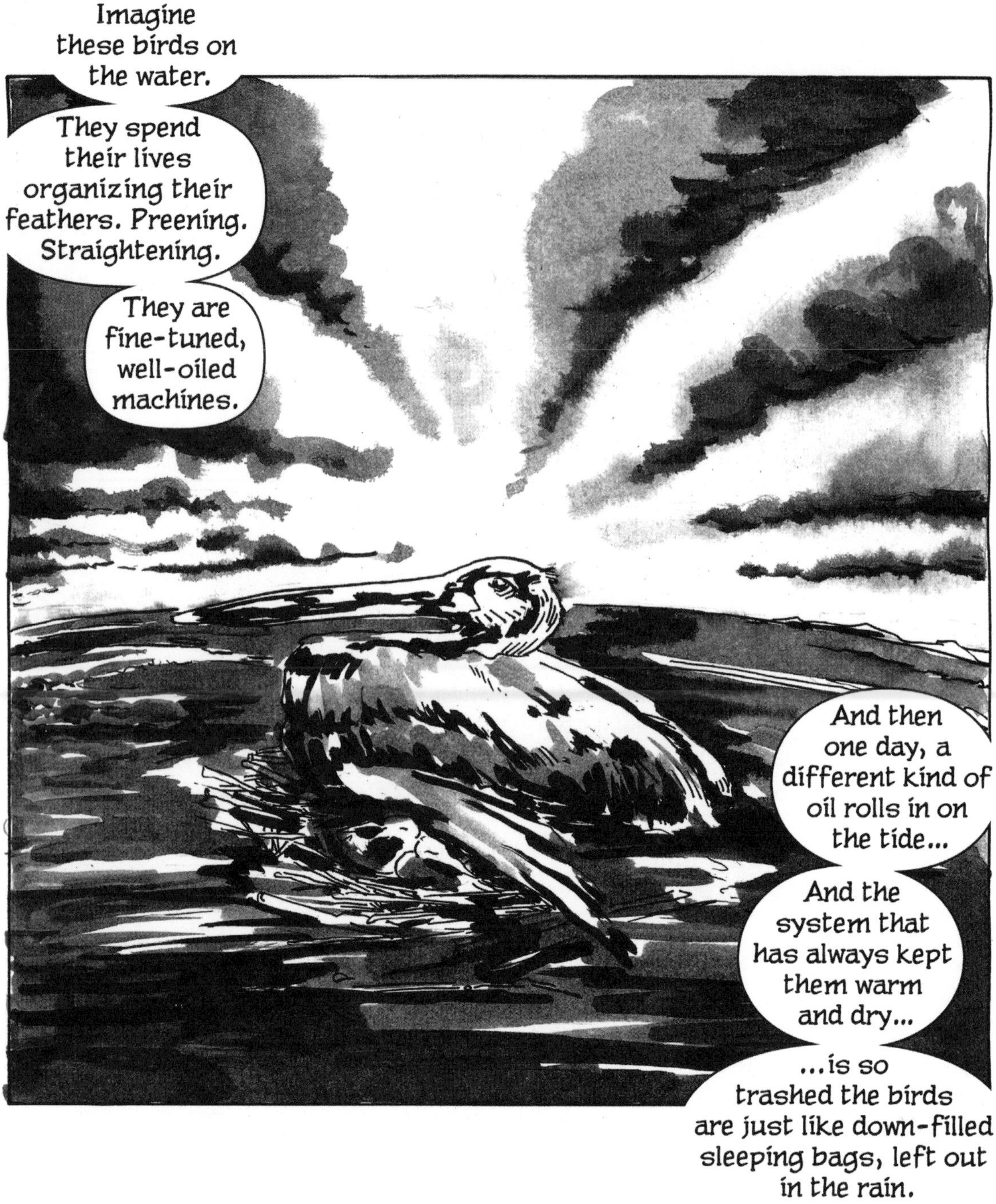
Imagine these birds on the water.
They spend their lives organizing their feathers. Preening. Straightening.
They are fine-tuned, well-oiled machines.
And then one day, a different kind of oil rolls in on the tide...
And the system that has always kept them warm and dry...
...is so trashed the birds are just like down-filled sleeping bags, left out in the rain.

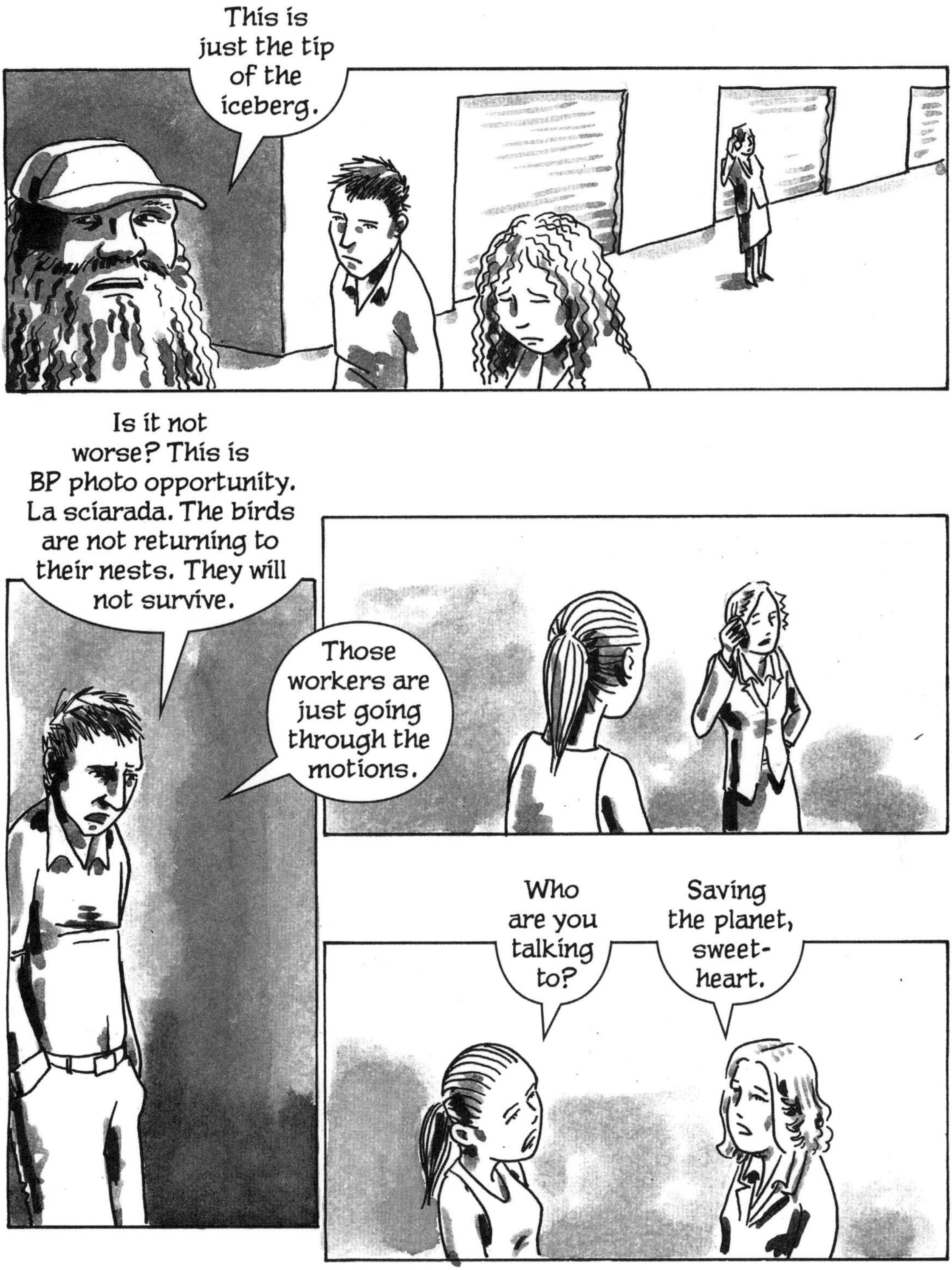
This is just the tip of the iceberg.
Is it not worse? This is BP photo opportunity. La sciarada. The birds are not returning to their nests. They will not survive.
Those workers are just going through the motions.
Who are you talking to?
Saving the planet, sweet-heart.

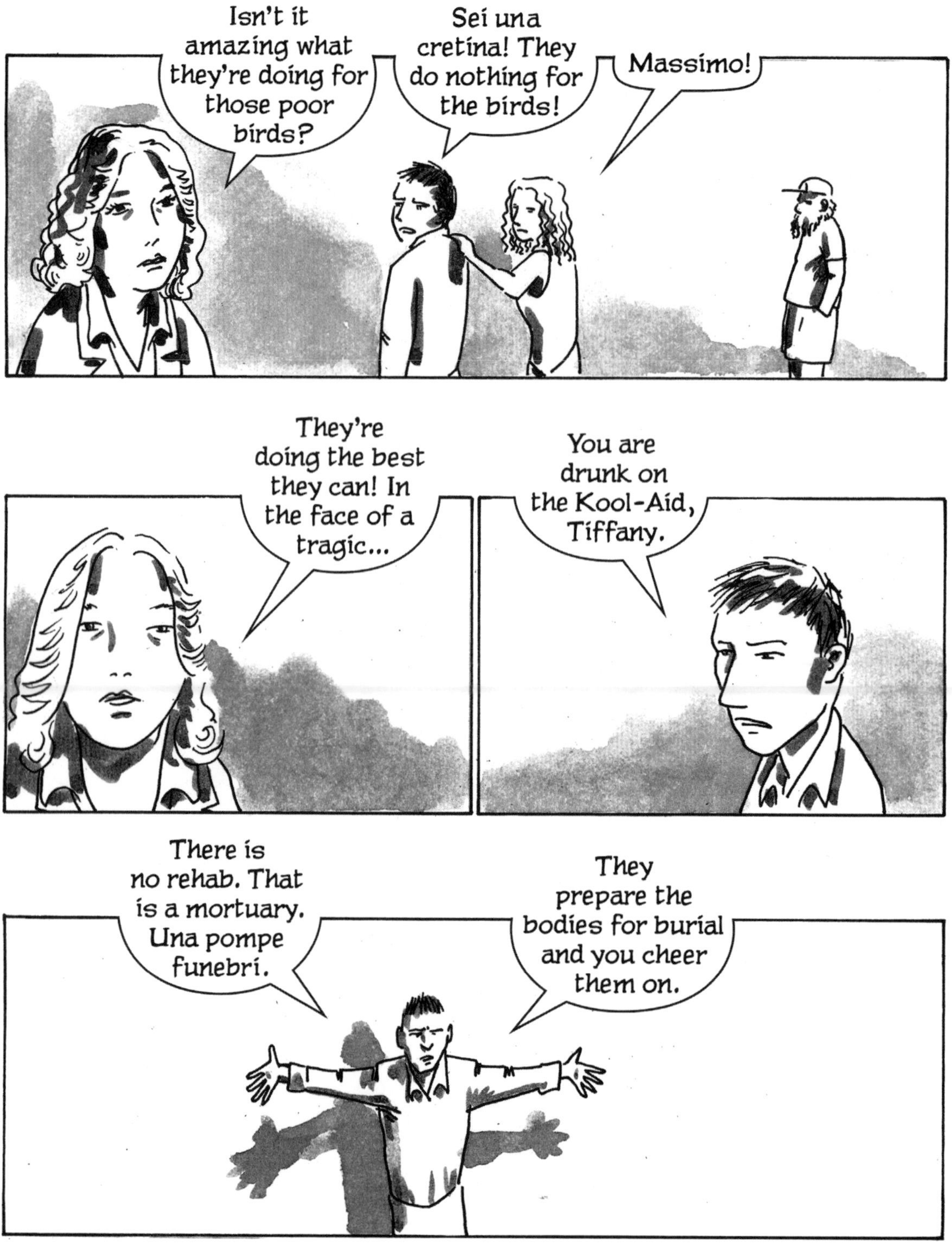
Isn't it amazing what they're doing for those poor birds?
Sei una cretina! They do nothing for the birds!
Massimo!
They're doing the best they can! In the face of a tragic...
You are drunk on the Kool-Aid, Tiffany.
There is no rehab. That is a mortuary. Una pompe funebri.
They prepare the bodies for burial and you cheer them on.

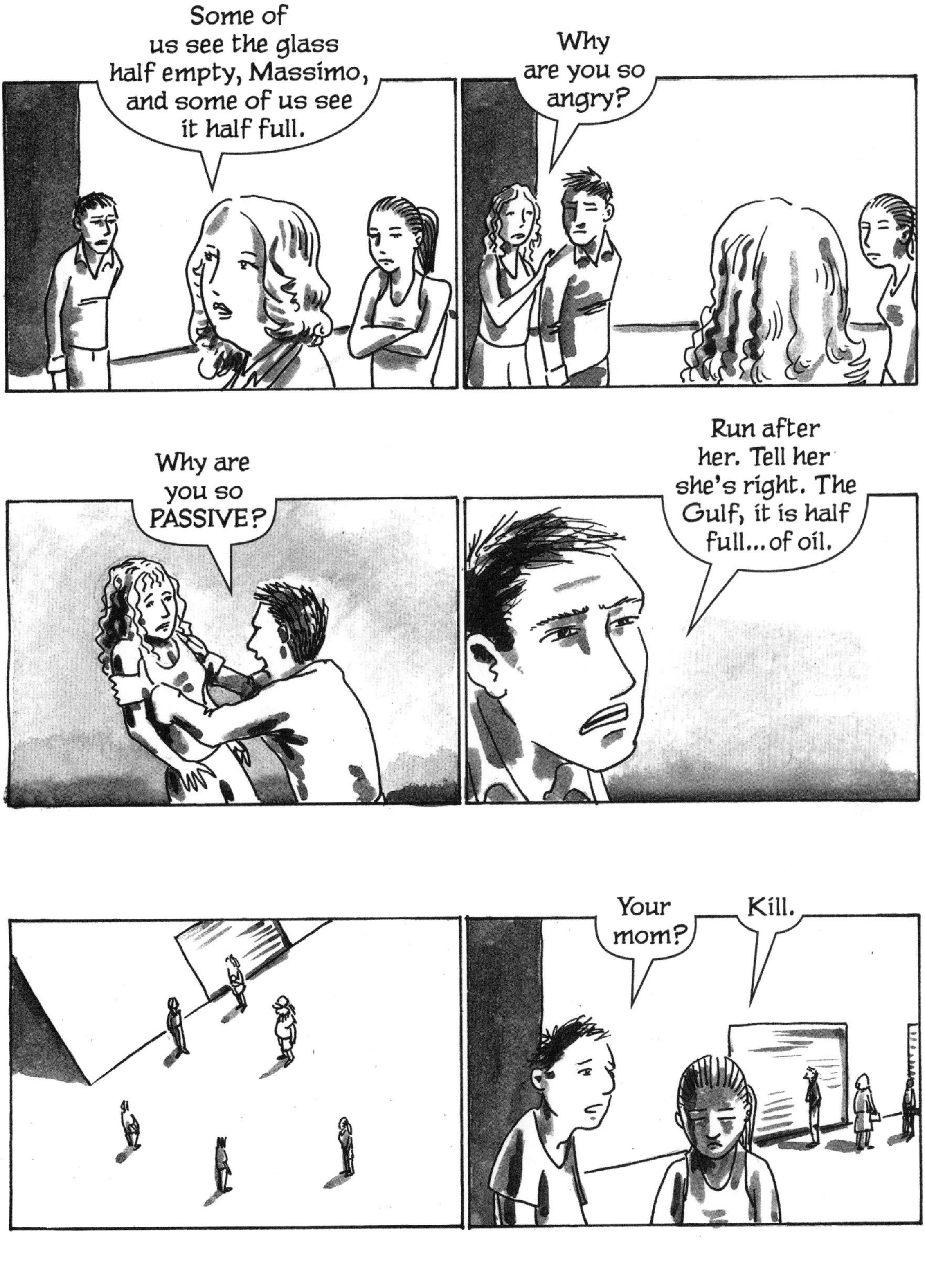
Some of us see the glass half empty, Massimo, and some of us see it half full.
Why are you so angry?
Why are you so PASSIVE?
Run after her. Tell her she's right. The Gulf, it is half full... of oil.
Your mom?
Kill.

On the Beach

Grand Isle, LA

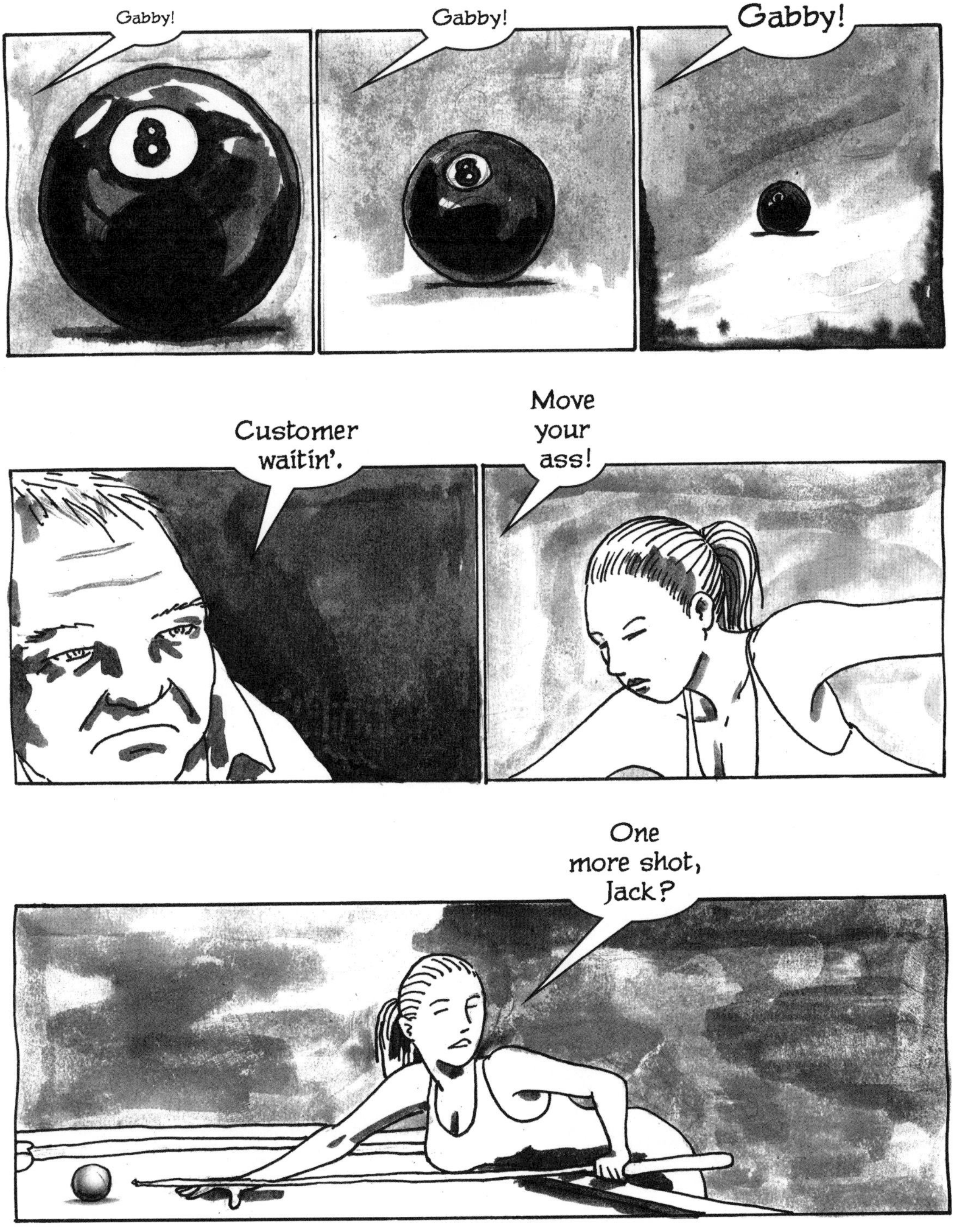
Gabby!
Gabby!
Gabby!
Customer waitin'.
Move your ass!
One more shot, Jack?

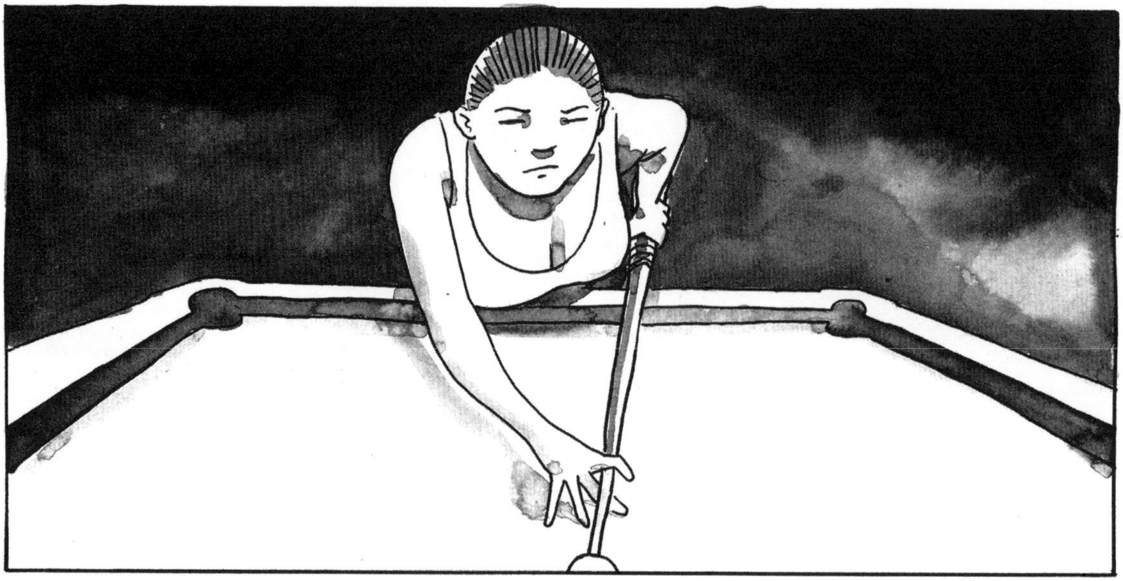

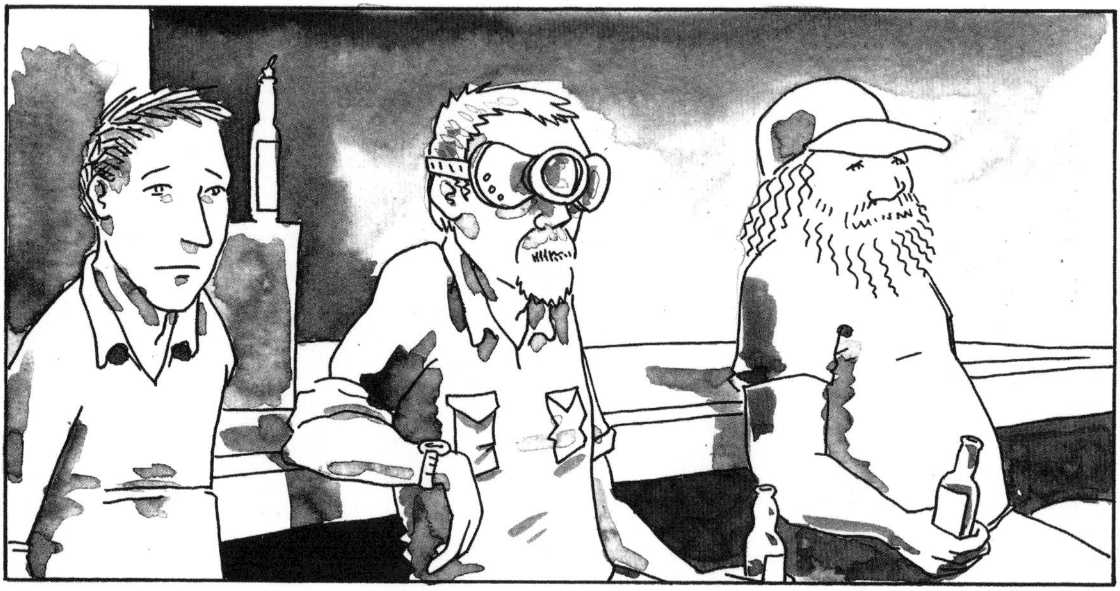

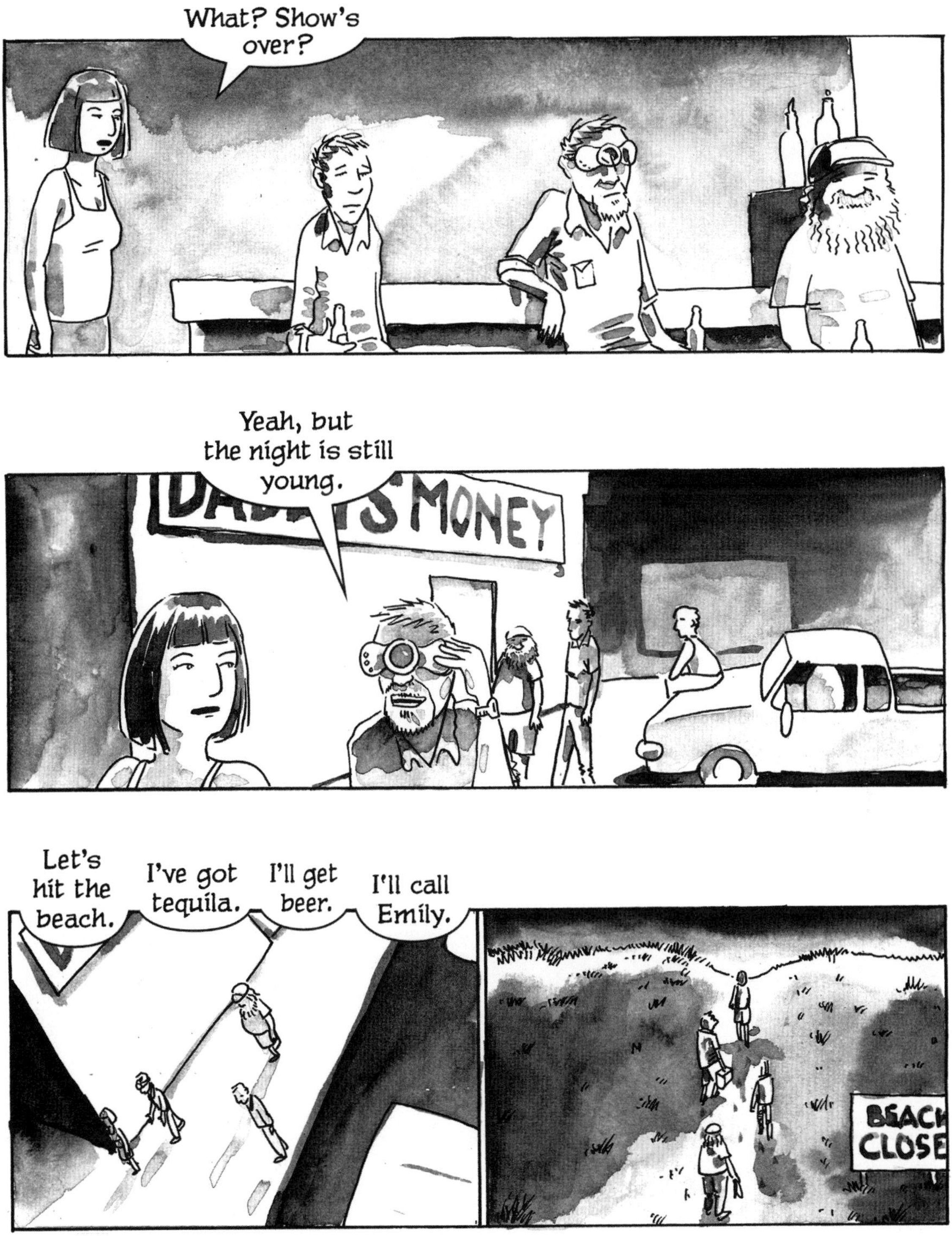
What? Show's over?
Yeah, but the night is still young.
MONEY
Let's hit the beach.
I've got tequila.
I'll get beer.
I'll call Emily.

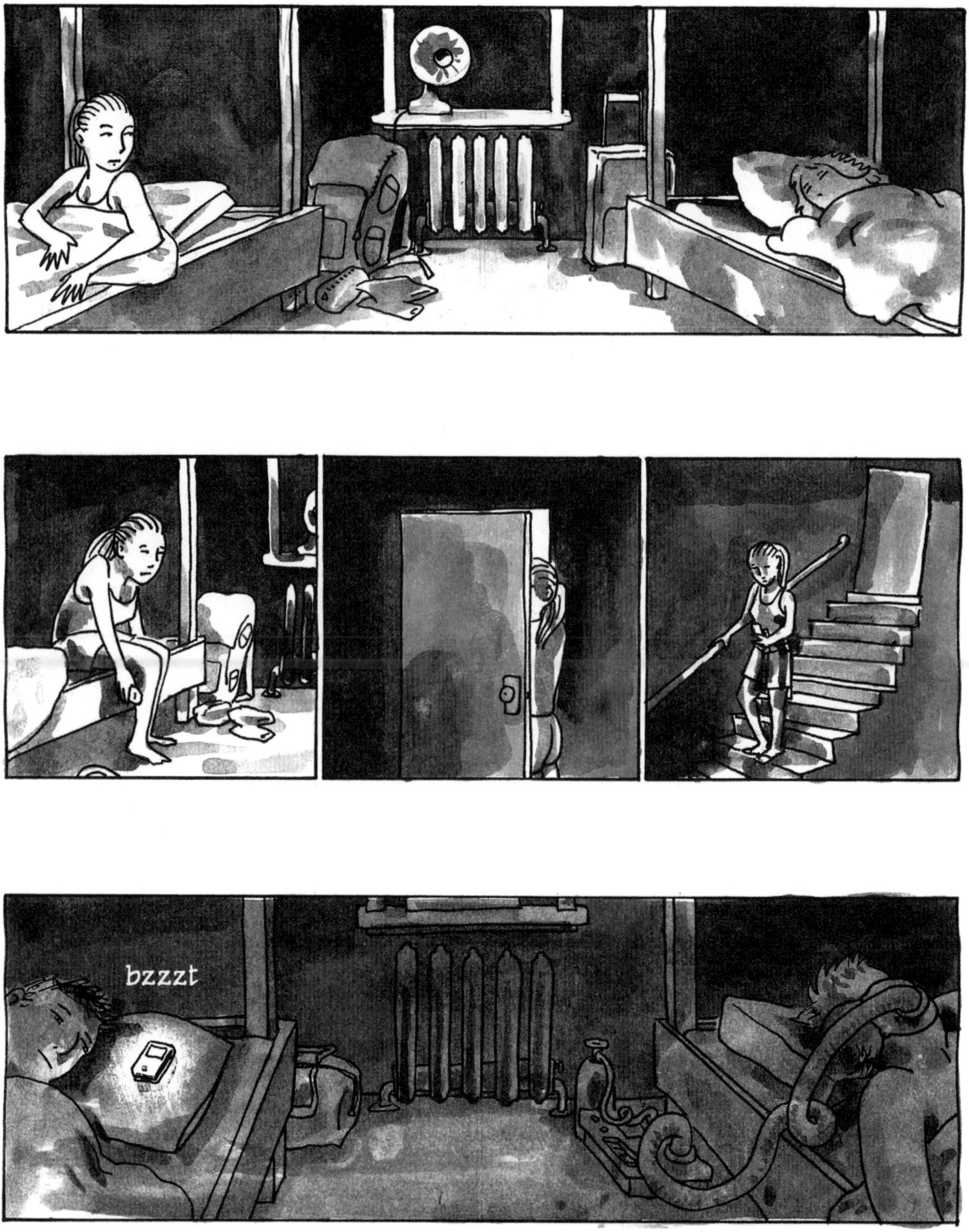
bzzzt

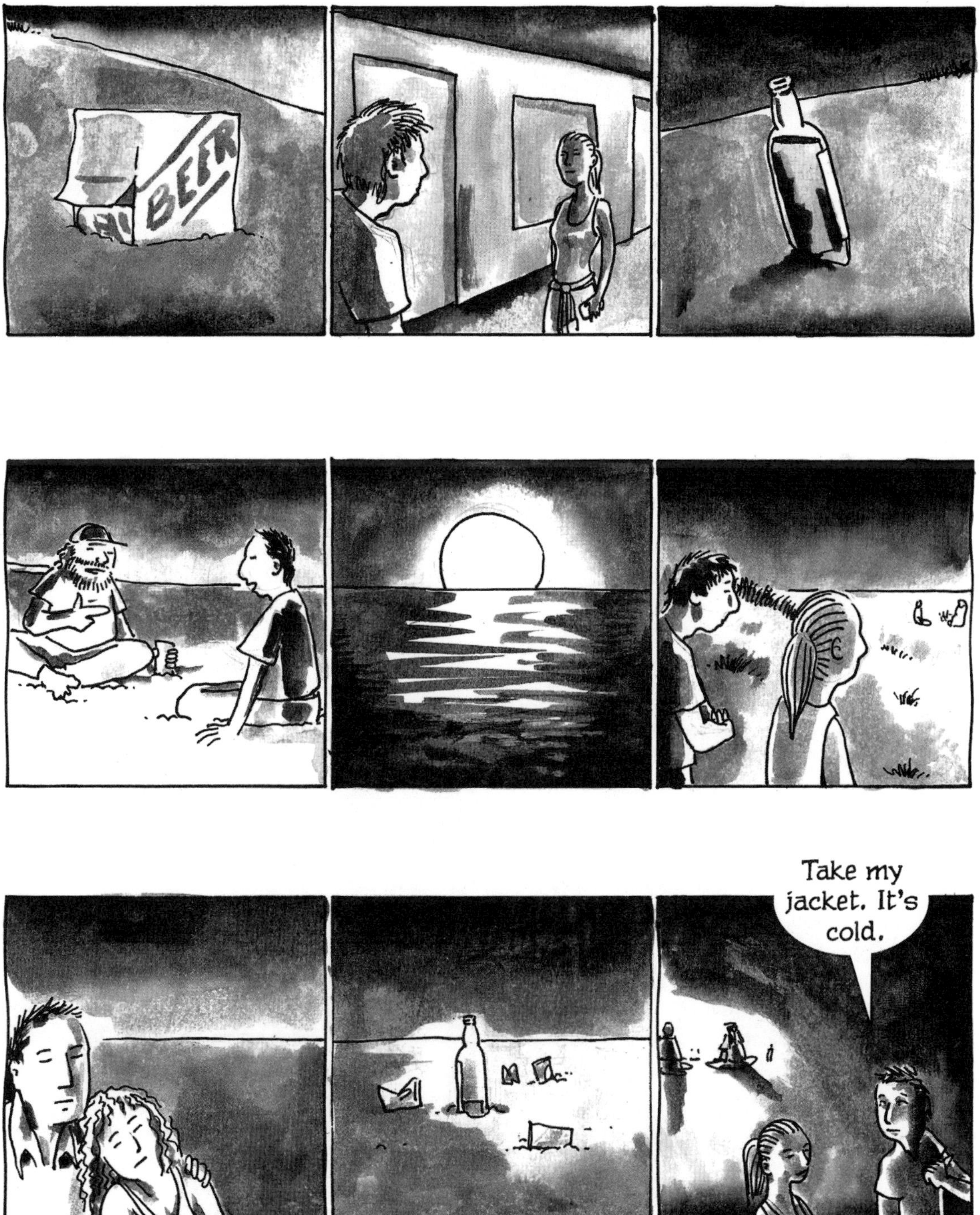
BEER
Take my jacket. It's cold.

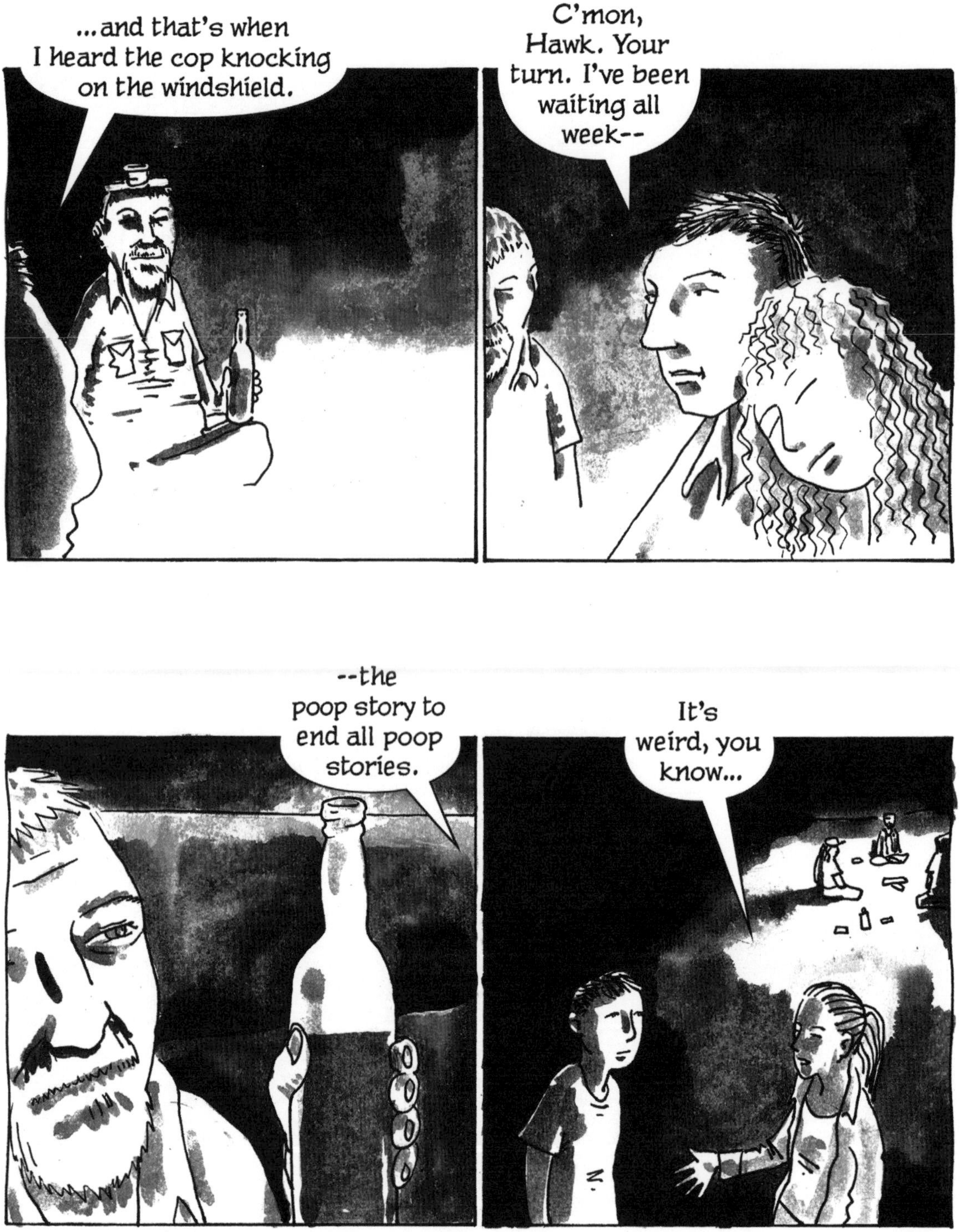

...and that's when I heard the cop knocking on the windshield.
C'mon, Hawk. Your turn. I've been waiting all week--
--the poop story to end all poop stories.
It's weird, you know...

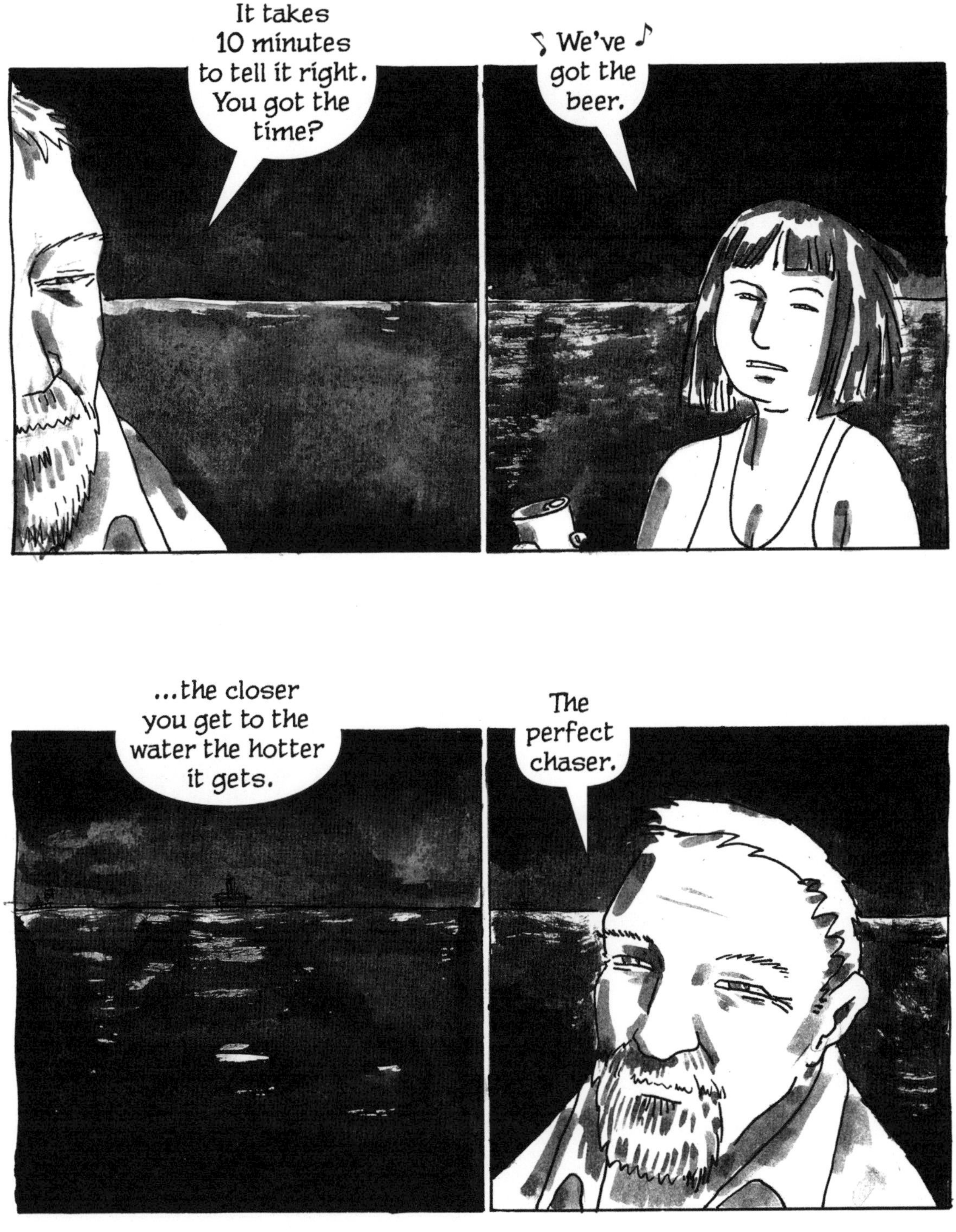
It takes 10 minutes to tell it right. You got the time?
♪ We've ♪ got the beer.
...the closer you get to the water the hotter it gets.
The perfect chaser.

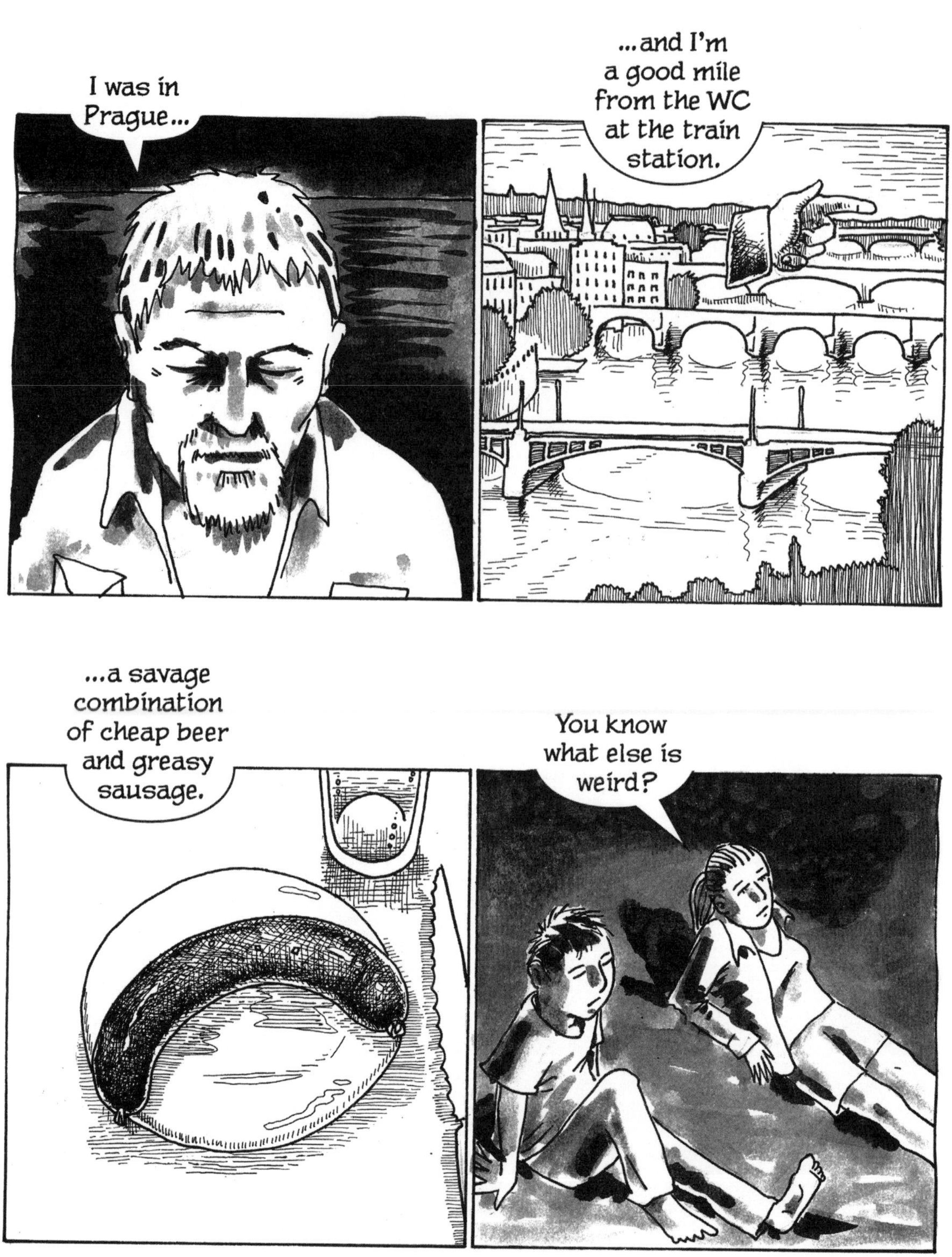
I was in Prague...
...and I'm a good mile from the WC at the train station.
...a savage combination of cheap beer and greasy sausage.
You know what else is weird?

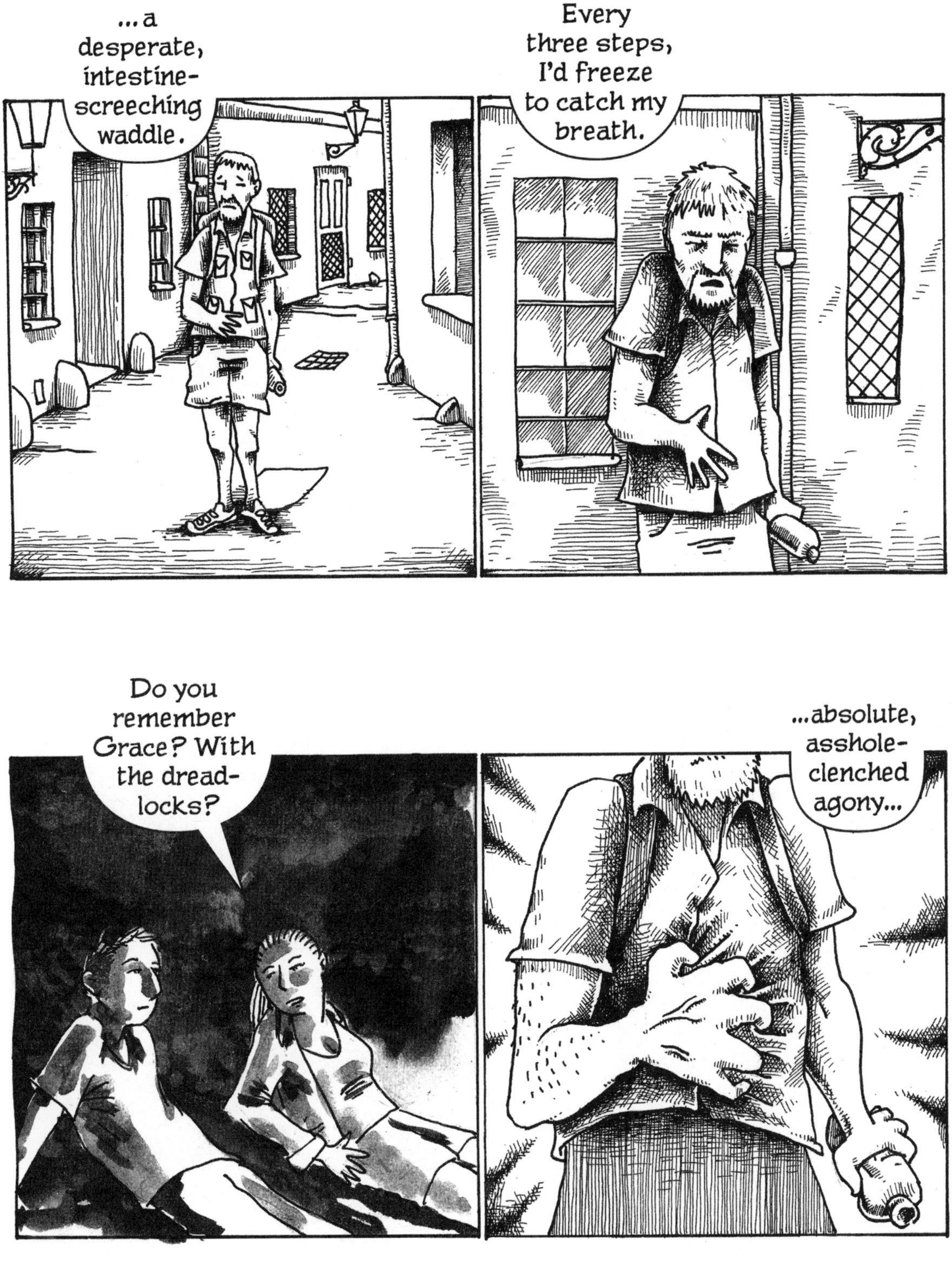
...a desperate, intestine-screeching waddle.
Every three steps, I'd freeze to catch my breath.
Do you remember Grace? With the dread-locks?
...absolute, asshole-clenched agony...

...I don't know how I finally made it...
...but as I stepped into the stall...
...painting the walls in 360-degrees of...
BLAT!
Am I the only one who knows she's gone?

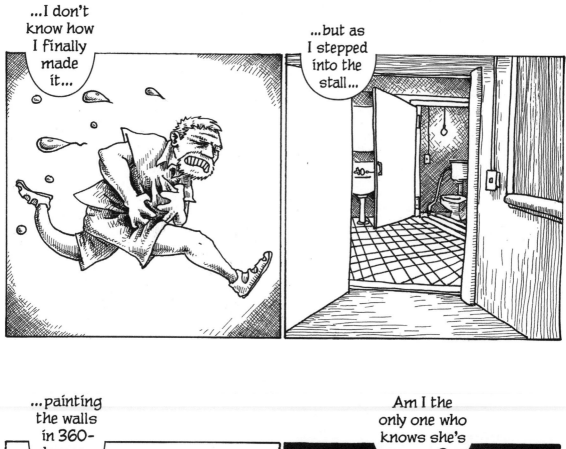

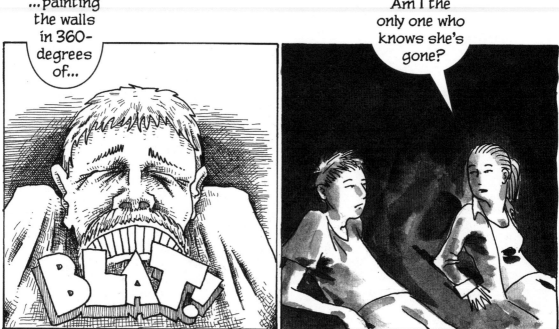

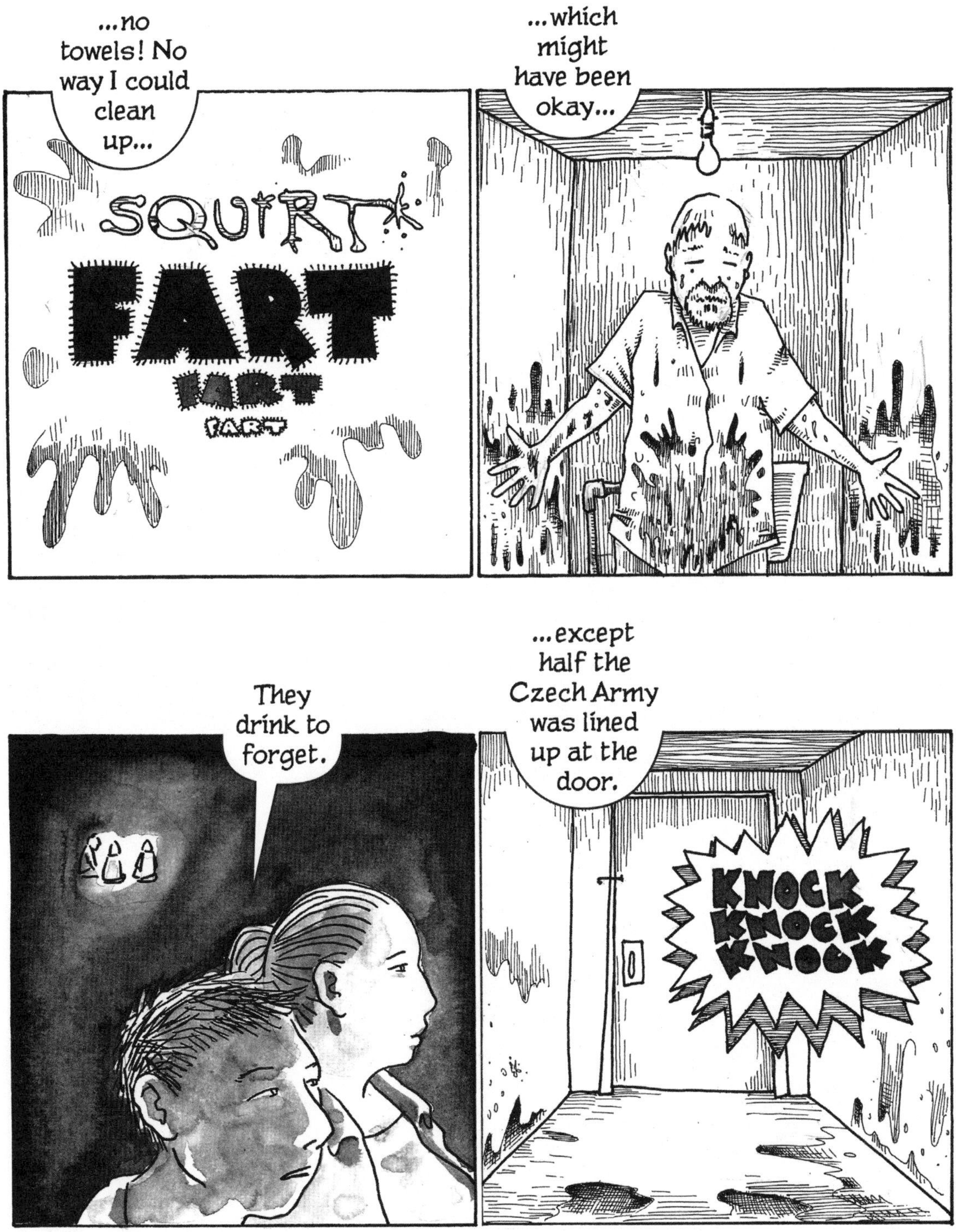
...no towels! No way I could clean up...
SQUIRT
FART
FART
FART
...which might have been okay...
They drink to forget.
...except half the Czech Army was lined up at the door.
KNOCK KNOCK KNOCK

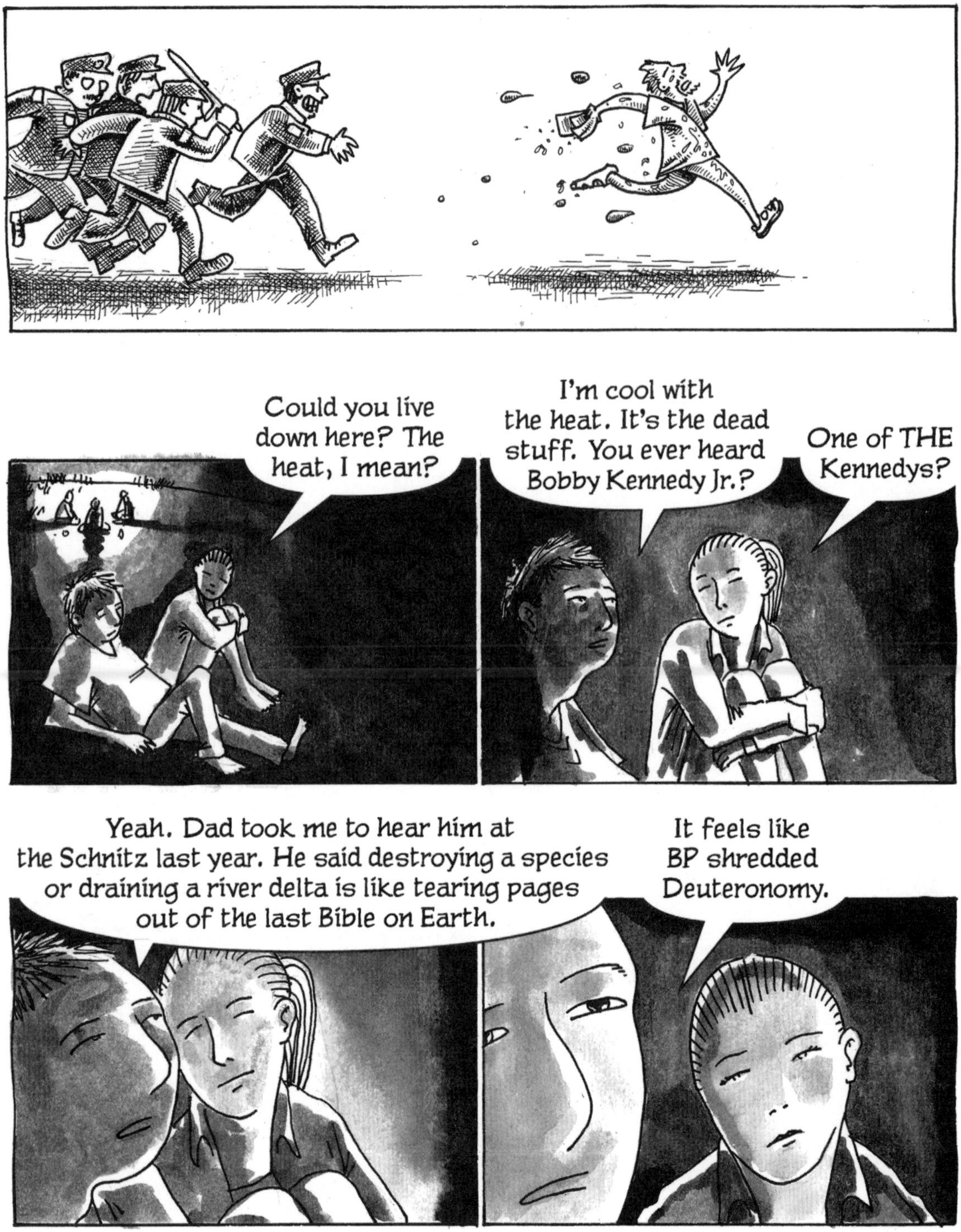
Could you live down here? The heat, I mean?
I'm cool with the heat. It's the dead stuff. You ever heard Bobby Kennedy Jr.?
One of THE Kennedys?
Yeah. Dad took me to hear him at the Schnitz last year. He said destroying a species or draining a river delta is like tearing pages out of the last Bible on Earth.
It feels like BP shredded Deuteronomy.

But it's another thing he said I've never forgotten.

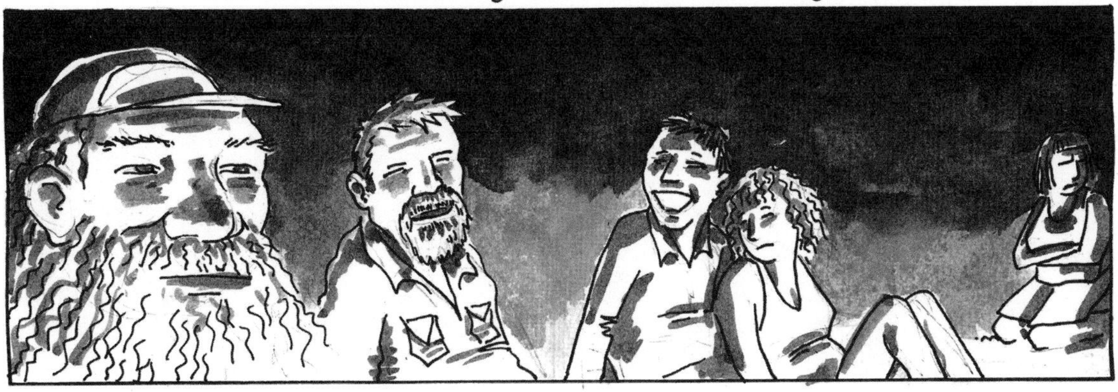

Life, he said, is all about proceeding to the next right thing.

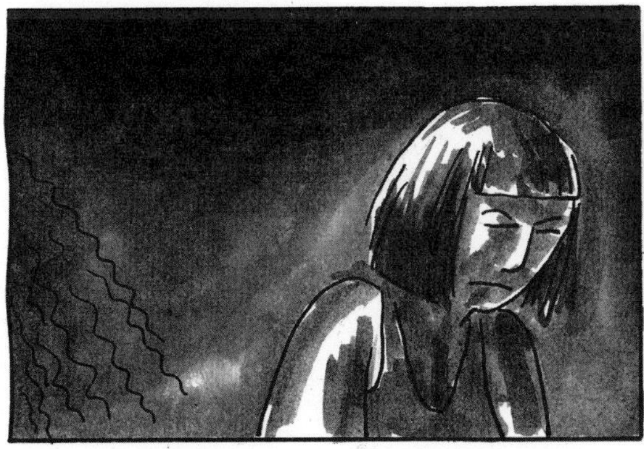

It doesn't have to be giving a speech or winning an election.

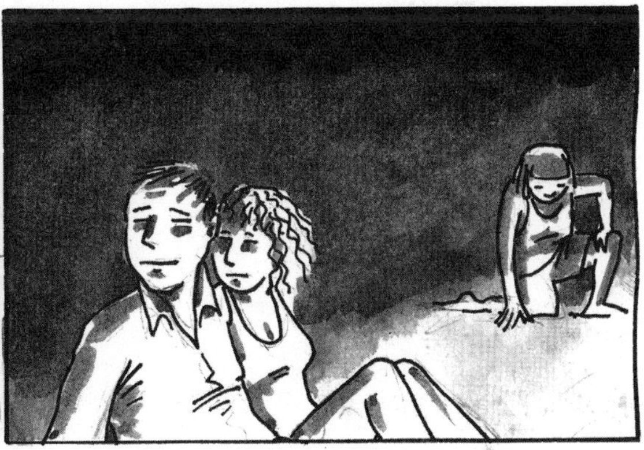

It's whether or not you empty the dishwasher before your parents get home from work.

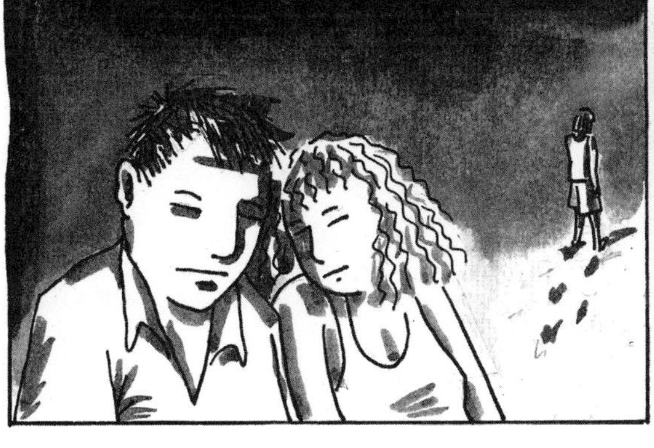

Whether you obey the speed limit.

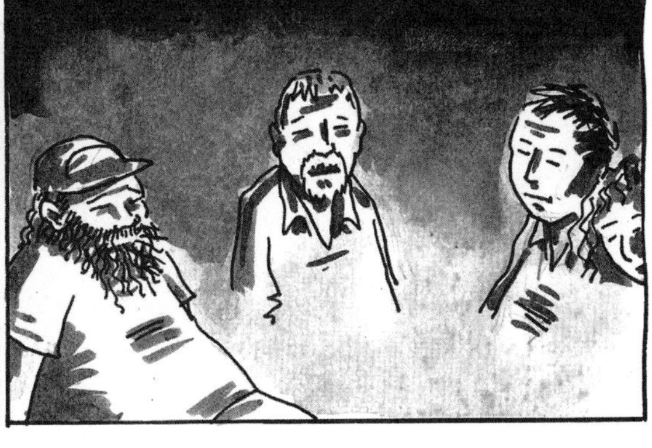

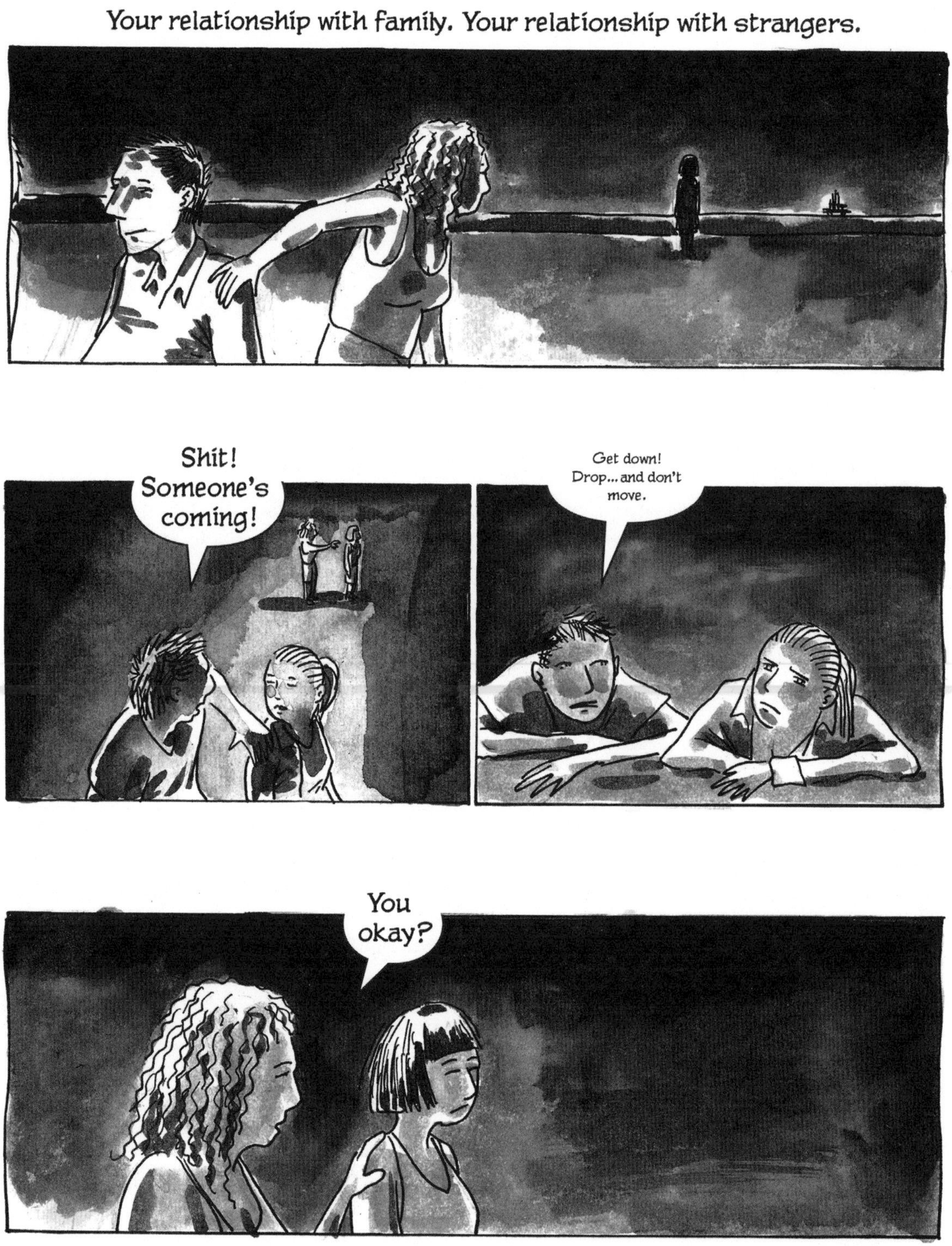
Your relationship with family. Your relationship with strangers.
Shit! Someone's coming!
Get down! Drop... and don't move.
You okay?

Assholes...
...and their raunchy stories.
They're drunk, Tess. They're guys.
There's so much left to do...
...and we're getting wasted on the beach.
You don't see the connection?
I... I can't believe how much I miss my kids.

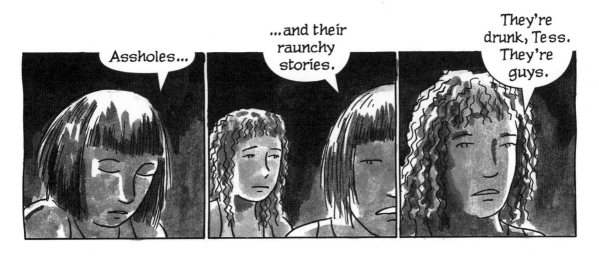

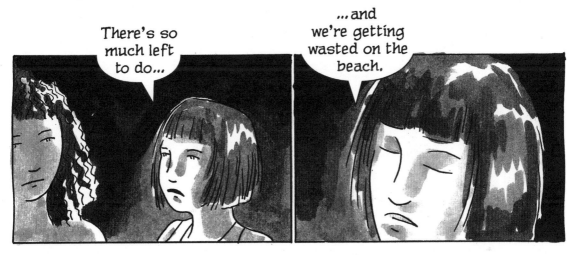

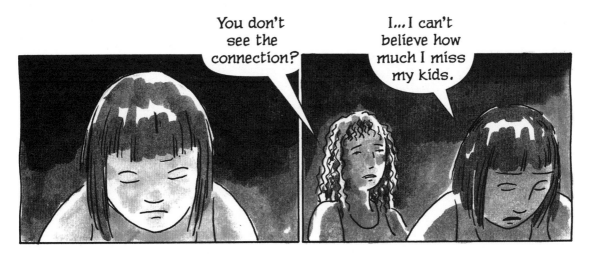

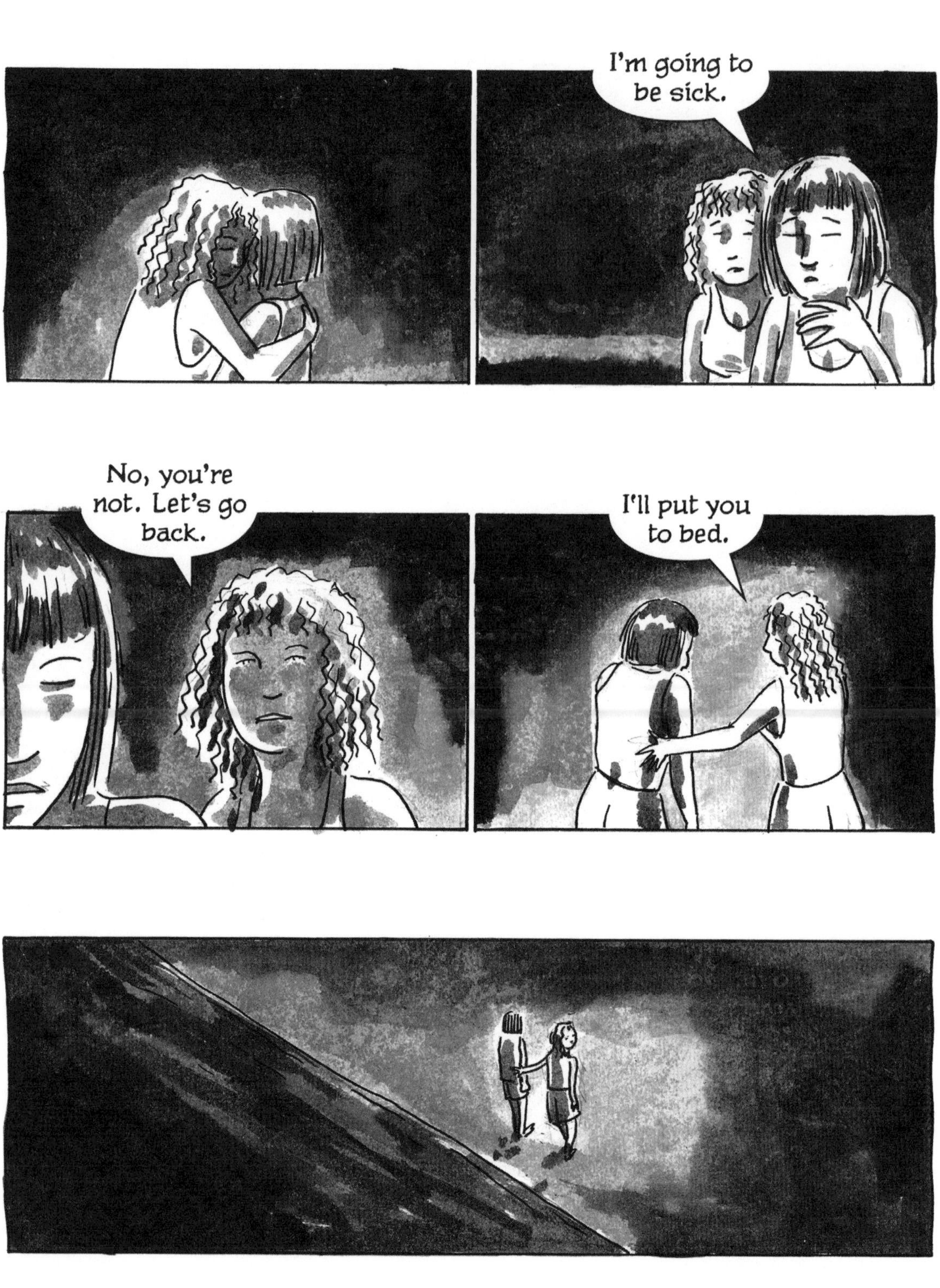
I'm going to be sick.
No, you're not. Let's go back.
I'll put you to bed.

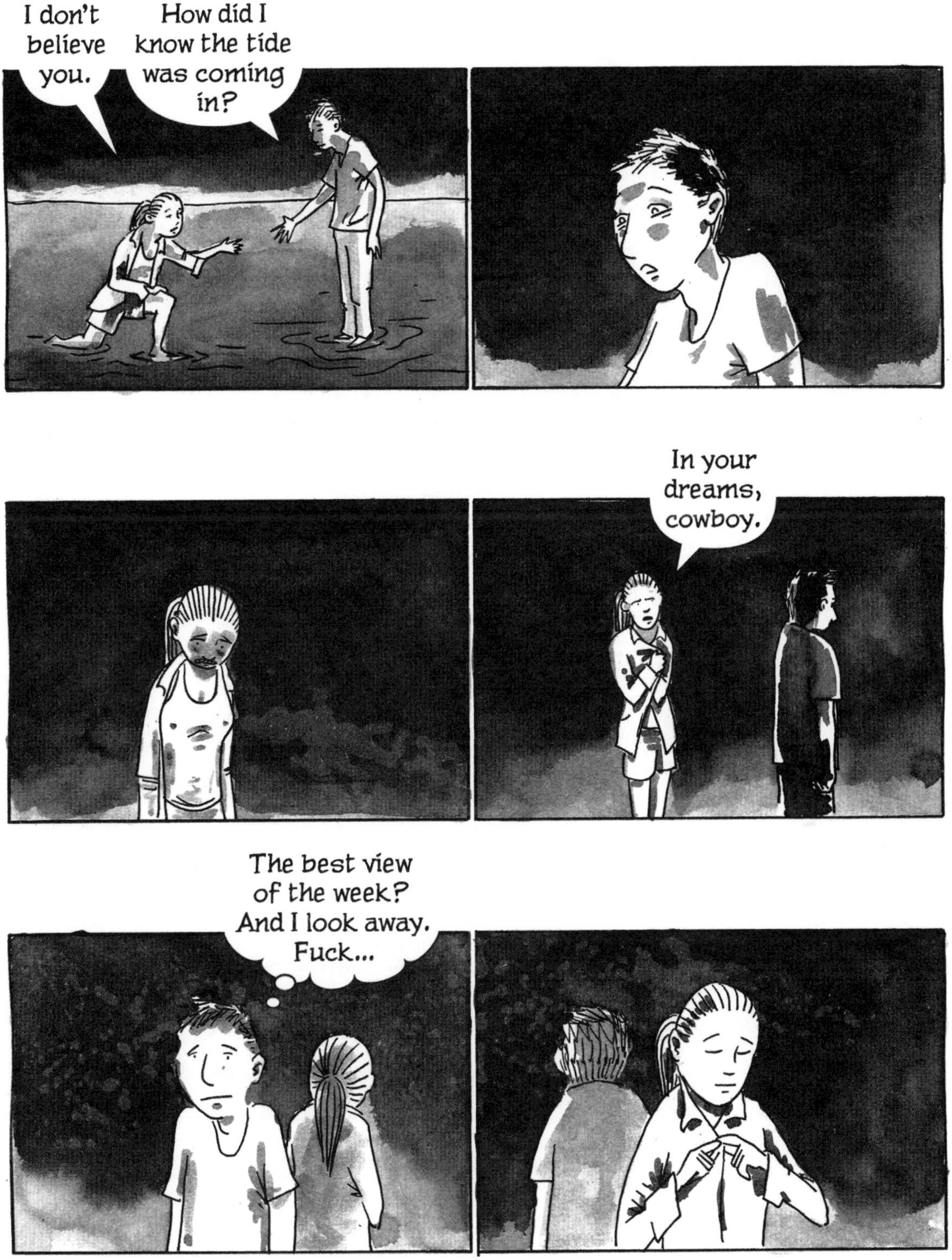
I don't believe you.
How did I know the tide was coming in?
In your dreams, cowboy.
The best view of the week? And I look away. Fuck...

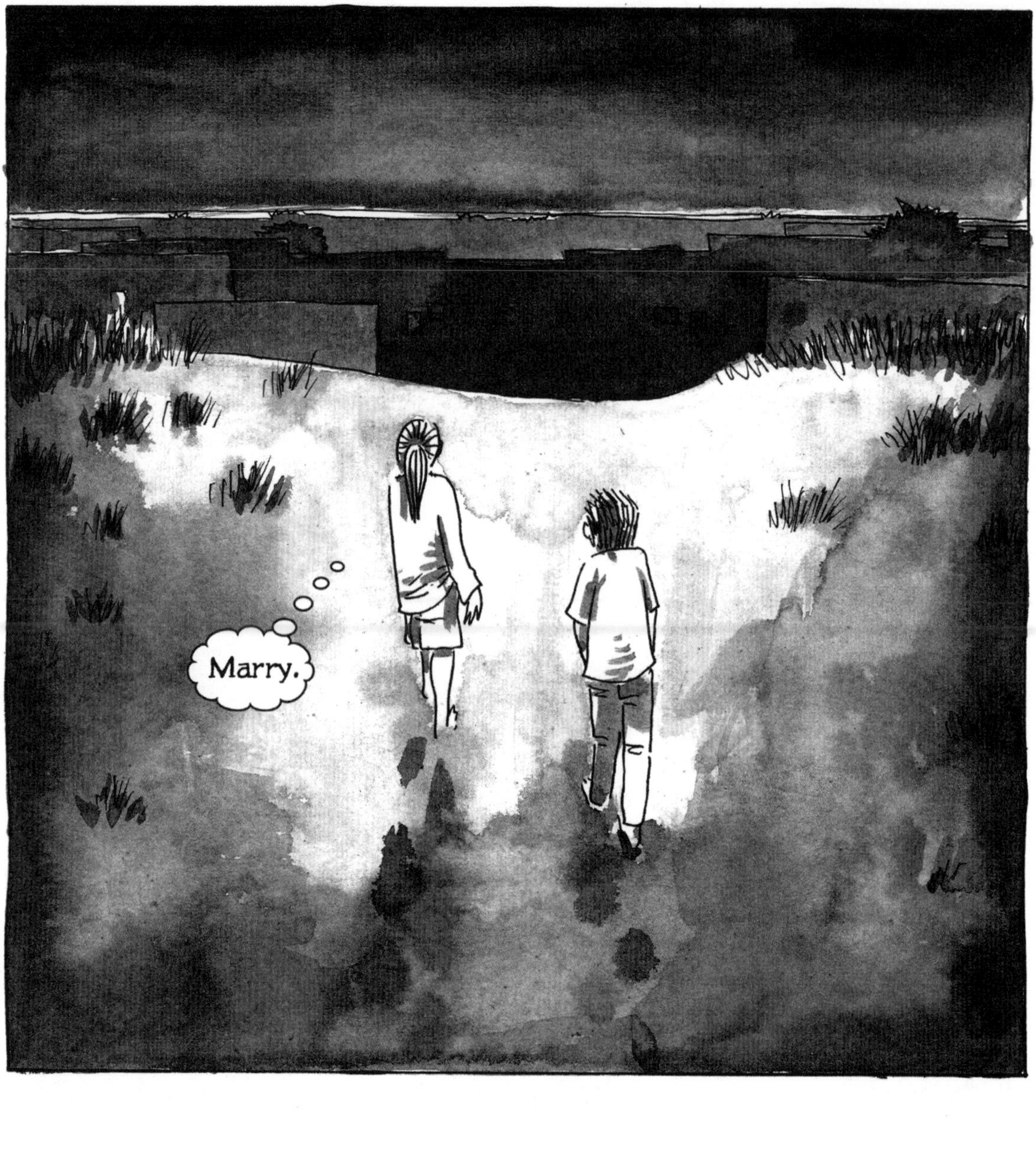
Marry.

On the Backs of Sea Turtles

Among the many victims of the Deepwater Horizon, sea turtles did most of their suffering in silence... at least until BP began carelessly trapping the marine marvels along with sheets of surface oil inside flame-resistant booms, then set the "burn boxes" ablaze.

Five of the world's seven sea turtle species nest along the Gulf Coast. All are endangered species. Of the more than 600 dead turtles recovered in the six months after the BP spill, almost 500 were Kemp's Ridley turtles, the smallest of the five species and the most endangered.

On many beaches, Unified Command scientists reasoned, contact with "weathered" oil posed little threat for the adult females digging their nests in the sand or for the hatchlings struggling to reach the water.

But not the beach at Grand Isle. The oil was too fresh and too thick.

To limit the damage, conservationists collected 70,000 sea turtle eggs from Gulf beaches in Florida and Alabama, mothered the eggs inside a hanger at the Kennedy Space Center until they hatched, then released almost 15,000 hatchlings into the Atlantic Ocean.

Ken Lohmann, a University of North Carolina biologist, questioned the effectiveness of the rescue operation. Lohmann long ago determined that sea turtles "imprint" on the magnetic fields of their beach as they gestate, which allows them to eventually find their way back to those beaches.

Lohmann was particularly disappointed that no one bothered to mark the hatchlings in order to determine how many turtles returned to the Gulf.

"The frustrating thing," Lohmann said, "is that the next time this happens, we're not going to be any wiser."

A credo of the BP oil spill, that.

Found

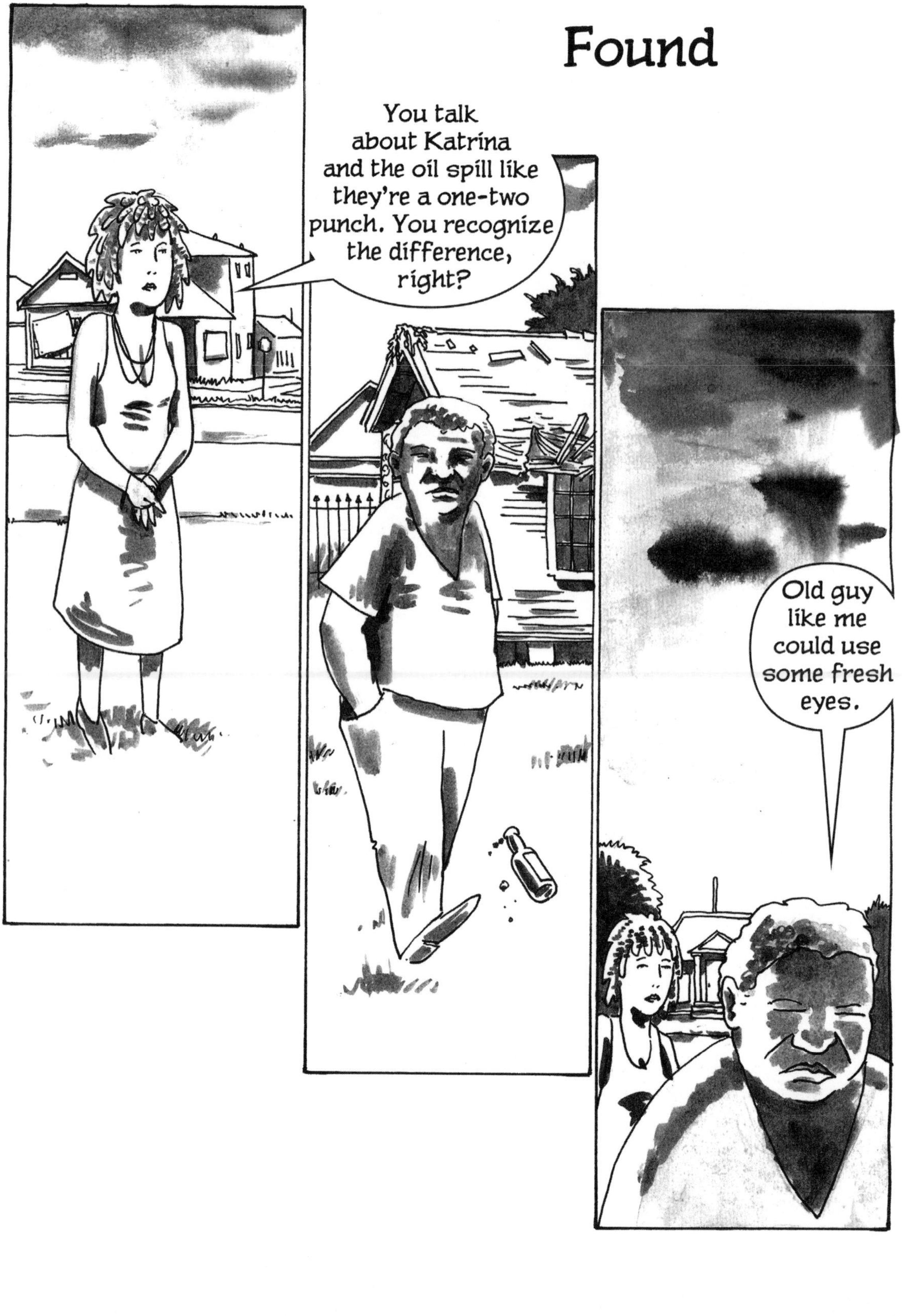
You talk about Katrina and the oil spill like they're a one-two punch. You recognize the difference, right?
Old guy like me could use some fresh eyes.

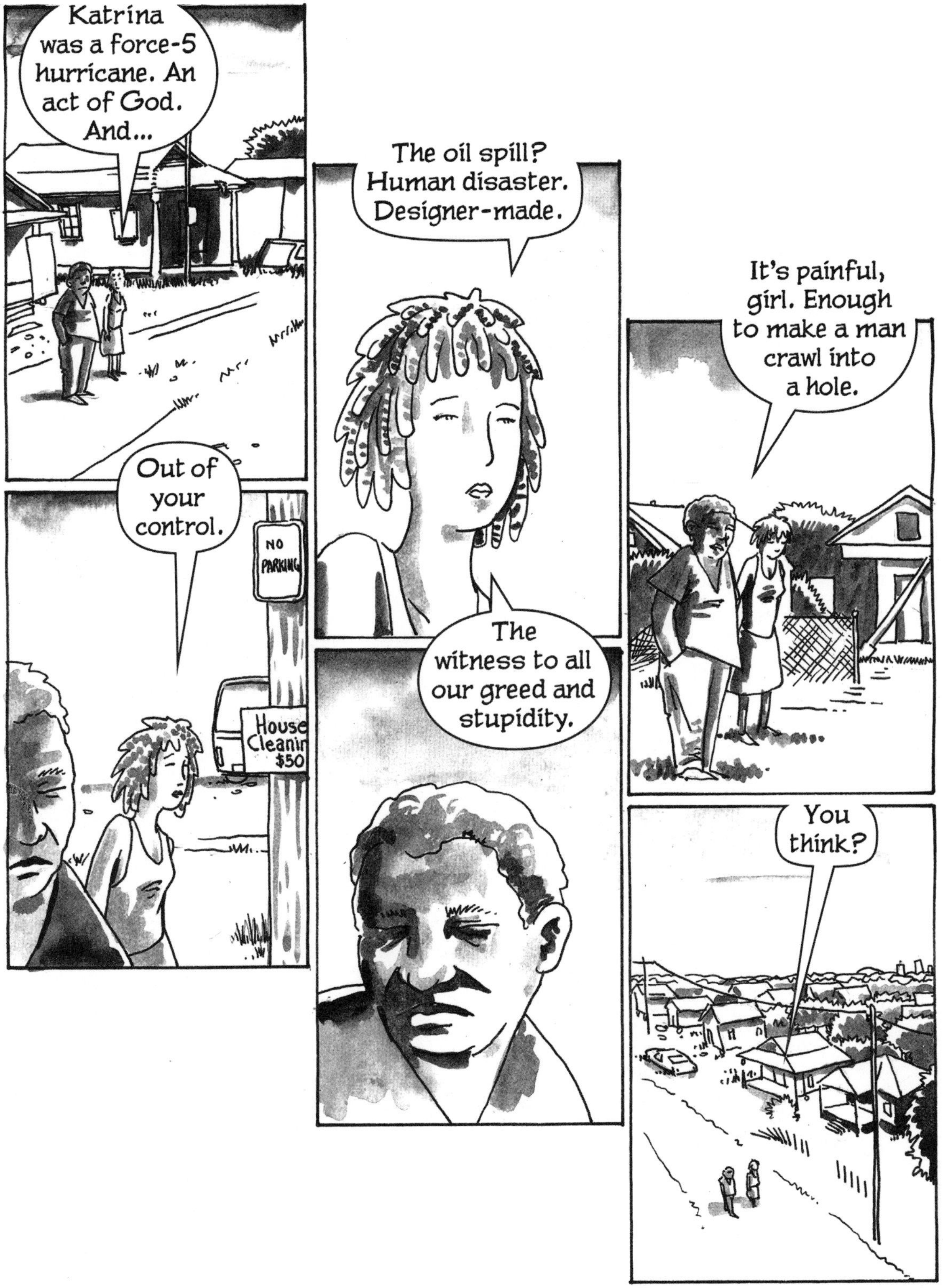
Katrina was a force-5 hurricane. An act of God. And...
Out of your control.
NO PARKING
House Cleanin $50
The oil spill? Human disaster. Designer-made.
The witness to all our greed and stupidity.
It's painful, girl. Enough to make a man crawl into a hole.
You think?

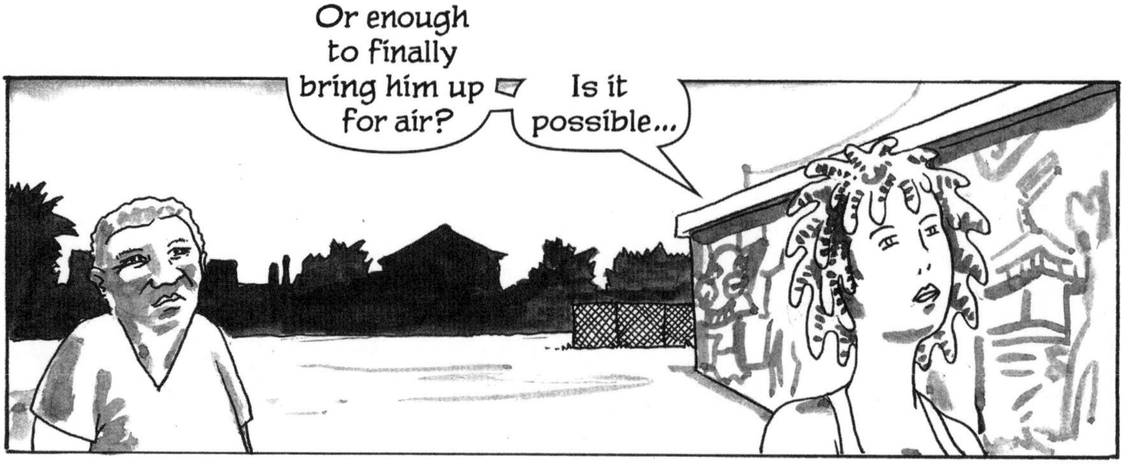
Is it possible...
Or enough to finally bring him up for air?

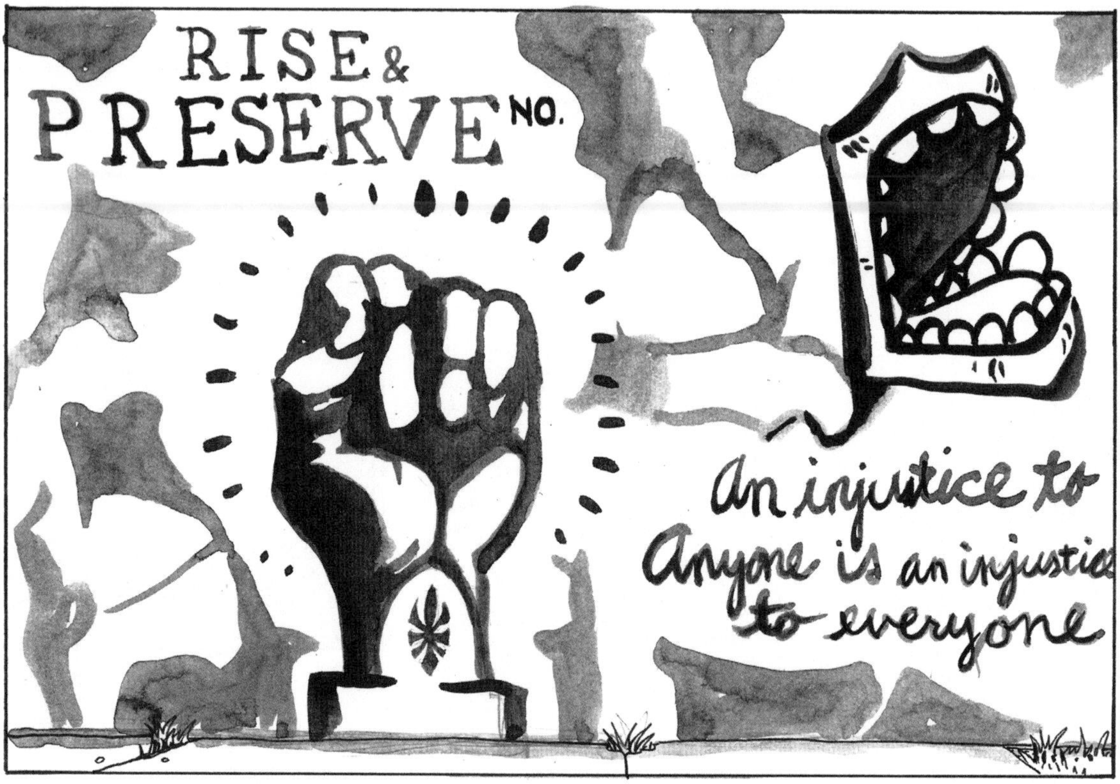
RISE &
PRESERVE NO.
An injustice to Anyone is an injustice to everyone

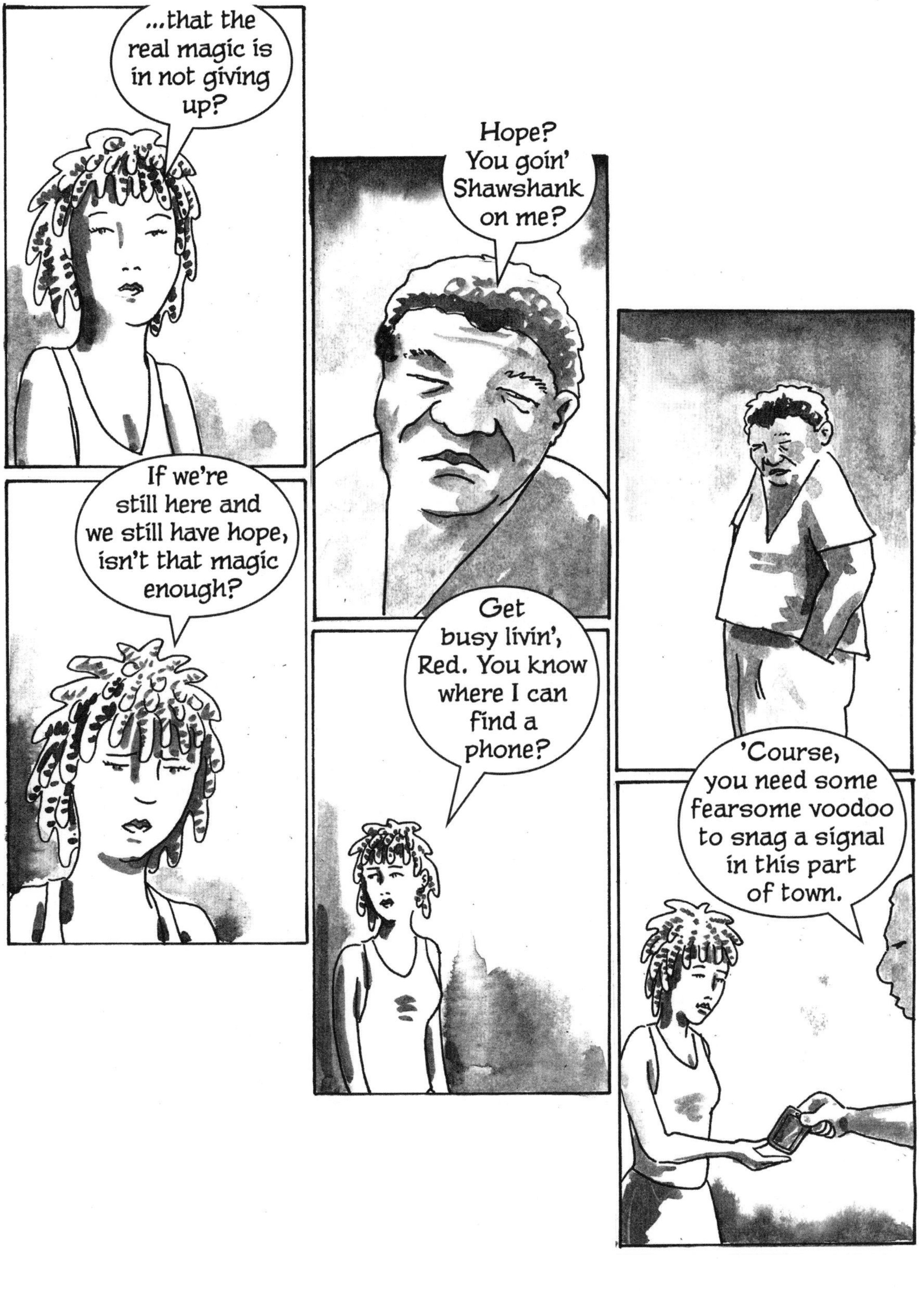
...that the real magic is in not giving up?
If we're still here and we still have hope, isn't that magic enough?
Hope? You goin' Shawshank on me?
Get busy livin', Red. You know where I can find a phone?
'Course, you need some fearsome voodoo to snag a signal in this part of town.

Catfish

D'Iberville, MS

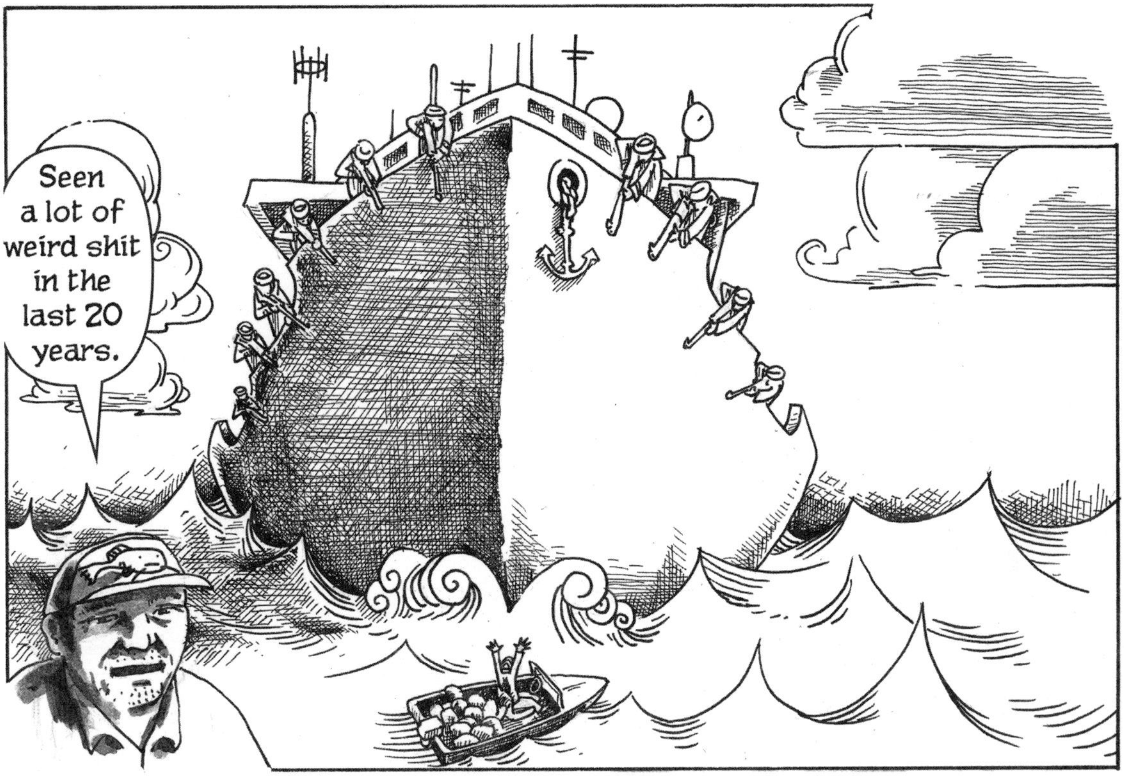
Seen a lot of weird shit in the last 20 years.

Shrimp disappear with the tide.

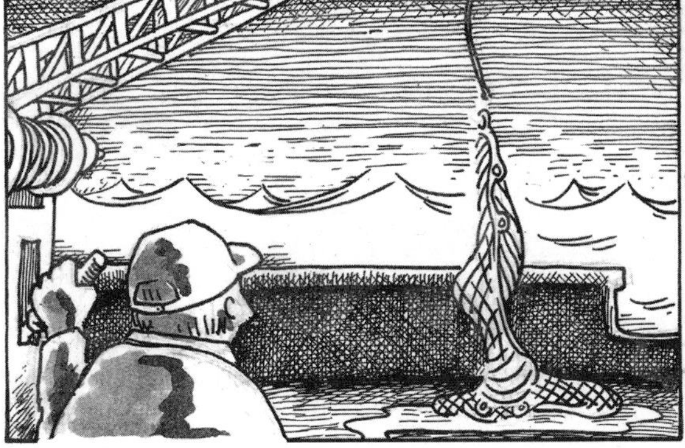

Viet Cong invade the gulf.

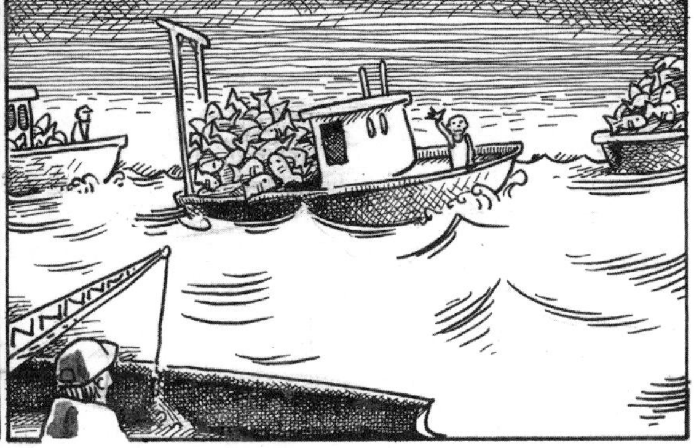

Coke going for $250 a gram.

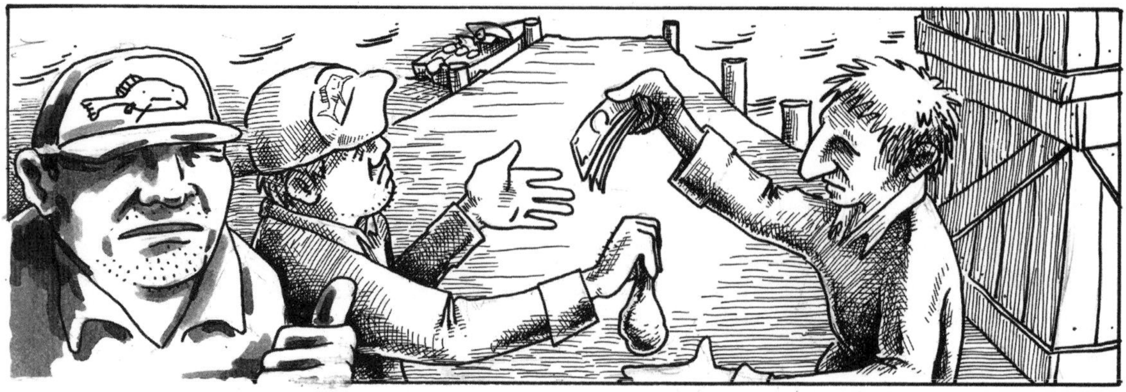

So, yeah, I can deal with a bunch of liberal whack jobs telling us to sing for our supper.

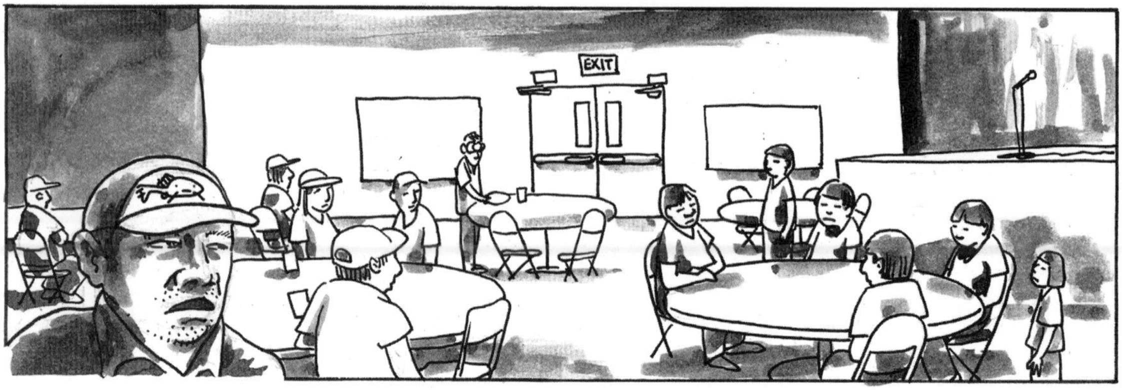
EXIT

Times like these... ...a free meal makes for strange bedfellows.

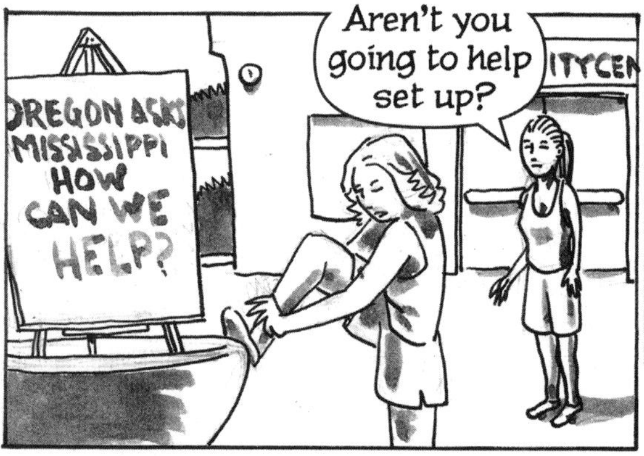
OREGON ASKS MISSISSIPPI HOW CAN WE HELP?
Aren't you going to help set up?

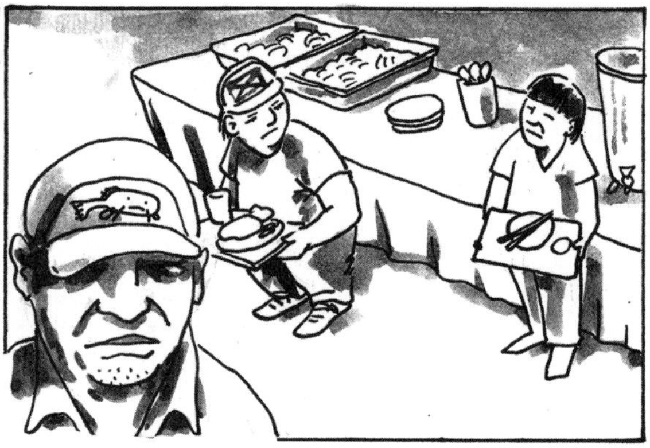

Me? They call me, 'Catfish.'
Everyone knows me 'round here.

I know where
the browns hide out.

Know where the whites
hunker down.

Know shrimpin' don't pay like drug-runnin'
on the bayou.

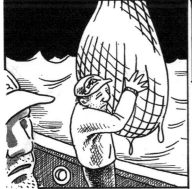

Made good money.

Served 39 months.

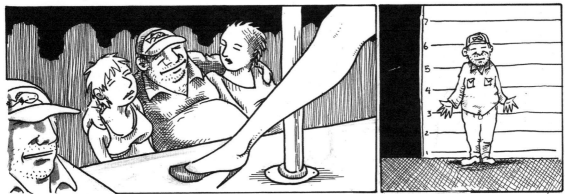

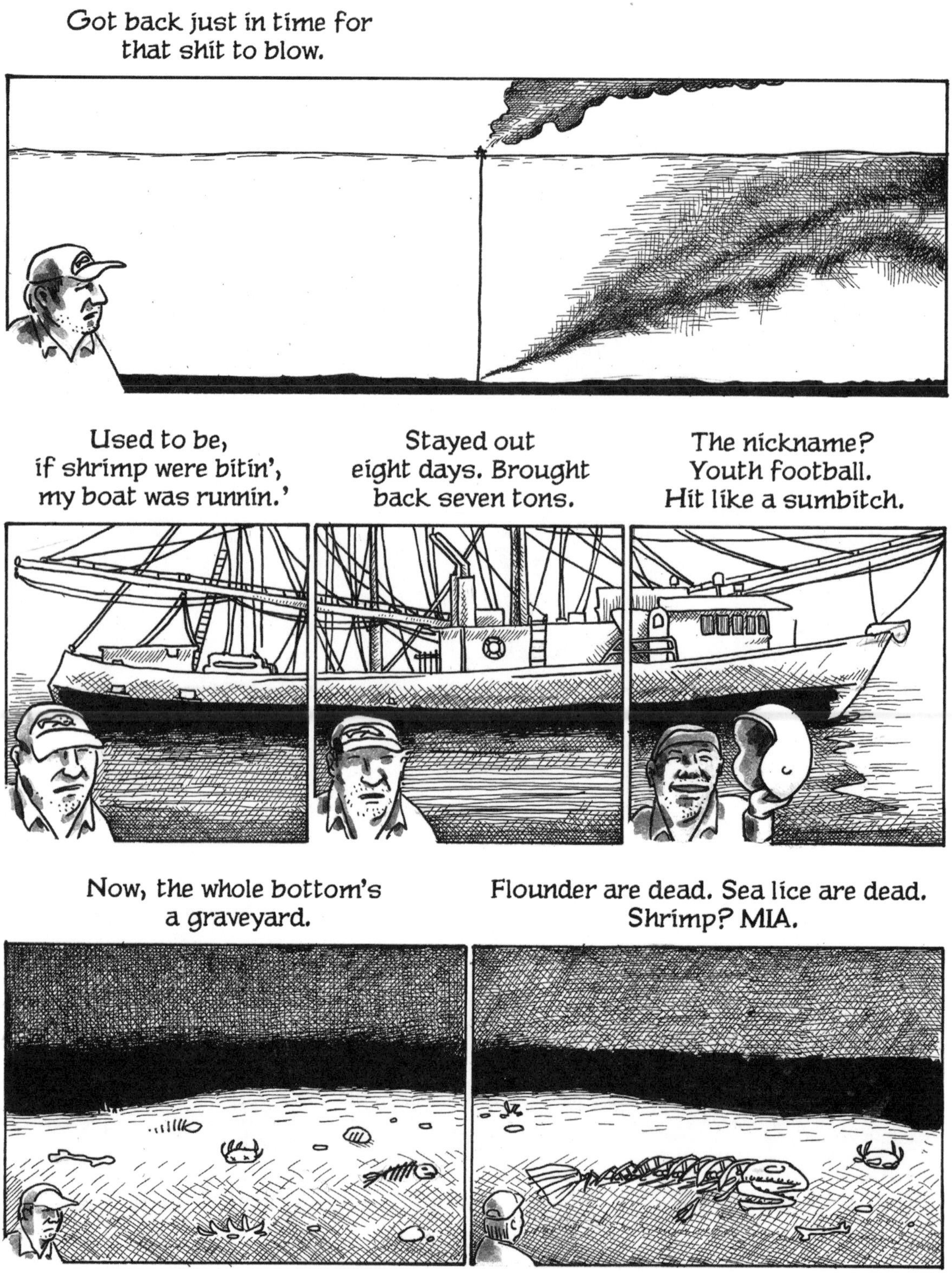

Got back just in time for that shit to blow.
Used to be, if shrimp were bitin', my boat was runnin.'
Stayed out eight days. Brought back seven tons.
The nickname? Youth football. Hit like a sumbitch.
Now, the whole bottom's a graveyard.
Flounder are dead. Sea lice are dead. Shrimp? MIA.

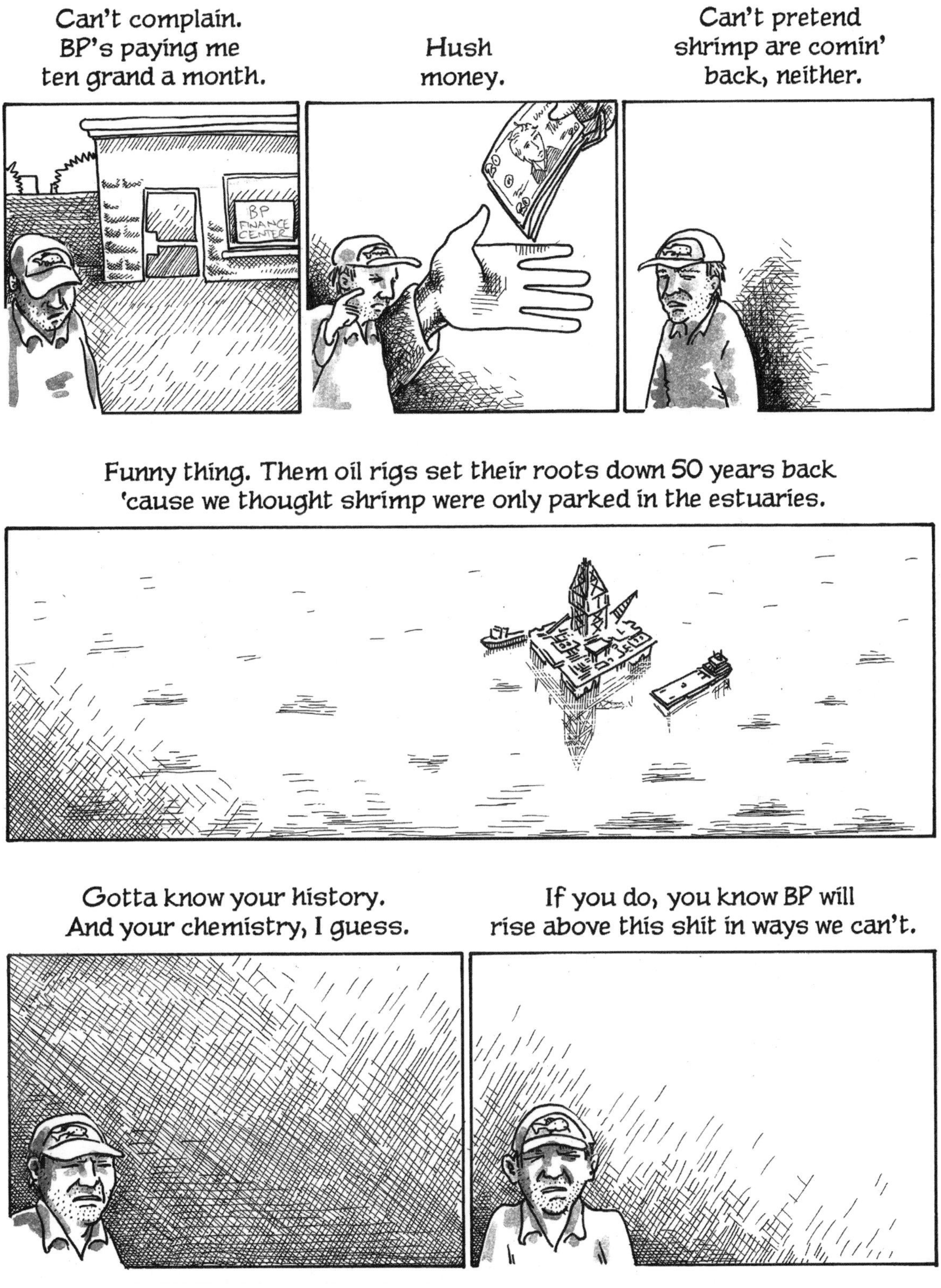
Can't complain. BP's paying me ten grand a month.
BP FINANCE CENTER
Hush money.
Can't pretend shrimp are comin' back, neither.
Funny thing. Them oil rigs set their roots down 50 years back 'cause we thought shrimp were only parked in the estuaries.
Gotta know your history. And your chemistry, I guess.
If you do, you know BP will rise above this shit in ways we can't.

We're screwed. All of us.

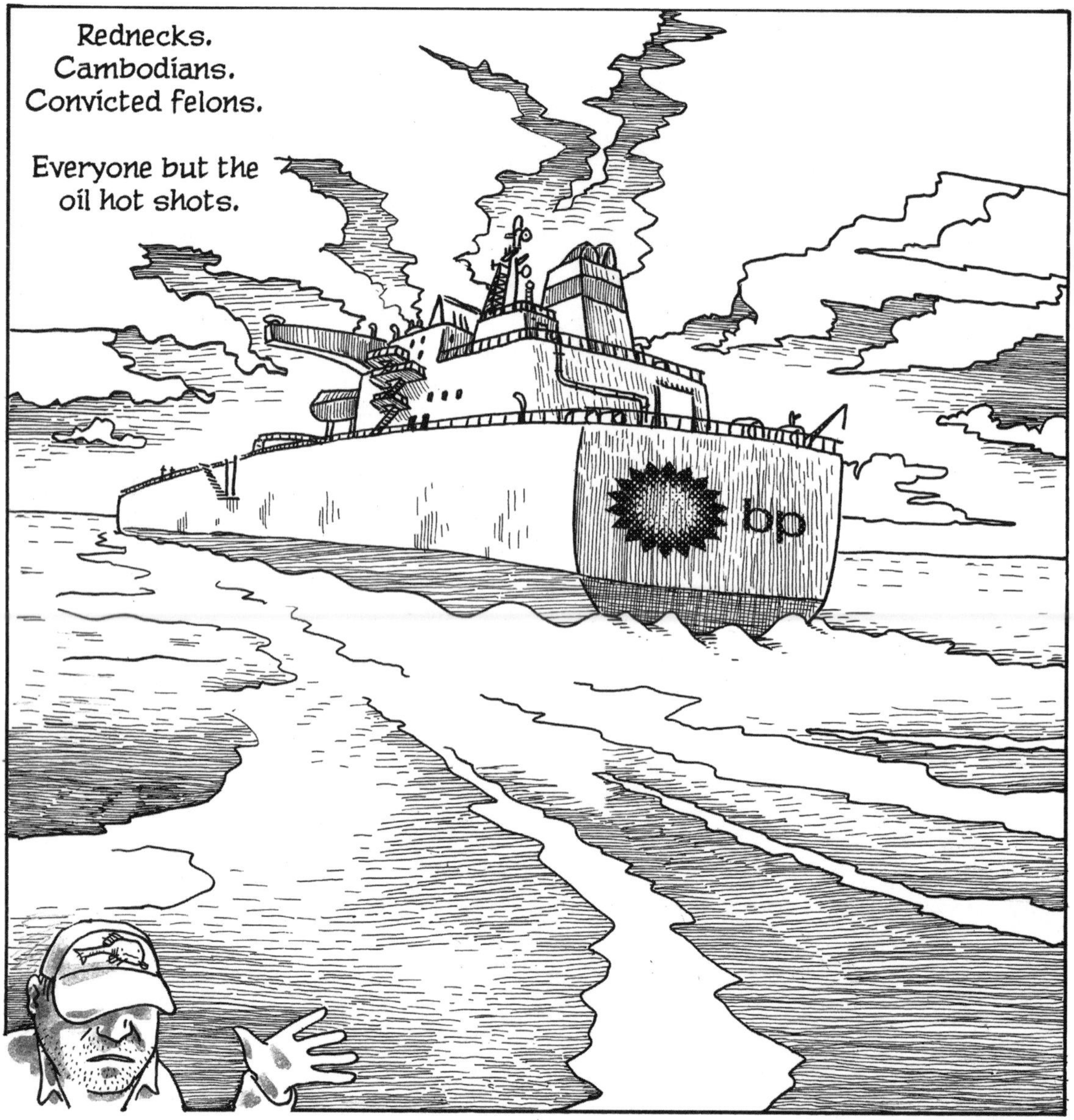
Rednecks.
Cambodians.
Convicted felons.
Everyone but the oil hot shots.
bp

BP. Hail, Brittania!

They still rule the waves.

The Hidden Menace

Have we mentioned the ticking time bomb? The delayed fuse?

The oil-soaked welcome wagon that will be waiting, come winter, come spring, for the millions upon millions of birds who return to the Gulf Coast to nest or to rest?

The bayous, estuaries and marshes here are in the flight path of the planet's greatest migration of birds: terns and rails, plovers and dowitchers, redhead scaups, American oystercatchers and Canadian geese.

And for years to come, oil from the Deepwater Horizon will lurk in the barrier islands, sea grass beds and food chain.

In nesting grounds or tiny ponds far beyond the reach of the clean-up crews, the thrush and frigatebirds will return to feed or gather strength. Wherever they turn, oil will rise from the water to grease their feathers, poison their food, blind their chicks.

The birds will die in numbers we can neither count nor imagine, invisible victims of this invasive spill.

Agida

Grand Bayou, LA

We drove to Grand Bayou looking for the Atakapa-Ishak tribe, but they had disappeared into the marshes. We were feeling useless, abbandonato, when the boat pulled in.

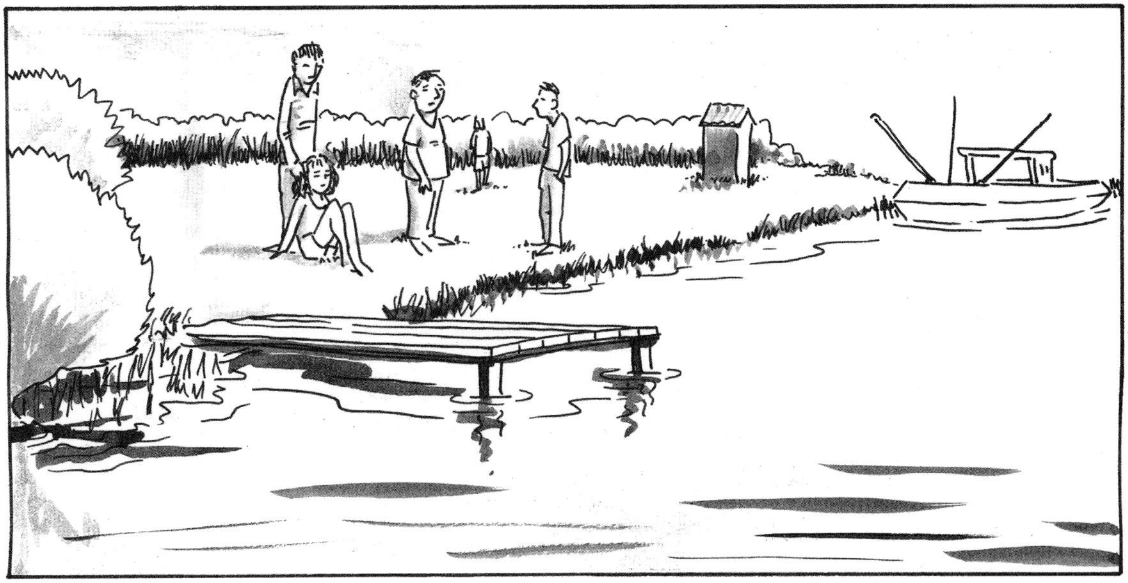

He was a crabber. Senza granchio.

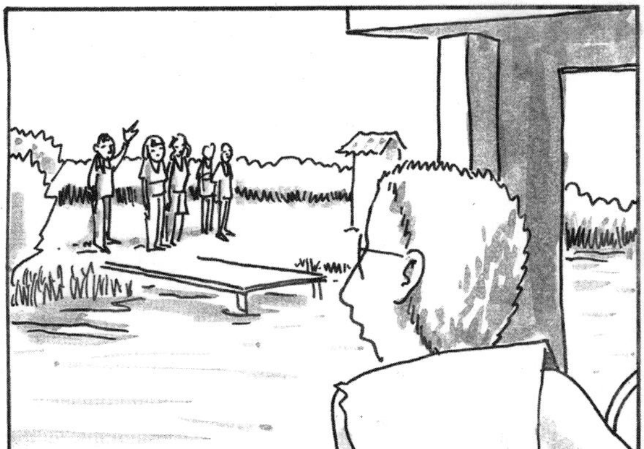

So, yes, for $100, he would take us out for an hour.

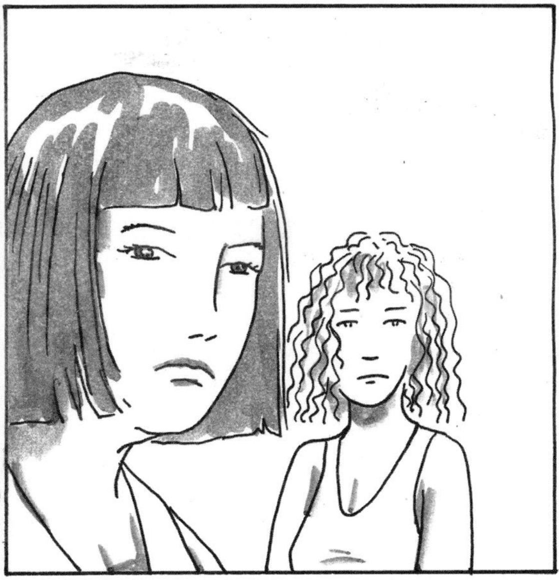

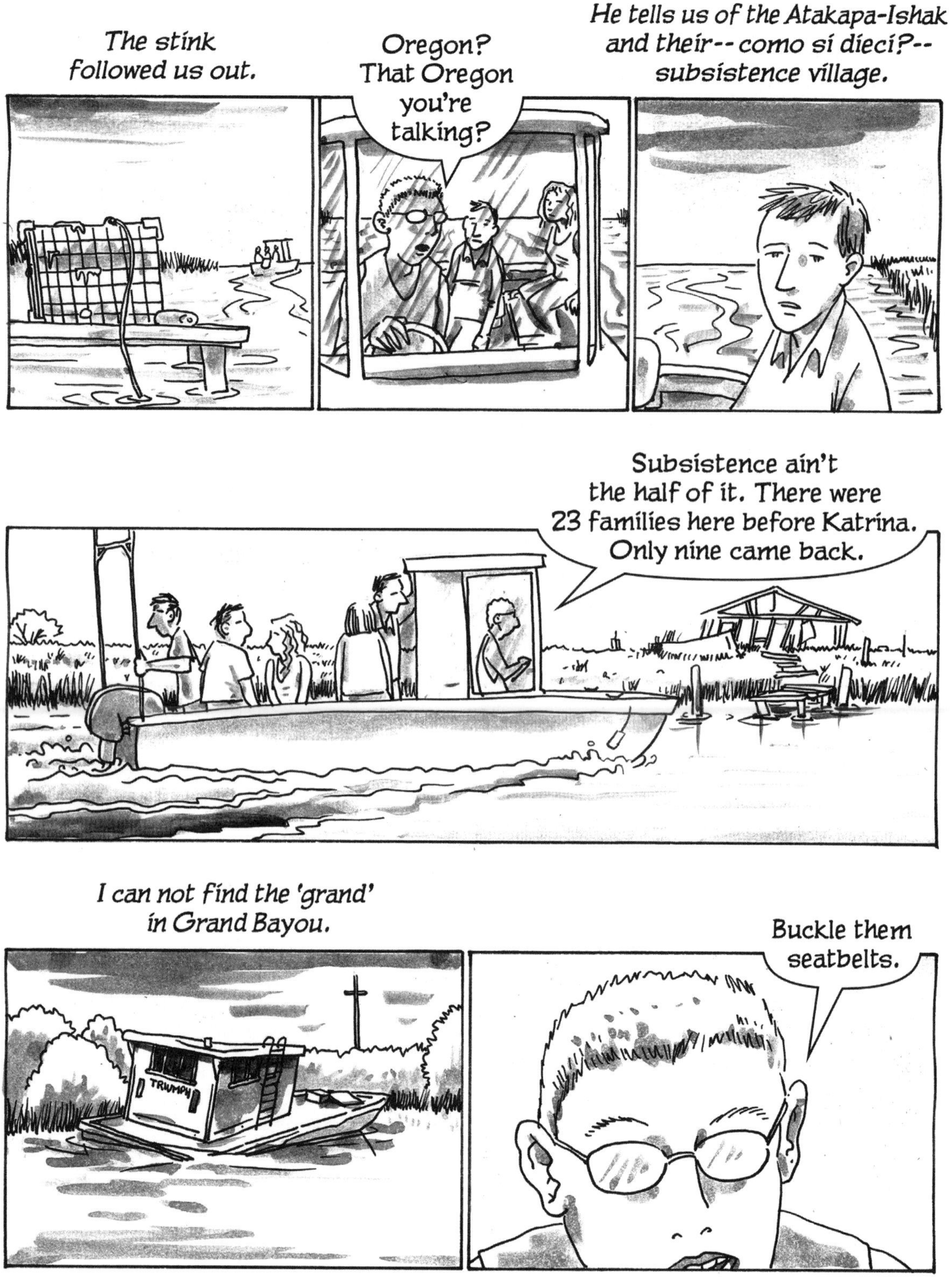
The stink followed us out.
Oregon? That Oregon you're talking?
He tells us of the Atakapa-Ishak and their-- como si dieci?-- subsistence village.
Subsistence ain't the half of it. There were 23 families here before Katrina. Only nine came back.
I can not find the 'grand' in Grand Bayou.
TRIUMPH
Buckle them seatbelts.

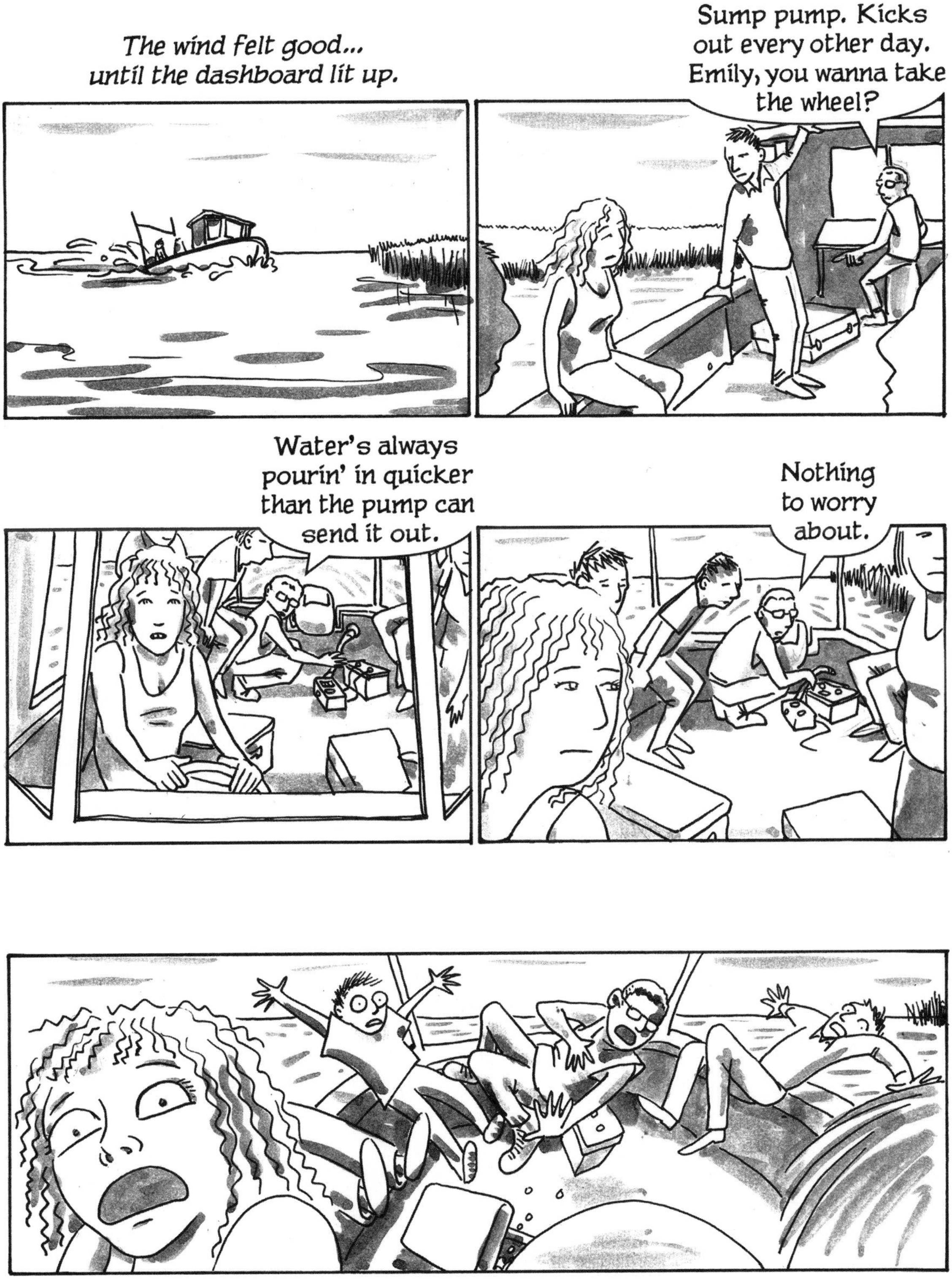
The wind felt good...
until the dashboard lit up.
Sump pump. Kicks out every other day. Emily, you wanna take the wheel?
Water's always pourin' in quicker than the pump can send it out.
Nothing to worry about.

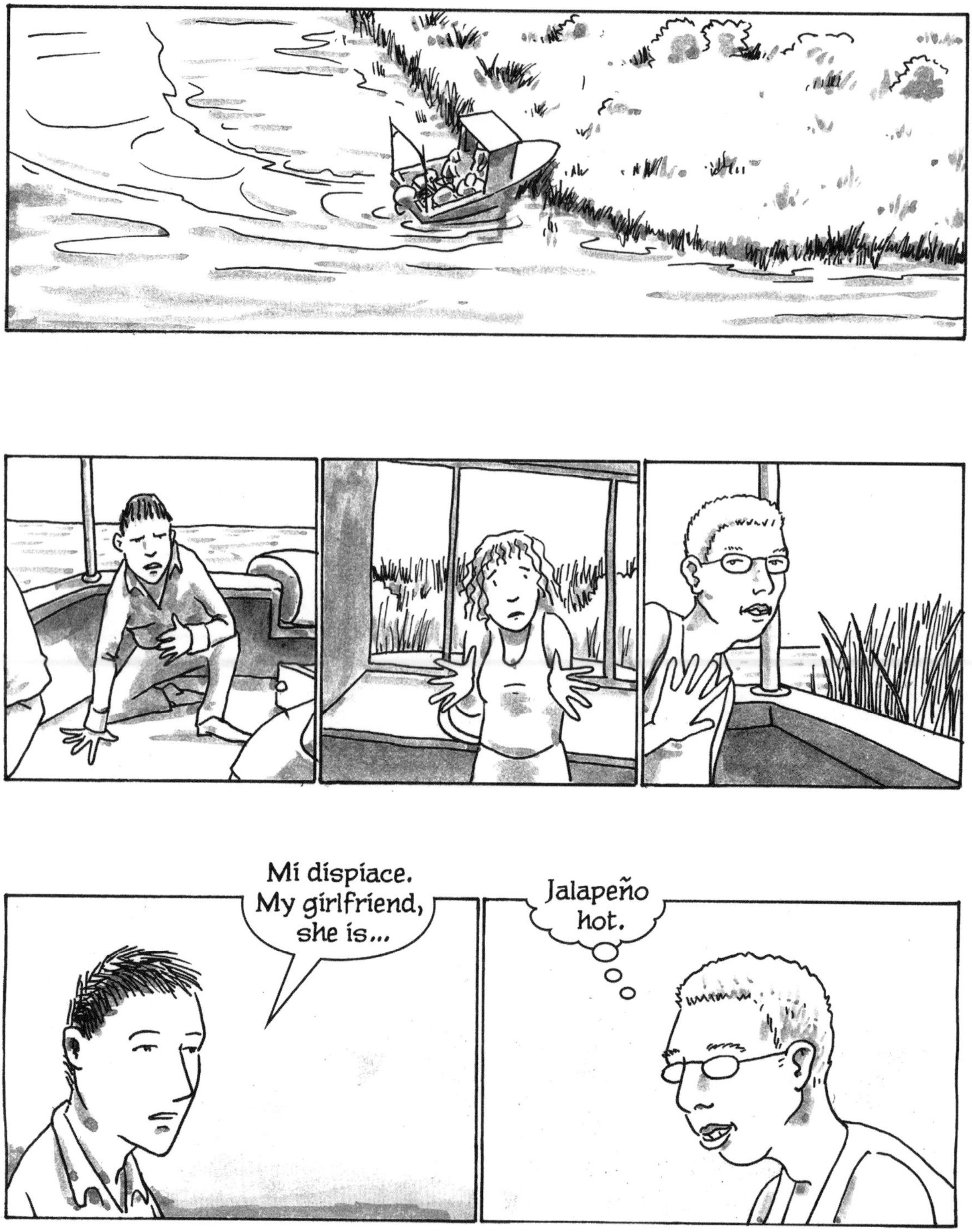
Mi dispiace. My girlfriend, she is...
Jalapeño hot.

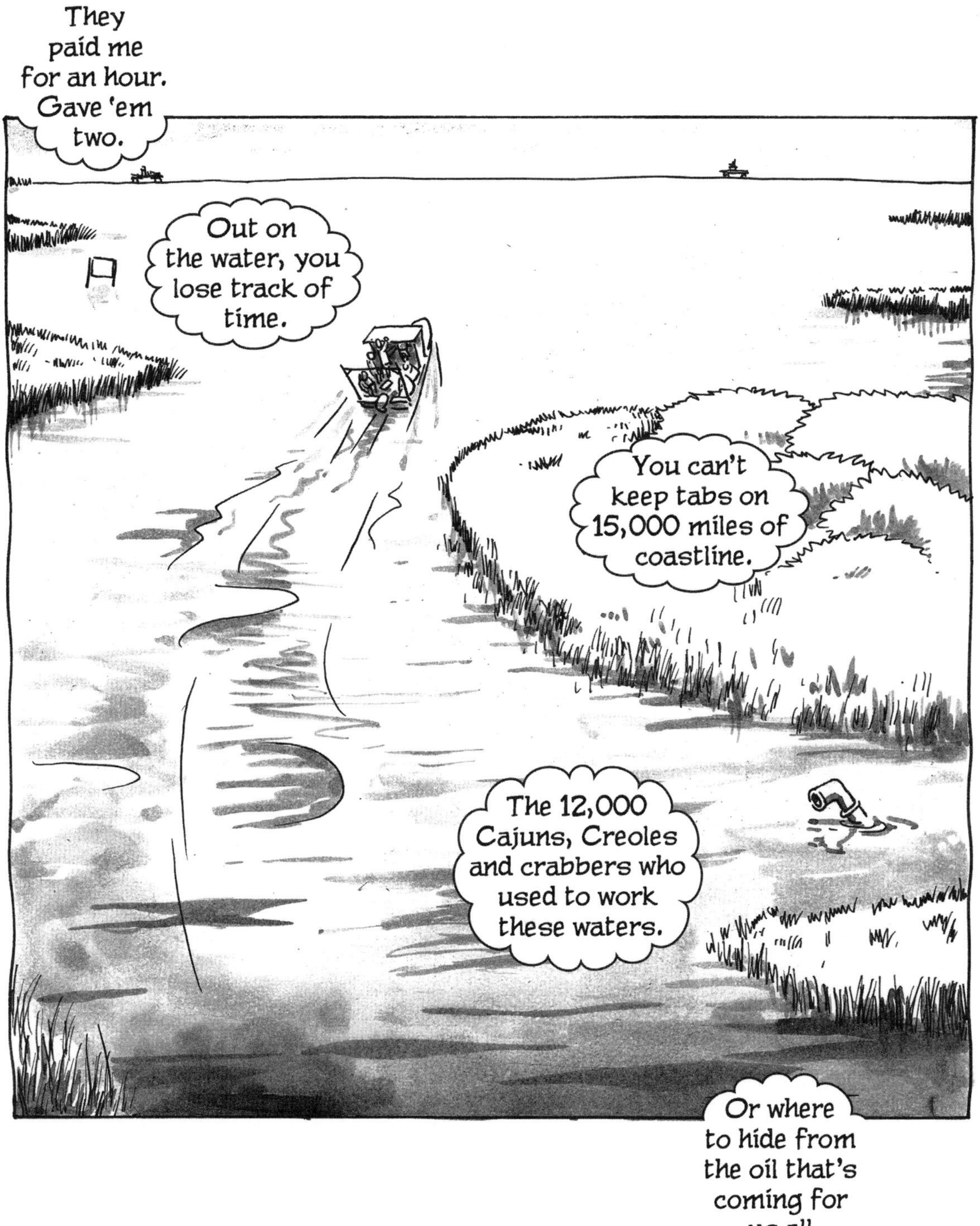
They paid me for an hour. Gave 'em two.
Out on the water, you lose track of time.
You can't keep tabs on 15,000 miles of coastline.
The 12,000 Cajuns, Creoles and crabbers who used to work these waters.
Or where to hide from the oil that's coming for us all.

"Nothing fired 'em up like the pipeline."

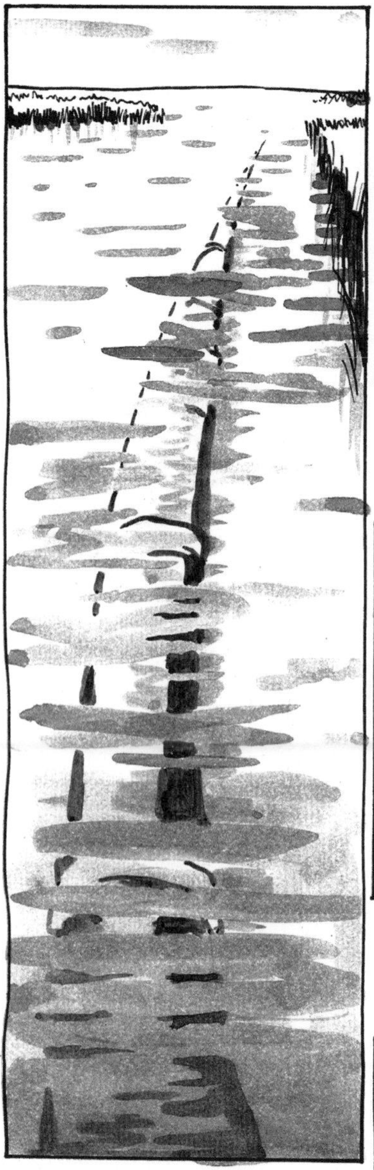

I stare at the snake under the water.

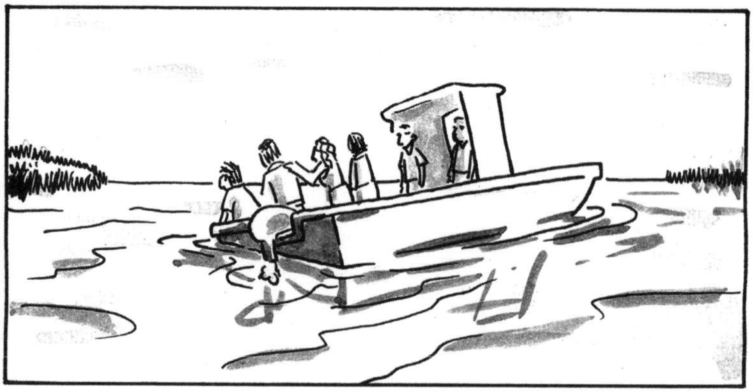

I listen to the agida in Brian's voice.

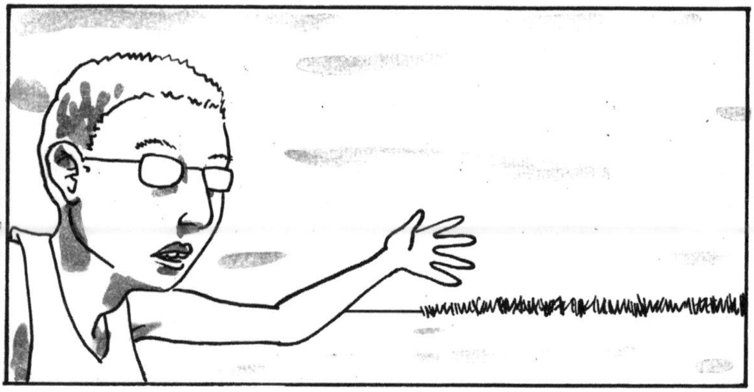

... and I do not capisce Louisiana.

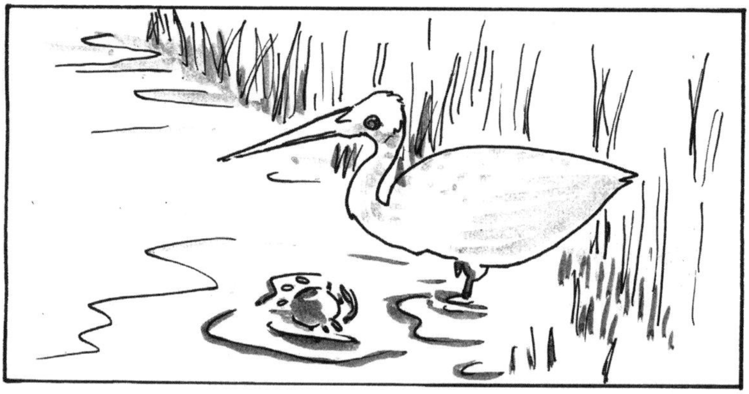

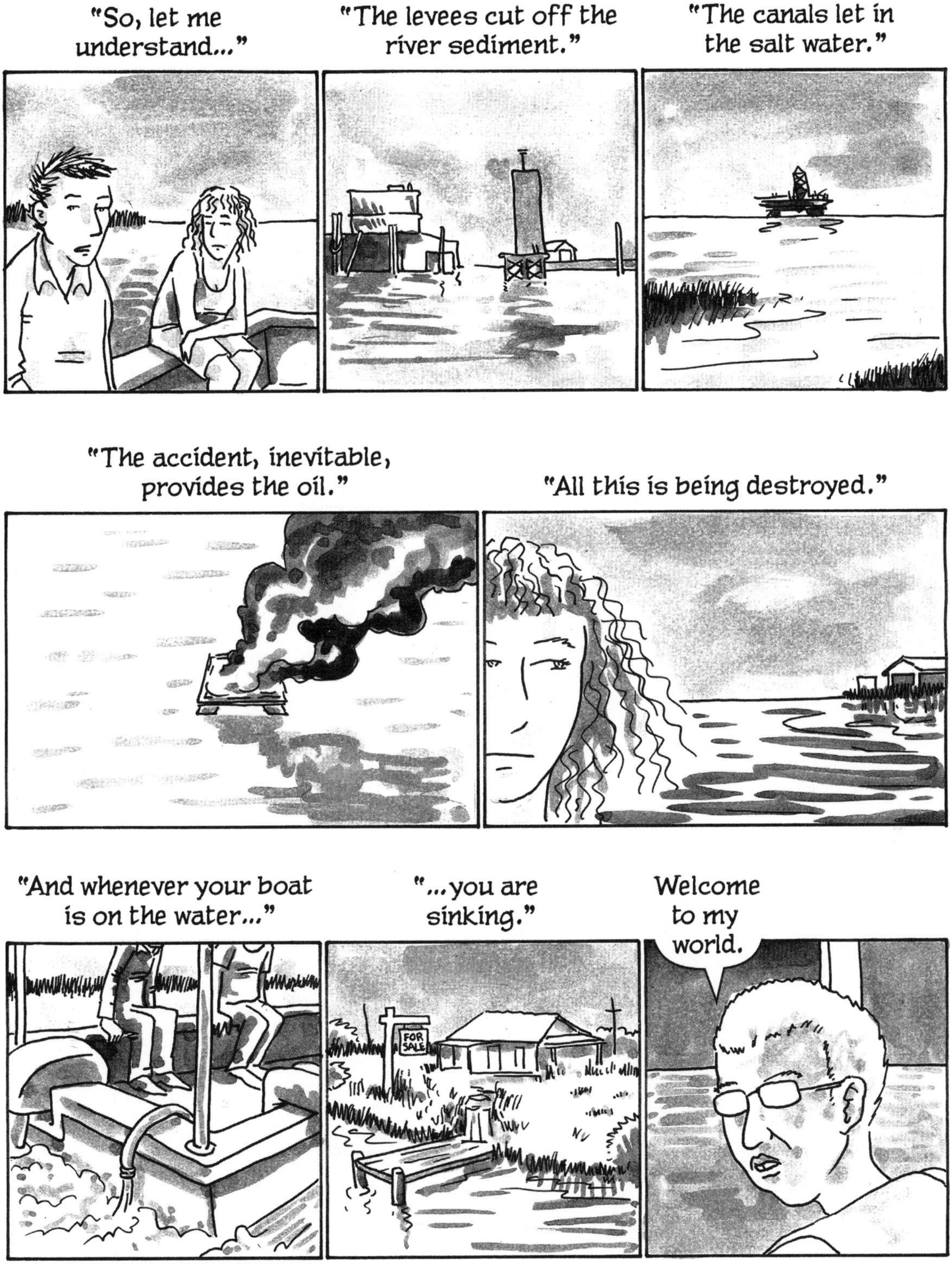
"So, let me understand..."
"The levees cut off the river sediment."
"The canals let in the salt water."
"The accident, inevitable, provides the oil."
"All this is being destroyed."
"And whenever your boat is on the water..."
"...you are sinking."
FOR SALE
Welcome to my world.

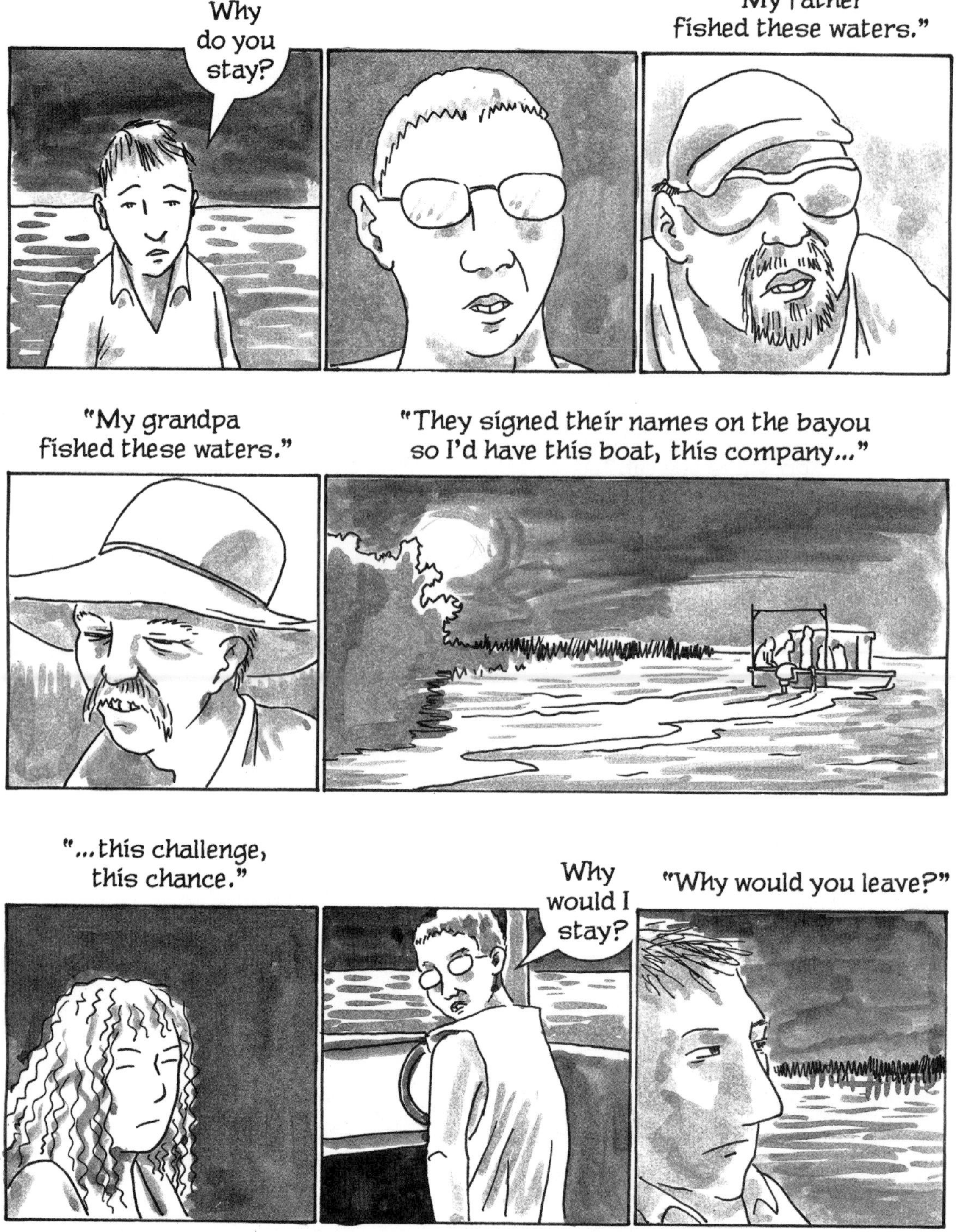

Why do you stay?
"My father fished these waters."
"My grandpa fished these waters."
"They signed their names on the bayou so I'd have this boat, this company..."
"...this challenge, this chance."
Why would I stay?
"Why would you leave?"

Oil is Another Matter

For the Atakapa-Ishak, the Faustian bargain comes in with the tide. The very water that sustains the Grand Bayou, La., tribe — with shrimp and blue crab, oyster and redfish — comes after them every five years or so with sullen, tempestuous fury.

The Category Five storms flood their homes. Crush their boats. Chases the weariest of them from the marshes.

Yet most of the subsistence fishing village hangs on. Water is the tribal members' lot, their lunch, their livelihood. For centuries, the Atakapa-Ishak have lived with it and lived on it.

But oil? Oil is another matter altogether.

The Atakapa-Ishak are not unfamiliar with the indignities imposed by neighboring cultures; tribal members refer to themselves as the "Ishak," since "Atakapa" — or "man-eaters" — is a Choctaw slur.

But imagine the survivors of this tribe, foraging just above the water line, and waiting for the oil from the Deepwater Horizon to seep into their crab pots and oyster beds, destroying everything they've built over the years and what little they have left.

Imagine moving to the edge of the world, or the eye of the hurricane, to escape our oil-fueled excesses… and discovering that wasn't far enough.

Home

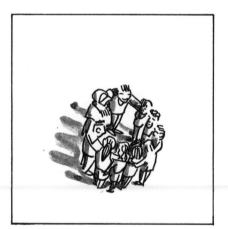

New Orleans, LA

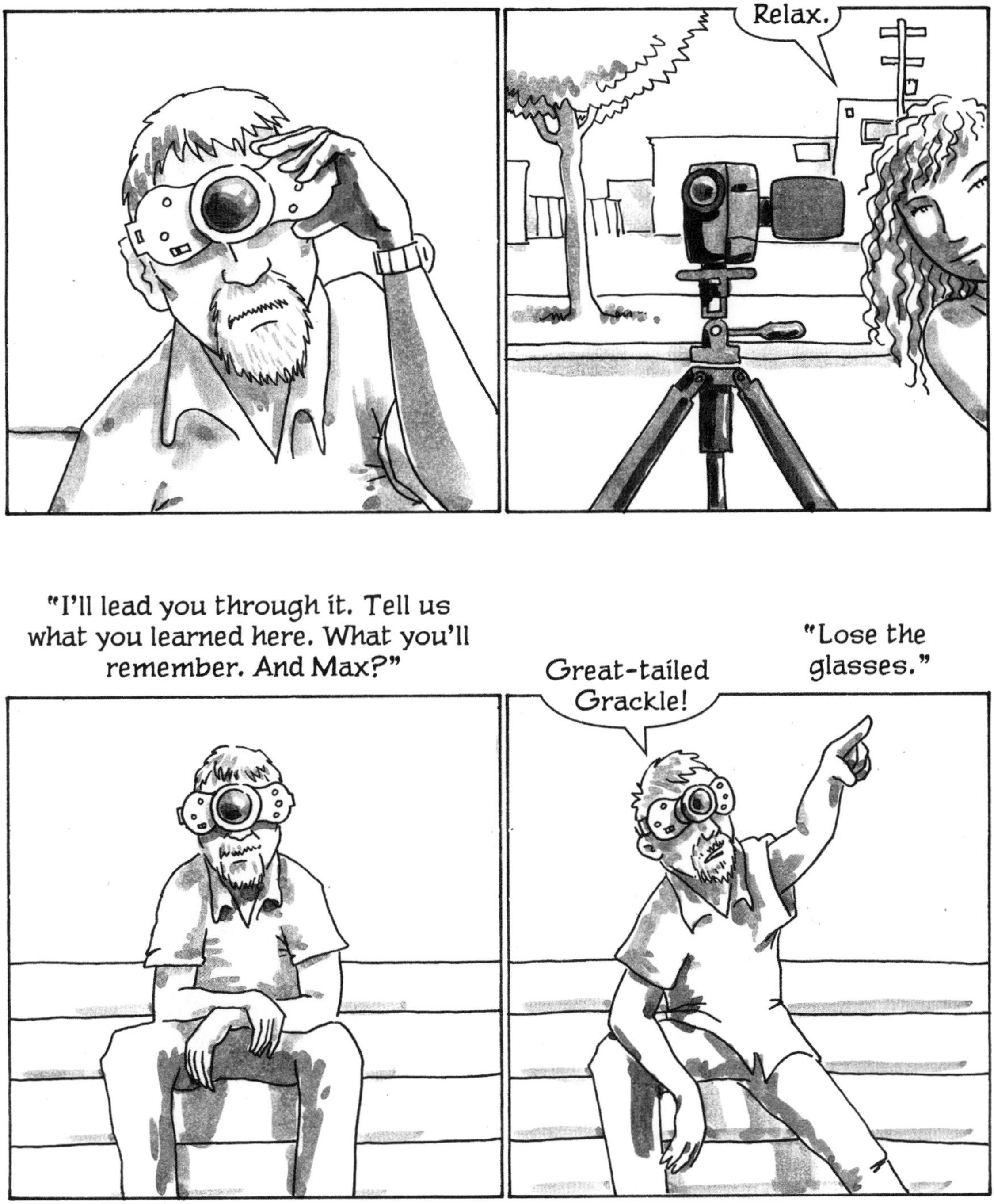
Relax.
"I'll lead you through it. Tell us what you learned here. What you'll remember. And Max?"
Great-tailed Grackle!
"Lose the glasses."

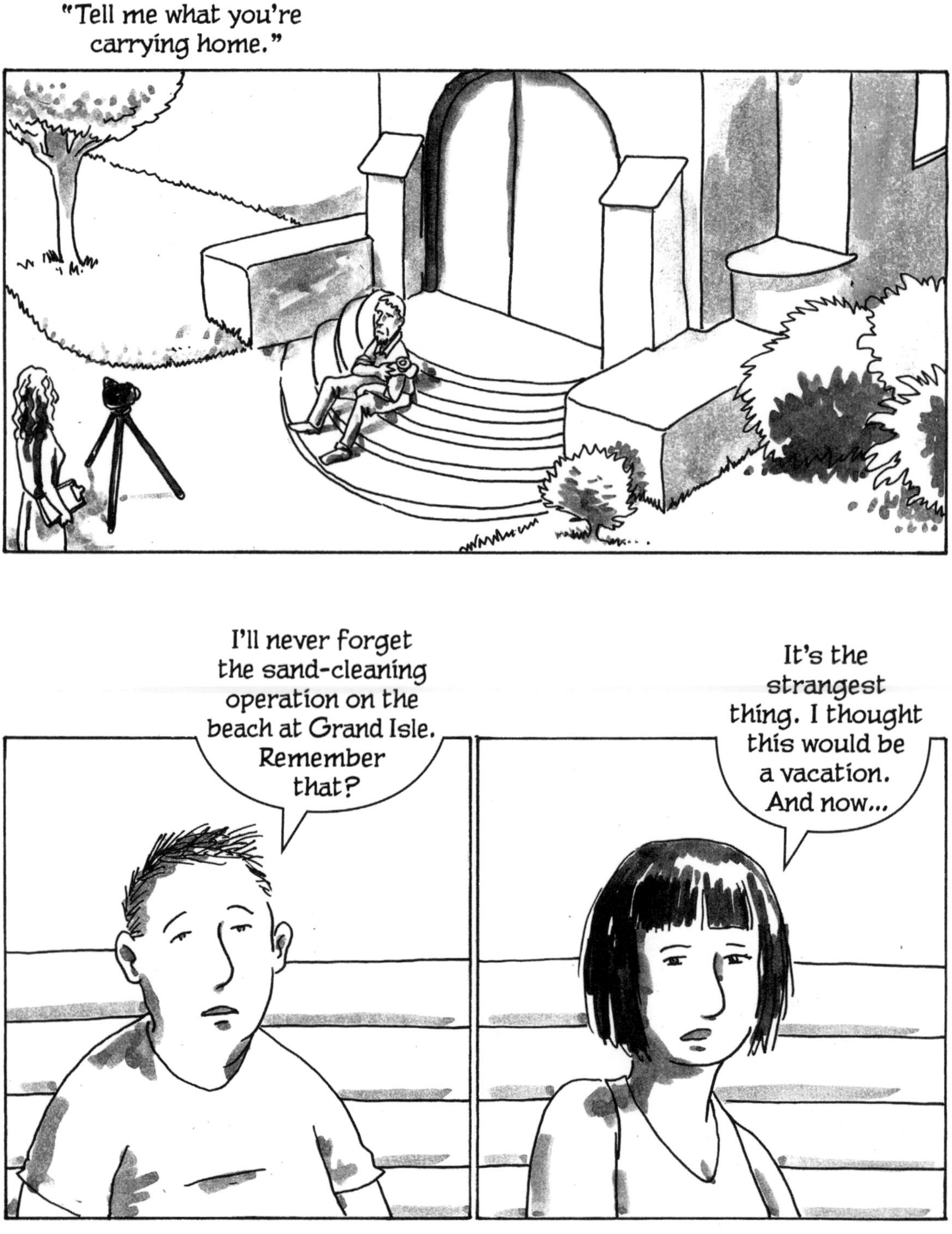
"Tell me what you're carrying home."
I'll never forget the sand-cleaning operation on the beach at Grand Isle. Remember that?
It's the strangest thing. I thought this would be a vacation. And now...

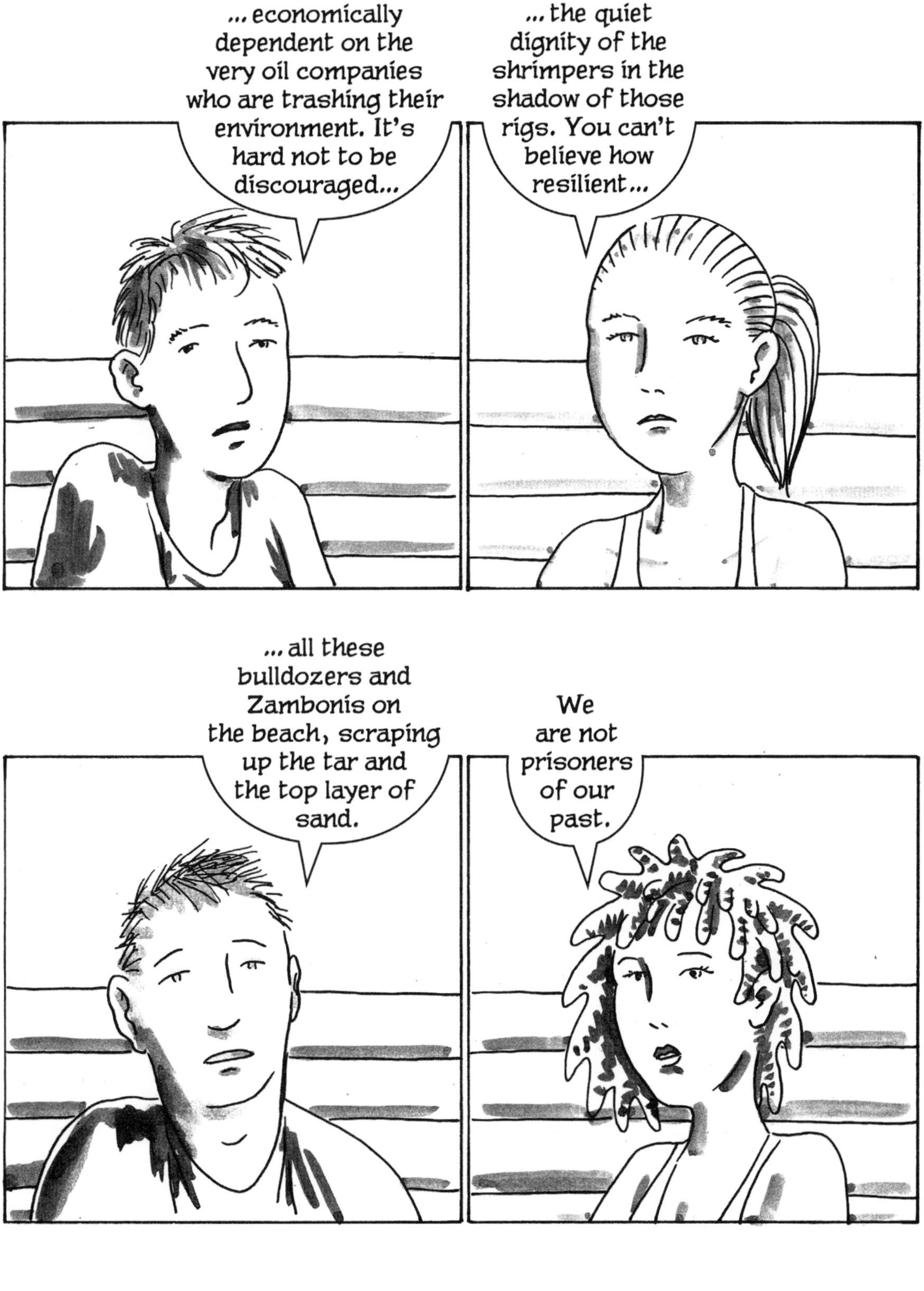
...economically dependent on the very oil companies who are trashing their environment. It's hard not to be discouraged...
...the quiet dignity of the shrimpers in the shadow of those rigs. You can't believe how resilient...
...all these bulldozers and Zambonis on the beach, scraping up the tar and the top layer of sand.
We are not prisoners of our past.

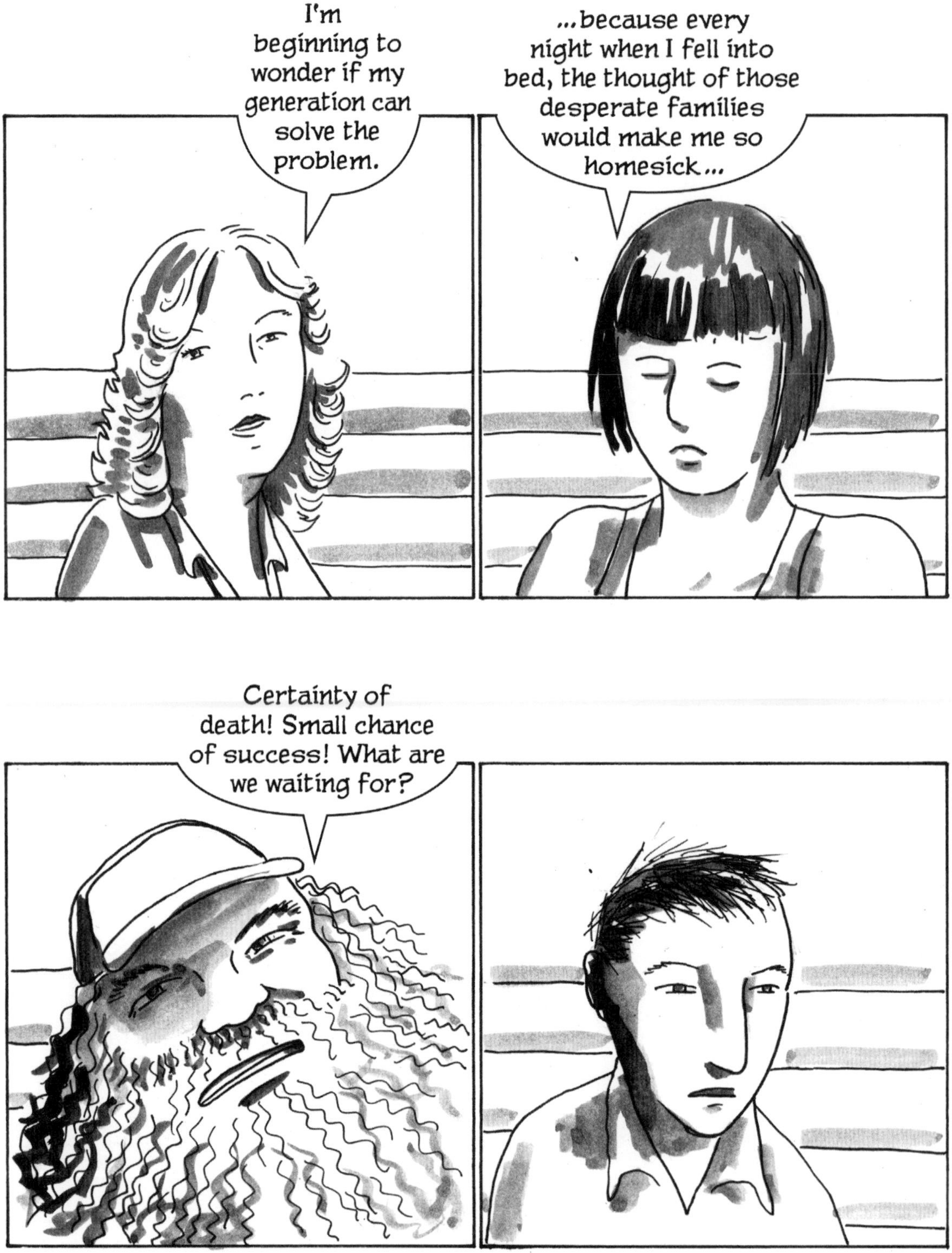
I'm beginning to wonder if my generation can solve the problem.
...because every night when I fell into bed, the thought of those desperate families would make me so homesick...
Certainty of death! Small chance of success! What are we waiting for?

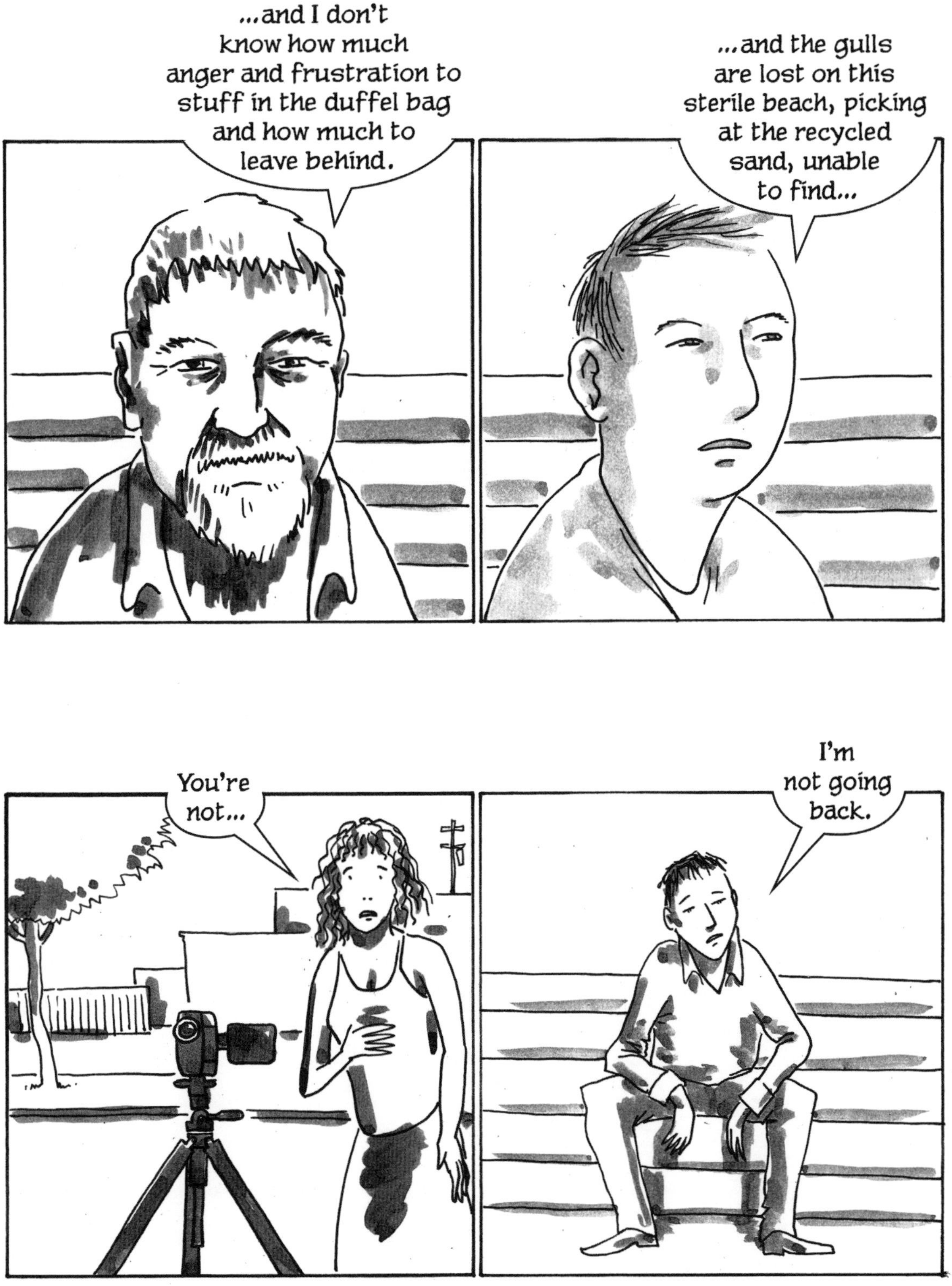
...and I don't know how much anger and frustration to stuff in the duffel bag and how much to leave behind.
...and the gulls are lost on this sterile beach, picking at the recycled sand, unable to find...
You're not...
I'm not going back.

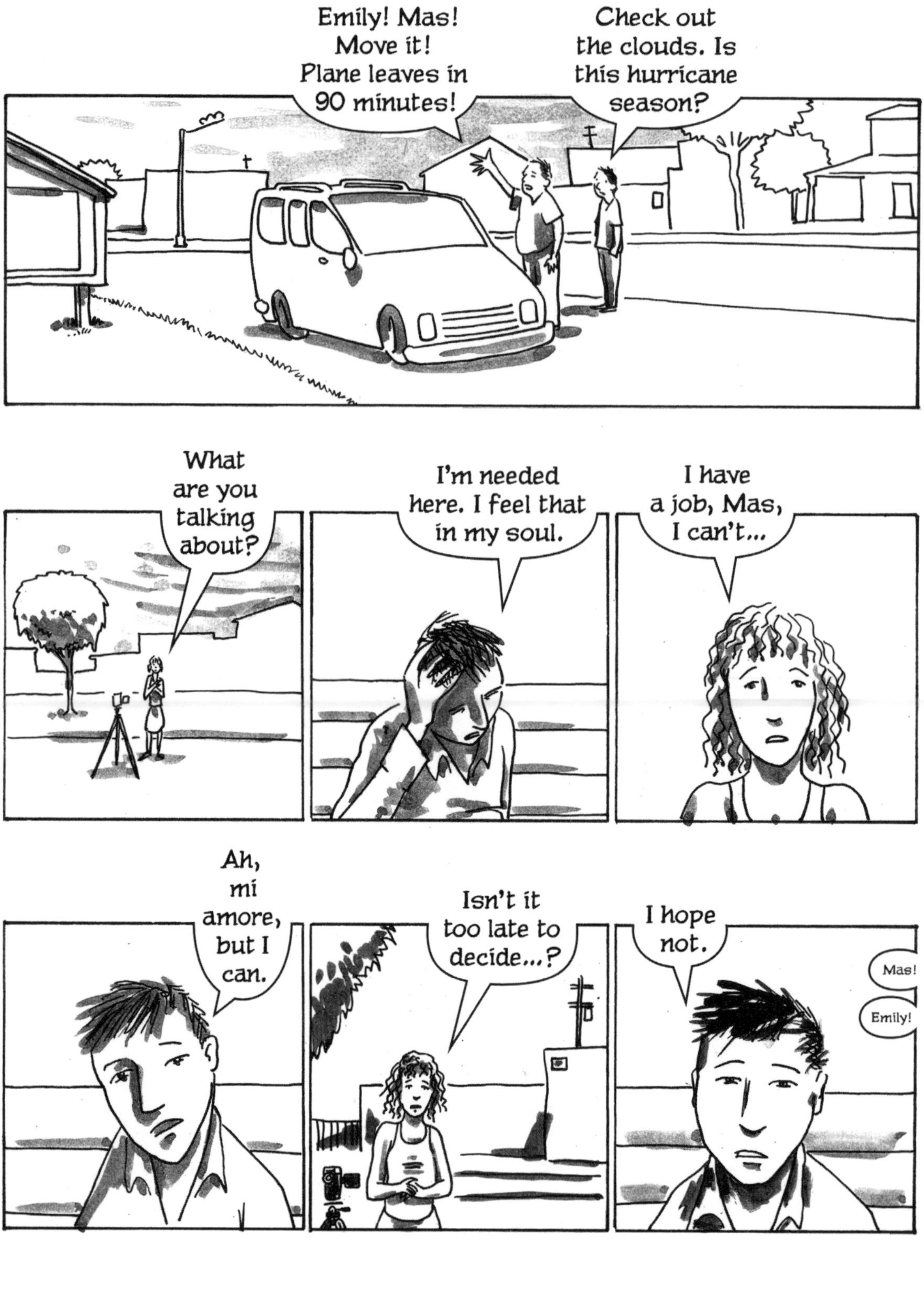
Emily! Mas! Move it! Plane leaves in 90 minutes!
Check out the clouds. Is this hurricane season?
What are you talking about?
I'm needed here. I feel that in my soul.
I have a job, Mas, I can't...
Ah, mi amore, but I can.
Isn't it too late to decide...?
I hope not.
Mas!
Emily!

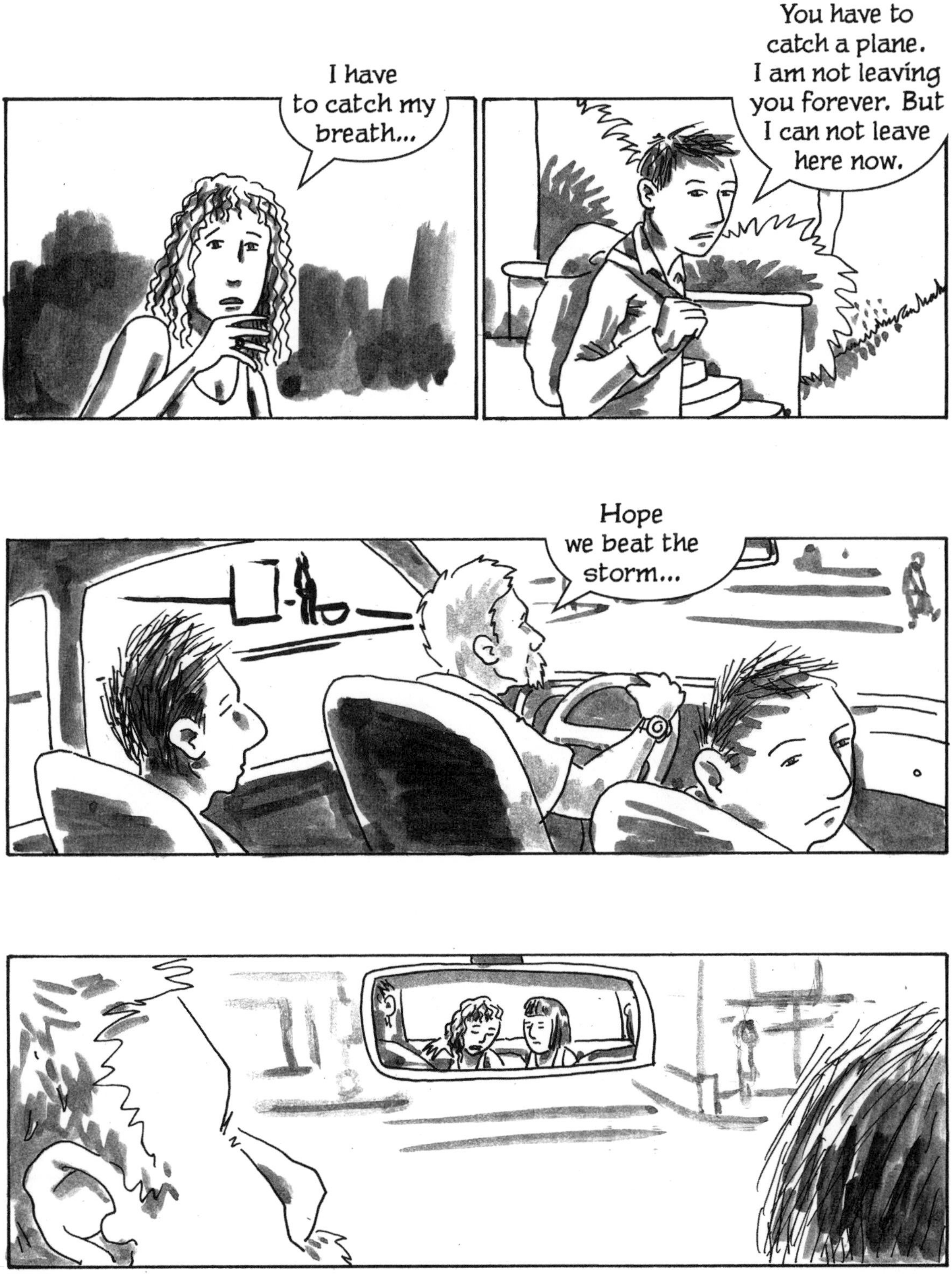
I have to catch my breath...
You have to catch a plane. I am not leaving you forever. But I can not leave here now.
Hope we beat the storm...

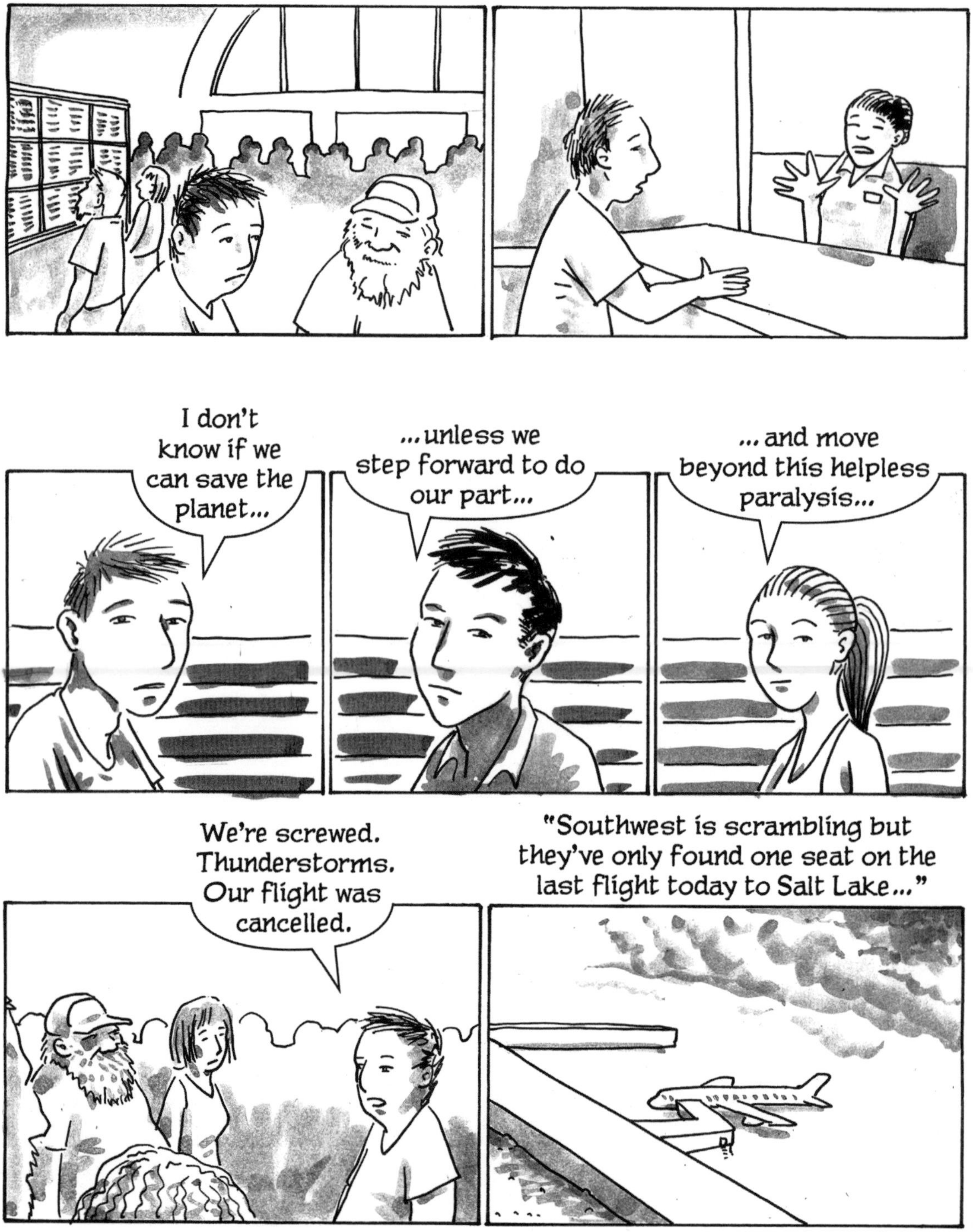

I don't know if we can save the planet...
...unless we step forward to do our part...
... and move beyond this helpless paralysis...
We're screwed. Thunderstorms. Our flight was cancelled.
"Southwest is scrambling but they've only found one seat on the last flight today to Salt Lake..."

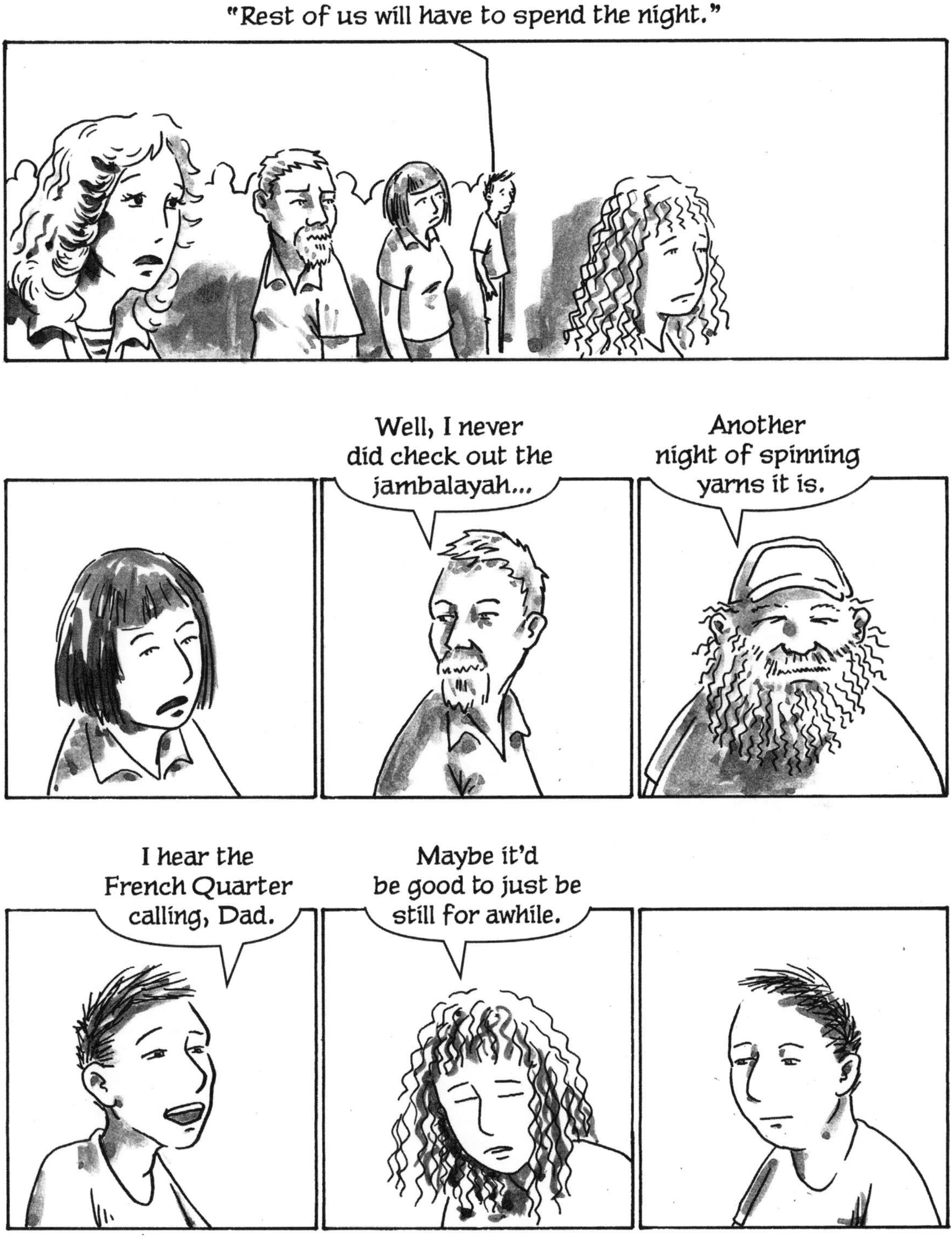
"Rest of us will have to spend the night."
Well, I never did check out the jambalayah...
Another night of spinning yarns it is.
I hear the French Quarter calling, Dad.
Maybe it'd be good to just be still for awhile.

"Safe travels, Tess."

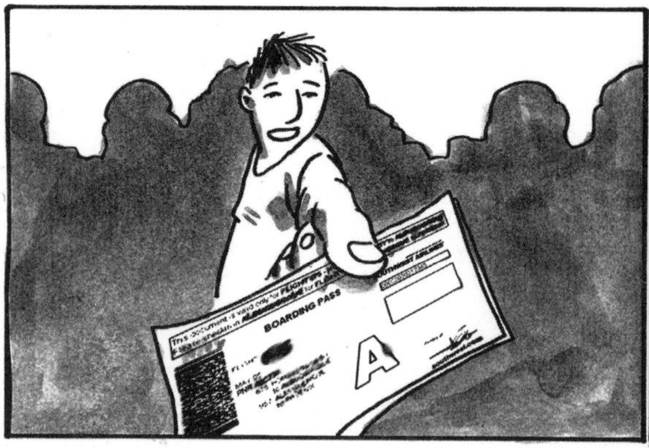
BOARDING PASS
A

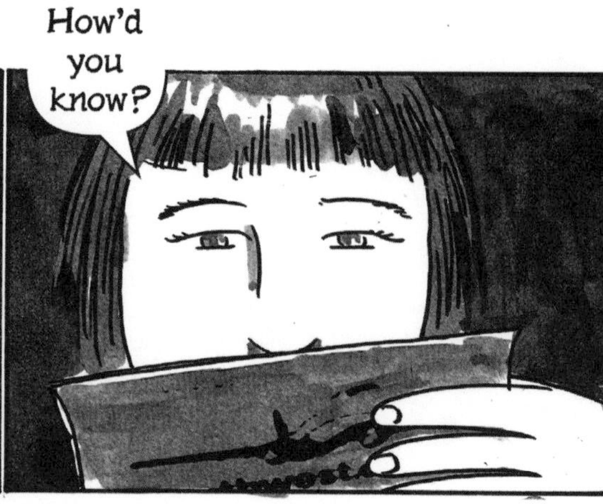
How'd you know?

"We all knew."

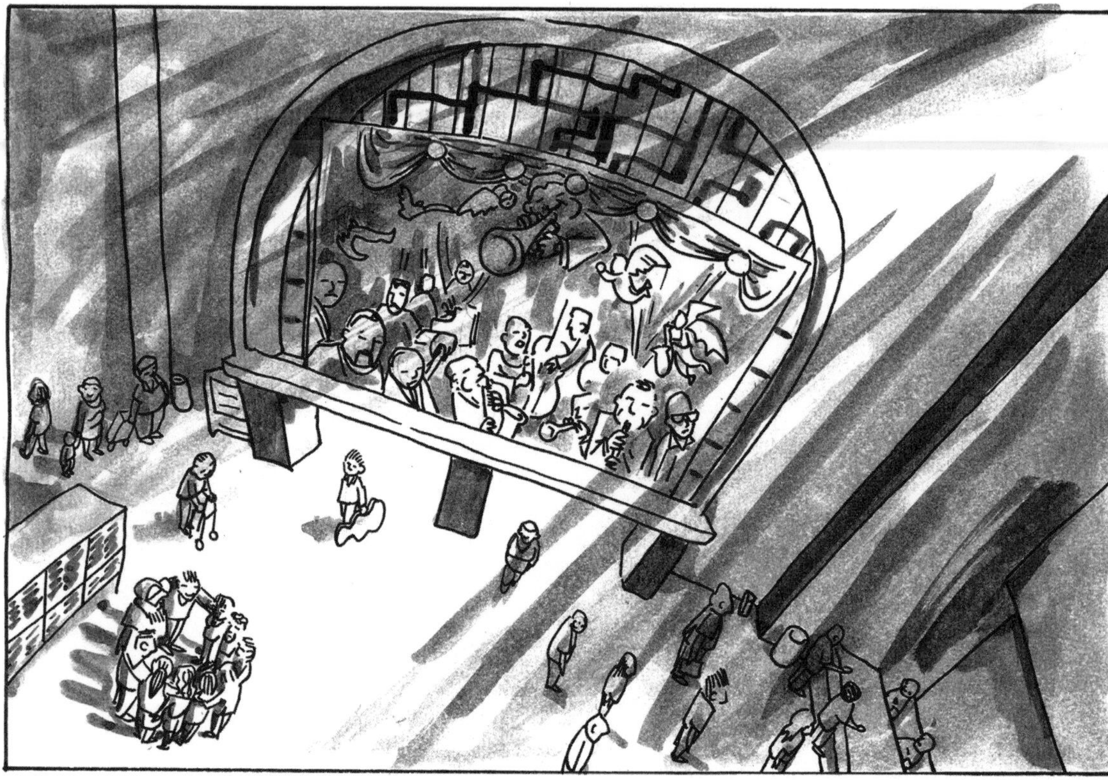

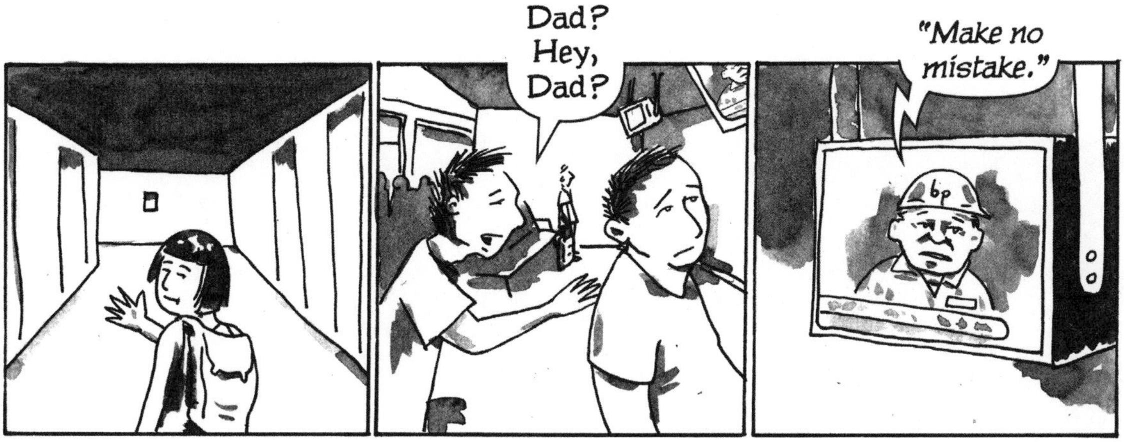
Dad? Hey, Dad?
"Make no mistake."

"BP will be here until all the oil is gone."

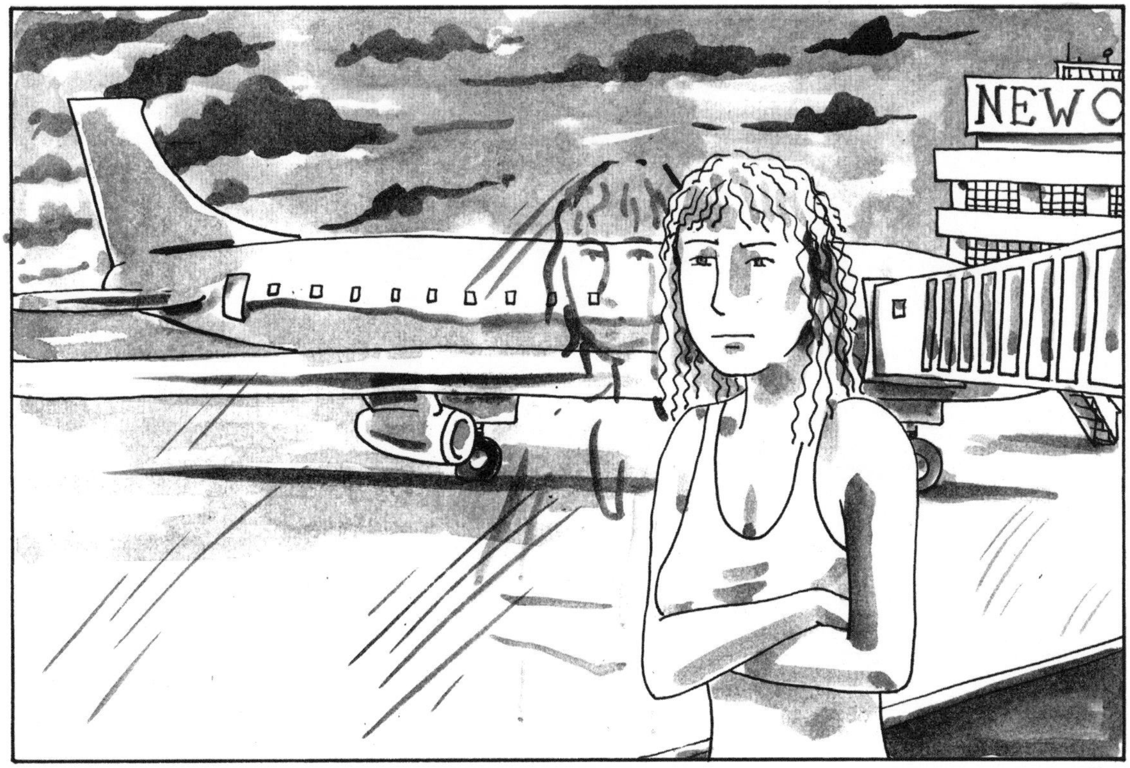
NEW O

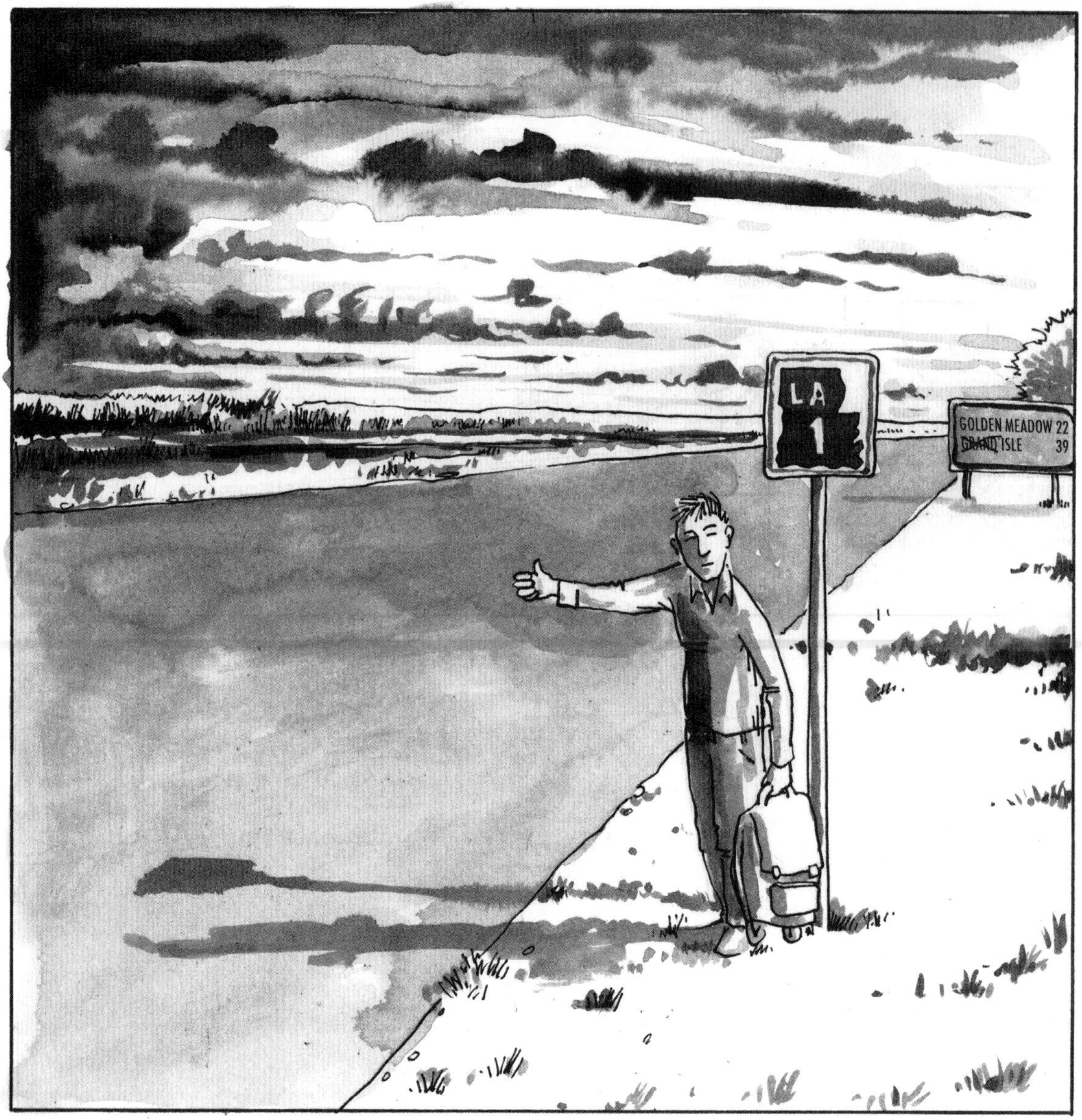
LA 1
GOLDEN MEADOW 22
GRAND ISLE 39